Fodor's

535 BEST

BEACHES

1st Edition

Fodor's Travel Publications · New York · Toronto · London · Sydney · Auckland

www.fodors.com

Be a Fodor's Correspondent

This new, full-color guide to the best beaches in the U.S., Caribbean, and Mexico is meant to inspire you to get out and find the beach of your dreams. We hope you'll peruse these pages and then go out and find your own bliss, whether your travels take you to the Pacific Northwest, the rugged coast of Maine, the surfing beaches of Oaxaca, the sunny shores of Florida, or the wave-splashed sands of Anguilla.

We are especially proud of this color edition. In this volume, you'll find our recommendations for the best beaches on every stretch of the U.S. coast in dozens of destinations. The result is the fruit of the labor of almost 60 different writers and a dozen of our in-house editors. We've filled the pages with more than 300 photographs so you can be inspired by the views and enthralled by the different hues of the water lapping onto more than 500 different shorelines. Regardless of where you're traveling, we know there's a beach out there to inspire you. And to enrich your explorations, we've also incorporated the very best of our illustrated features on everything from the Napali Coast of Kaua'i to whale-watching in Cape Cod.

We also invite you to join the travel conversation. Your opinion matters to us, and to your fellow travelers. Come to Fodors.com to plan your trip, share an experience, ask a question, submit a photograph, post a review, or write a trip report. Tell our editors about your trip. They want to know what went well and how we can make this guide even better.

We know that everyone has his or her different idea of what the best beach is. If our writers haven't quite captured the essence of a place, tell us how you'd do it differently. If any of our descriptions are inaccurate or inadequate, we'll incorporate your changes in the next edition and will correct factual errors at Fodors.com immediately. Share your opinions at our feedback center at fodors.com/feedback, or e-mail us at editors@fodors.com with the subject line "535 Best Beaches Editor." You might find your comment published in a future Fodor's guide. We look forward to hearing from you.

Happy Traveling!

Tim Jarrell, Publisher

CONTENTS

Experience the
Best Beaches

BEST BEACHES PLANNER

What to Bring

If you are planning to stay in a large resort, then it's a waste of space to pack beach towels, water toys, and snorkeling equipment (unless you are a very serious snorkeler). The resort will have all these items on hand. However, if you are planning to stay in a hotel or bed-and-breakfast, you may need to bring more equipment with you or buy it once you arrive at your destination (weigh the cost of the item you need to have with the cost of checking the bag big enough to carry it).

When to Reserve

School holiday periods are the busiest times. Winter is also high season, especially for beaches in warmer climes. But in popular mass-market destinations throughout the Caribbean, Mexico, and the United States, you could probably find something even a couple of weeks in advance. Paradoxically, it's easier to find an acceptable room in the busiest destinations by sheer virtue of the number of rooms available at any given time. Waiting until the last minute doesn't always net a bargain because last-minute airfares to resort destinations can be expensive.

Fees and Add-ons

Almost every destination charges an accommodations tax ranging from 7% to 15%. In addition, many hotels and resorts tack on a service fee (especially in the Caribbean, Mexico, and sometimes even in resort destinations in the United States and Hawai'i), usually around 10%. The service fee isn't quite the same as a tip for service, and it is customary at most resorts to tip the staff even if a service charge is added to the cost of your room. The latest growing trend is the "resort fee." You can encounter this almost anywhere. The fee presumably covers costs like housekeeping (though you might sometimes see this on your bill, too, especially for villa rentals), utilities, and use of resort facilities. Figure $5 to $50 per night, but know that this is generally restricted to larger hotels and defies generalization since it depends more on the individual resort or hotel chain than the destination itself. These additional costs aren't always mentioned when you book, so be sure to enquire. When all these taxes and charges are added, expect to pay at least 20% above and beyond the base rate for a resort room, at least 10% above and beyond the base rate for a non-resort room.

Picking the Best Room

On virtually every beach destination, especially at beachfront lodgings, the better the beach access or ocean view, the higher the price. You can save up to $100 or more per night simply by choosing a garden-, mountain-, or town-view room. But regardless of view, be sure to ask about the property's layout. For example, if you want to be close to the "action" at many larger resorts, whether you have mobility concerns or just need to satisfy your gambling or beach-gamboling itch, the trade-off might be noise, whether from screaming kids jumping in the pool or DJs pumping and thumping music in the bar. Likewise, saving that $100 may not be worth it if your room faces a busy thoroughfare. This is your vacation, so if you have any specific desires or dislikes, discuss them thoroughly with the reservations staff.

Where to Stay

Beachgoers can find every conceivable type of accommodation for every taste and budget. Most beach destinations offer the gamut of glitzy resorts, boutique-chic hotels, historic hostelries, family-run B&Bs, condo resorts, self-catering apartments, and private villas and homes.

Resorts: Most prevalent in beach destinations (especially in the warmer climates) are large resorts, including all-inclusives, usually strategically positioned on the beach. These include golf/spa resorts and name-brand chain hotels in various price categories from Ritz-Carlton to Comfort Suites. Jamaica, Mexico, and the Dominican Republic specialize in the all-inclusive experience, but outside of Mexico and the Caribbean, all-inclusive resorts are very rare indeed. Some destinations abound in cookie-cutter tour-group hotels that look like they could be plunked down anywhere. You'll find these everywhere from Cape Cod to Honolulu to South Padre Island to Hilton Head.

Condos and Times-Shares: Condo resorts are increasingly popular in all areas and can offer both extra space and superior savings for families with kitchens, sofa beds, and more. In fact, they dominate the scene in some destinations like parts of the Florida Panhandle, Maui, Grand Cayman, and Myrtle Beach. Some time-share properties are good values and don't require you to sit through a sales pitch.

Private Villas and Homes: Another increasingly popular option for families or those seeking a surprising bargain: private villas and homes. Self-catering means saving on dining out in more-expensive destinations, like St. Barth (where villas usually cost much less than hotels), though a car is usually necessary. Along the Alabama and Mississippi Gulf coast and in the Outer Banks of North Carolina private homes are the predominant lodging option.

Inns and B&Bs: Historic inns come in all shapes and sizes and can be found along all the coasts of the United States, especially in New England and the Pacific Northwest. Inns can be found in the Caribbean and even in Mexico and Hawai'i in some of the older areas that weren't developed solely for tourists.

Motels: Especially in the United States, there are reasonably priced, limited-service hotels and motels in almost every conceivable beach destination. While the location may not always be directly on the sand, almost every destination from Miami to Oregon offers this option. If you are on a budget and willing to forego organized activities and hotel services, a motel may be the cheapest option you'll find.

Drive or Fly?

The rising costs of airfare cannot be underestimated, but in the Continental United States, driving is almost always an option. Regardless of how expensive gasoline gets, if you own your own car, it's almost always cheaper to drive to your destination if more than two people are traveling, especially when you consider the costs of checking luggage, meals in transit, and renting a car. Of course, driving can take considerably longer than flying, and you may have to spend a night or two on the road, which comes with its own costs.

Food Costs

Restaurants in resort areas are usually more expensive than those at home. In places like Hawai'i and much of the Caribbean, food costs can be as much as 40% higher than at home. One way to save on food is to find a hotel or resort that includes breakfast in the rate. If you can subsist on fast food, you'll save some money, but keeping a few lunch items in your room's refrigerator (assuming there is one) can be another way to keep food costs down. And cooking on your own in a rented apartment or house can save money, too. Families, whether staying close to home or traveling farther afield, should consider bringing well-loved food items for the kids just in case they can't be found in the local supermarket.

WHEN TO GO

The tropical high season (for South Florida, Mexico, Hawai'i, the Bahamas, and the Caribbean) is traditionally winter—from December 15 to April 14, after which prices drop. Winter is rainy in Southern California, where the beach season starts in early spring and runs through late summer; this season is also the best time to visit the beaches of the Carolinas and Georgia, northern Florida, and the Gulf Coast. Once you move farther north, the summer season starts later. The traditional summer season starts on Memorial Day and runs through Labor Day in most of the other coastal regions. But you'll be hard-pressed to find many beachgoers in Northern California or Cape Cod until mid- to late June, and on the West Coast summer fog north of San Francisco in July and August can make the weather feel more like winter in Southern California.

Climate

It's hard to generalize about climate when you're talking about an area as large as the United States, Caribbean, and Mexico combined. The tropical climate is fairly constant, but even as far north as Miami and Puerto Vallarta you can experience chilly winter temperatures. And while winter temperatures are generally mild in the mid-Atlantic, Gulf Coast, and California, you can still experience some cold, especially in January and February. The Pacific Northwest experiences much more moderate winters than the Northeast, but winters in the Northwest are very wet. Hawai'i has less variation in temperatures, with December, January, and February being the coolest months (and, because visitors are generally fleeing much colder temperatures in the United States, are the most expensive months to visit); however, it never gets cold in most of Hawai'i.

Hurricanes occasionally sweep through the Caribbean between June and November; during this period hurricanes can also affect the Pacific Coast of Mexico and the United States and Hawai'i.

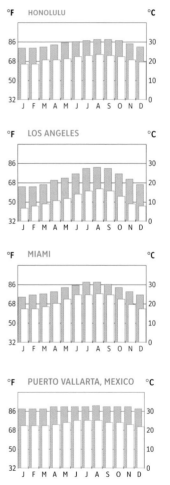

HURRICANE SEASON

The Atlantic hurricane season lasts from June 1 through November 30, but it's fairly rare to see a large storm in either June or November. The Central Pacific hurricane season (affecting Hawai'i and Mexico's Pacific Coast) is generally at the same time.

Avoiding the Storms: Keep in mind that hurricanes are rarer the farther south you go. The ABC Islands (Aruba, Bonaire, and Curaçao) as well as Trinidad and Tobago are the least likely to see a direct hit by a Caribbean hurricane, while the area south of Los Cabos along Mexico's Pacific Coast is least likely to be struck by a hurricane. However, all these areas are still susceptible to strong storms, and even the periphery of a large storm can bring heavy wind and rain, putting a damper on any beach vacation.

Airlines: Airports are usually closed during hurricanes and many flights canceled, which results in a disruption of the steady flow of tourists in and out of affected islands. If you are scheduled to fly into an area where a hurricane is expected, check with your airline regularly and often. If flights are disrupted, airlines will usually allow you to rebook at a later date, but you will not get a refund if you have booked a nonrefundable ticket, nor in most cases will you be allowed to change your ticket to a different destination; rather, you will be expected to reschedule your trip for a later date.

Hotels and Resorts: If a hurricane warning is issued and flights disrupted to your destination, virtually every resort will waive cancellation and change penalties and will allow you to rebook your trip for a later date; some will allow you to cancel if a hurricane threatens to strike, even if flights aren't canceled. Some will give you a refund if you have prepaid for your stay; others will expect you to rebook your trip for a later date. Some large resort companies—including Sandals and SuperClubs—have "hurricane guarantees," but these apply only when flights have been canceled or when a hurricane is sure to strike.

Travel Insurance: If you plan to travel to a beach destination during the hurricane season, it is wise to buy travel insurance that allows you to cancel for any reason. This kind of coverage can be expensive (up to 10% of the value of the trip), but if you have to prepay far in advance for an expensive vacation package, the peace of mind may be worth it. Just be sure to read the fine print; some policies don't kick in unless flights are canceled and the hurricane makes a direct hit on the island to which you have chosen to travel, something you may not be assured of until the day you plan to travel. In order to get a complete cancellation policy, you must usually buy your insurance within a week of booking your trip. If you wait until after the hurricane warning is issued to purchase insurance, it will be too late.

Track Those Hurricanes: The obsessive and naturally curious keep a close eye on the Caribbean during hurricane season. You can, too. Several Web sites track hurricanes during the season, including ⊕ *weather.com*, ⊕ *www.hurricanetrack. com*, and ⊕ *www.accuweather.com*.

IF YOU LIKE

Warm Water and Soft Sand

What makes a great beach can depend on personal preference. You might want to sift your toes in soft white sand. You may want your beach to be empty but for the occasional palm tree. You may want to be surrounded by a hundred pairs of beautiful limbs, all smelling slightly of coconut oil. Part of the fun of taking a beach vacation is discovering your own favorites, which are sometimes the ones you'd least suspect. Here are a few of our favorite tropical beach destinations.

■ **Abaco, Bahamas.** Treasure Cay Beach is one of the widest stretches of powdery sand to be found in the Bahamas, and parts are often deserted.

■ **Eagle Beach, Aruba.** Once undeveloped, this beach on Aruba's southwestern coast is now hopping and happening.

■ **Grand Cayman, Cayman Islands.** Seven Mile Beach is free of litter and peddlers; the best northern sections rank among the best beachfront areas of the Caribbean.

■ **Harbour Island, Bahamas.** Three-mile-long Pink Sand Beach is one of the world's most dazzling beaches and is a favorite of many travelers.

■ **Kaua'i, Hawai'i.** The island has miles of breathtaking beaches, but Hanalei Bay Beach Park is the island's (and one of the state's) best.

■ **Negril, Jamaica.** Seven miles of sand lined by bars, restaurants, and hotels in westernmost Jamaica have been popular for decades.

■ **Puerto Escondido, Oaxaca, Mexico.** In a region full of beautiful beaches, Playa Carrizalillo can still take your breath away, and it's only a short drive from town.

Strolling and Beachcombing

Not all beaches are made for swimming and sunning. Sometimes what you want is to stroll along a nice long stretch of beach and enjoy the views, perhaps watch some whales frolic in the waters, or simply stare off at the sunset. Maybe you don't mind slipping on a sweater to ease the cold and chill, or perhaps you love to dig for clams or wade through tidal pools. Here are some beaches that we recommend when you aren't into swimming.

■ **Assateague Island, Maryland.** The national seashore has abundant wildlife and hiking trails.

■ **Big Sur, California.** Julia Pfeiffer Burns State Park provides some fine hiking, from an easy ½-mi stroll with marvelous coastal views to a strenuous 6-mi trek through the redwoods.

■ **Fort Bragg, California.** Glass Beach likely has more sea glass than you've ever seen in one place before.

■ **Kennebunk, Maine.** Three-mile-long Goose Rocks, a few minutes' drive north of town off Route 9, has plenty of shallow pools for exploring and a good long stretch of smooth sand.

■ **Olympic National Park, Washington.** Miles of spectacular, rugged coastline dotted with tidal pools and driftwood hem the edges of the Olympic Peninsula. Some of the best beaches are near La Push.

■ **Sanibel Island, Florida.** Walk the length of Bowman's Beach and leave humanity behind, finding some of the area's greatest concentrations of shells along the way.

■ **Seaside, Oregon.** Eight miles south of Seaside, U.S. 101 passes the entrance to Ecola State Park, a playground of sea-sculpted rocks, sandy shoreline, green headlands, and panoramic views.

Diving and Snorkeling

Many people would rather spend their days under the sea rather than on the beach. Generally, the best conditions for diving—clear water and lots of marine life—are also good for snorkelers, though you won't see as much from the surface looking down. If you haven't been certified yet, take a resort course. After learning the basics in a pool, you can often do a short dive from shore. Here are some of our favorite diving and snorkeling destinations. Nor surprisingly, these are often in tropical climates.

■ **Anegada, British Virgin Islands.** The reefs surrounding this flat coral and limestone atoll are a sailor's nightmare but a scuba diver's dream.

■ **Bimini, Bahamas.** The rocks at Bimini Beach, which have abundant sea life, lie in just 20 feet of water.

■ **Cozumel, Mexico.** Because reefs are abundant and close to shore, most swimmers don masks and snorkels even if they're just paddling about beside the beach at their hotel.

■ **Florida Keys, Florida.** Long Key offers great snorkeling as well as bonefishing.

■ **Maui, Hawai'i.** The island's Molokini Crater is a snorkeler's dream.

■ **San Diego, California.** La Jolla Cove has some of the best shore diving in Southern California.

■ **Tobago Cays, St. Vincent and the Grenadines.** A group of five uninhabited islands surrounds a beautiful lagoon studded with sponges, coral formations, and countless colorful fish.

■ **Turks and Caicos Islands.** The world's third-largest coral reef is visible from the air and packed with exotic marine life,

dramatic wall drop-offs, colorful fans, and pristine coral formations.

Golf

What's better than playing the back 9 shaded by swaying palm trees with a view of the crashing surf? What about teeing off above a sheer cliff as the waves crash on the shore below? Golfers are drawn to courses with stunning views, often attached to comfortable and luxurious resorts, where the rest of the family can lounge by the pool while you head off for a morning or afternoon round of golf. Here are a few of our favorite golf destinations that happen to be along beautiful beaches.

■ **Cape Charles, Virginia.** Clean, uncrowded public beaches beckon, as do a marina and renowned golf courses.

■ **Lana'i, Hawai'i.** The island has just three courses, but they are all good.

■ **Los Cabos, Mexico.** Los Cabos has become one of the world's top golf destinations, with championship courses that combine lush greens and desert terrain.

■ **Myrtle Beach, South Carolina.** Some 120 golf courses at all skill levels meander through pine forests, dunes, and marshes.

■ **Naples, Florida.** With several good courses, Naples is a good place to combine a beach and golf vacation.

■ **Nevis, St. Kitts and Nevis.** Robert Trent Jones Jr.'s wicked layout at the Four Seasons Resort incorporates ravines and sugar mills, making this island well above par.

■ **Punta Cana, Dominican Republic.** The first of three Jack Nicklaus–designed courses at the new Cap Cana development in Punta Cana has already hosted one PGA championship event.

IF YOU LIKE

History

Since civilizations often evolve around the coast, it's not surprising that there's history to be discovered near some of North America's best beaches. Here are some of the more interesting beach destinations that are near important historic sights.

■ **Antigua.** An impeccable restoration of Lord Horatio Nelson's 18th-century headquarters has delightful hotels, restaurants, and crafts shops.

■ **Cape Cod, Massachusetts.** At Eastham's popular First Encounter Beach, a bronze plaque marks the spot where Myles Standish and his *Mayflower* buddies first encountered Native Americans in 1620.

■ **Charleston, South Carolina.** In addition to some nice beaches at Kiawah Island and Isle of Palms, Charleston has historic Ft. Sumter.

■ **Curaçao.** The Kurá Hulanda Museum is at the heart of a rebirth for Curaçao.

■ **Kure Beach, North Carolina.** This area offers Fort Fisher State Historic Site as well as one of North Carolina's three aquariums. The Wright Brothers first took flight in Kitty Hawk.

■ **Montego Bay, Jamaica.** Jamaica is home to many former plantation great houses but none with as rich a history as Rose Hall. Appleton Estate offers a terrific guided tour on the history of rum making.

■ **Tulum, Mexico.** The biggest draw to Tulum's beaches is the fact they are surrounded by ancient Mayan ruins.

Nightlife

A beach vacation doesn't end at sundown. If you are looking for something to spice up your nights as well as your days, these beach destinations may do the trick.

■ **Aruba.** While it's not everyone's cup of tea, Aruba has a vibrant nighttime scene. You definitely do not have to wait until spring to break free here.

■ **Honolulu, Hawai'i.** The largest city in Hawai'i has hot restaurants and lively nightlife as well as gorgeous white-sand beaches.

■ **Jamaica.** Reggae Sumfest is the big summer music festival. Both Montego Bay's so-called Hip Strip and Negril's Norman Manley Boulevard are lined with bars and clubs.

■ **Los Angeles, California.** Both Venice and Santa Monica are within easy striking distance of the city's famed nightlife, and both offer great beaches.

■ **Miami, Florida.** Vacations here are as much about lifestyle as locale, so prepare for power shopping, club hopping, and decadent dining.

■ **Puerto Rico.** With a full range of bars, nightclubs, and every form of entertainment, San Juan is a big small city that never sleeps.

■ **Puerto Vallarta, Mexico.** Ecotour opportunities abound, but most people come to party—outside of Acapulco, PV has the Pacific Coast's most sophisticated nightlife.

■ **Seaside Heights, New Jersey.** Seaside Heights is a showcase of debauchery and nightclub mayhem, the wildest town on the Jersey Shore.

Shopping

The second-most popular activity on a vacation (other than sightseeing) is shopping. Many people who go on a beach vacation still want to escape to the outlet mall or find a unique boutique to spend their money on something other than taffy or a postcard. If you want to bring home

more than just a vial of sand, here are some beach destinations that also offer great shopping opportunities.

■ **Bandon, Oregon.** The town is famous for its cranberry products and its cheese factory, as well as its artists' colony, complete with galleries and shops.

■ **Kittery, Maine.** Known as the "Gateway to Maine," Kittery has come to more recent light as a major shopping destination thanks to its complex of factory outlets.

■ **Lewes and Rehoboth Beach, Delaware.** Along Route 1, from Lewes to Rehoboth, are three large outlet centers with name-brand stores.

■ **Nassau, Bahamas.** With its proximity to Paradise Island, Nassau's famous straw market draws tourists for bargains on locally made crafts.

■ **Newport Beach, California.** This tony retreat for the über-wealthy has good beaches as well as great upscale shopping opportunities, and nearby outlet malls cater to the less-well-heeled.

■ **San Juan, Puerto Rico.** From the boutiques of Old San Juan to ateliers of the young designers elsewhere in metro San Juan to galleries scattered all over the island, there's plenty to see and buy.

■ **St. Barthélemy.** Without a doubt, the shopping here for luxury goods and fashion is the best in the Caribbean.

■ **St. Thomas, U.S. Virgin Islands.** Main Street in Charlotte Amalie is well known for numerous duty-free shops, selling everything from rum to designer fashions and gems.

Staying Active

There's much more to do on a vacation than simply lie on the beach, sip a cool drink, or play a round of golf. If you would rather hike, kayak, sail, or windsurf than lie on the beach all day, consider these popular beach destinations that have more activities to offer.

■ **Cabarete, Dominican Republic.** The windsurfing capital of the DR's North Shore, Cabarete has great resorts as well as beautiful beaches.

■ **Florida, Keys, Florida.** The Keys are nirvana for anglers, divers, book lovers, and Jimmy Buffet wannabes.

■ **Maui, Hawai'i.** Maui is the most diversified Hawaiian island, perfect for families with divergent interests and offering every activity imaginable.

■ **Ocho Rios, Jamaica.** Headquartered at the Ocho Rios polo fields, Chukka Caribbean Adventures is now Jamaica's top soft-adventure outfitter, having added canopy tours, river rafting, and more to its excellent horseback-riding program.

■ **Orange County, California.** Doheny State Beach is one of Southern California's top surfing destinations.

■ **Seattle, Washington.** Alki Beach is always busy with in-line skaters, joggers, and cyclists sharing the walkway, and sun-loving singles playing volleyball and flirting.

■ **Ventura, California.** Miles of beautiful beaches attract both athletes—bodysurfers and boogie-boarders, runners and bikers—and those who'd rather doze beneath a rented umbrella all day.

■ **Vieques, Puerto Rico.** Vieques's bioluminescent bay is best experienced on a kayak tour on a moonless night, when every stroke makes the water light up.

■ **Virginia Beach, Virginia.** A wide variety of water sports is available, including diving, kayaking, and fishing from several local outfitters.

IF YOU LIKE

Staying on a Budget

Going to the beach isn't all about five-star resorts. Here are some destinations where you can sleep for much less and still have a great time.

- **Big Island, Hawai'i.** If you don't mind staying off the beach, the Big Island has plenty of accommodating lodges and guesthouses that can help you keep costs down, and there are hundreds of condo rentals in Kailua-Kona.

- **Cancún, Mexico.** A favorable exchange rate, excellent restored beaches, and wide choice of hotels in all price ranges makes Cancún a good value, especially for Americans.

- **Cannon Beach, Oregon.** One of the most charming hamlets on the coast, the town has beachfront homes and hotels, and a weathered-cedar downtown shopping district.

- **Daytona Beach, Florida.** Proximity to NASCAR and great beaches means there is a lot to do, and a wide range of accommodations options keeps costs down.

- **Dominican Republic.** The best value in the Caribbean offers great beaches and a host of all-inclusive and non-inclusive resort options at all price levels.

- **Gulf Shores, Alabama.** The soft, white sandy beaches rival those in Florida. But with fewer crowds, they can provide an ideal spot for family vacations.

- **Pismo Beach, California.** With 20 mi of sandy shoreline and a wide variety of accommodations options, this resort area attracts many locals, especially from the Central Valley.

Sleeping in the Lap of Luxury

The most luxurious resorts are worlds unto themselves. If you are looking to splurge, these are the best places to do it.

- **Anguilla.** Known for its luxury resorts, beautiful beaches, and good restaurants, Anguilla is one of the best Caribbean islands to splurge.

- **Barbados.** Elegant and stylish upscale resorts are the specialty of this very British Caribbean destination.

- **The Hamptons, New York.** The playground of New York City's rich and famous offers luxurious house rentals, upscale hotels, and extravagant restaurants.

- **Harbour Island, Bahamas.** With some of the country's best beaches and most luxurious resorts, Harbour Island has been called the Nantucket of the Bahamas.

- **Kaua'i, Hawai'i.** Kaua'i's excellent resorts offer complete indulgence in a paradisiacal tropical setting.

- **Los Cabos, Mexico.** With expensive spa resorts and excellent golf courses, Los Cabos is the best place in Mexico to pull out your platinum card.

- **Monterey Peninsula, California.** Luxurious small inns and larger resorts, proximity to an excellent golf course, and a great deal of charm make the Monterey Peninsula a great place to splurge.

- **Palm Beach, Florida.** With Gatsby-era architecture, extravagant resorts, and highbrow shops, Palm Beach is Florida's ultimate place to splurge.

- **St. Barthélemy.** St. Barth's hotels are all small, expensive, and exclusive, but they offer pampering service, proximity to good restaurants, and great low-key nightlife—all for a price.

The Perfect Honeymoon Destination

Swaying palms, moonlight strolls on the beach, candlelit dinners: no wonder the beach is a favorite honeymoon destination. Whatever you are looking for in a honeymoon—seclusion, privacy, or more

active fun—you can certainly find it, and it will usually be on a perfect beach. Our favorites run the gamut, so if you need a place with easy access, or if you want to really get away from it all, we have the perfect spot.

■ **Amelia Island, Florida.** The shores of Amelia Island puts you close to nature, and a great resort keeps you comfortable.

■ **The Grenadines.** Several private-island resorts offer the perfect private getaway for a honeymoon.

■ **Maui, Hawai'i.** Offering a little bit of everything, including myriad activities and both luxurious resorts and more reasonably priced condos, Maui is the perfect tropical retreat.

■ **Nantucket, Massachusetts.** Small inns help you get away from the crowds while increasingly good restaurants are a short trip away.

■ **Riviera Maya, Mexico.** Quieter than Cancún or Cozumel but still with lovely beaches, great resorts, and even a bit of history, the Riviera Maya is a great destination for honeymooners.

■ **St. Lucia.** One of the Caribbean's top honeymoon destinations offers dazzling scenery, good beaches, and great diving.

■ **Turks and Caicos Islands.** Some of the most beautiful beaches in the Caribbean and luxury accommodations offer an ideal spot for a warm getaway.

Eating Well

For many people, eating at great restaurants is every bit as important as lounging on a beautiful beach. Great restaurants aren't always expensive, but they generally make the most use of fresh local ingredients. For those who want both, here are some of our favorite destinations with great food.

■ **Anguilla.** This small island is known for three things: excellent soft-sand beaches, exquisite luxury resorts, and great independent restaurants. In a Caribbean increasingly turned over to mediocre all-inclusive resorts, the lively dining scene here is welcome.

■ **Cape Cod, Massachusetts.** While Cape restaurants aren't always upscale, the variety of locally caught seafood is abundant and abundantly good

■ **Cayman Islands.** Grand Cayman's best restaurants include a Caribbean outpost of a New York City four-star chef and just about anything else you can imagine, from the freshest fish to the elegant atmosphere of the Grand Old House.

■ **Los Angeles, California.** With one of the widest selections of restaurants in the state (as well as some of the best beaches in Southern California), L.A. is a great destination for foodies, regardless of their preferences.

■ **Maui, Hawai'i.** In the mid-1990s, Maui emerged as a gastronomic force, the birthplace of Hawaiian regional cuisine, and many of the original chefs involved in the movement still live and operate their own restaurants on Maui.

■ **Miami, Florida.** The stand-out city in South Florida's dining scene offers Latin-accented food as well as every other option under the sun.

■ **St. Maarten/St. Martin.** The island's French side is renowned for its cuisine capital, Grand Case, but there are some excellent restaurants on the Dutch side as well.

BEACH SAFETY

Ocean safety is of the utmost importance when visiting any beach destination. Don't swim alone, and follow the international signage posted at beaches that alerts swimmers to strong currents, dangerous sea creatures, sharp coral, high surf, and dangerous shore breaks.

Coral. Coral is sharp and should be avoided; if you scratch yourself on coral (even if it's a relatively small scratch), be sure to get medical attention since these wounds can become infected easily. So-called "fire coral" (which are not true corals at all but related to jellyfish) have a painful sting.

Crime. Despite the beauty of the beach, crime does still occur in beach destinations. When visiting remote beaches, don't leave any valuables in your car. And while on the beach, don't leave valuables on the sand while you dash into the water. If someone can't stay behind, consider a waterproof plastic box to carry cards and some money. Wear a waterproof watch that you don't have to leave behind, and consider not bringing cameras or valuable electronics.

Insects. The worst insects you will encounter in any beach destination may well be the tiny no-see-ums (sand fleas) that appear especially after a rain, near swampy ground, and at the beach around sunset; there are no sand fleas in Hawai'i, however. Mosquitoes can also be annoying and, more important, may be carriers of dengue fever, a viral disease that is a growing concern in many warm climates of the northern hemisphere. Malaria has been reported in some areas of the Caribbean and Mexico, but malaria is not a pervasive problem in most of the tourist areas.

Rip Currents. If you plan to swim, note the water's condition. Rip currents, caused when the tide rushes out through a narrow break in the water, can overpower even the strongest swimmer. If you do get caught in one, resist the urge to swim straight to shore—you'll tire long before you make it. Instead, swim parallel to the shoreline until you are outside the current's pull, then head to shore.

Sea Urchins. Watch out for black spiny sea urchins that live on the rocky sea floor in both shallow and deep waters. Stepping on one is guaranteed to be painful for quite some time, as the urchin releases its spikes into the offending body. To remove a spike, simply pull it out and apply an antiseptic. To remove an embedded spike, first apply some warm oil (preferably olive oil) to soften and dilate the skin and then remove the spike with a sterile needle.

Sharks. Despite what you may believe from seeing *Shark Week* television shows, shark attacks are rare, though they do happen, especially in Hawai'i and Florida. Be aware of your surroundings and heed any warnings that are posted.

Sunburn. The major health risk in most beach destinations isn't sharks or riptides, it's sunburn or sunstroke. Having available a long-sleeve shirt, a hat, and a beach wrap is essential on a boat or midday at any beach, especially in warmer climates that are closer to the equator. Use sunscreen with an SPF of at least 15 (preferably 30 or more) and apply it liberally to your nose, ears, and other sensitive and exposed areas. Reapply sunscreen whenever you go in the water.

Best Beaches on the West Coast

WHAT'S WHERE

1 San Diego. San Diego's historic Gaslamp Quarter and Mexican-theme Old Town have a human scale—but it's big-ticket animal attractions like SeaWorld and the San Diego Zoo that pull in planeloads of visitors.

2 Orange County. The real OC is a diverse destination with premium resorts, first-rate restaurants, strollable waterfront communities, and kid-friendly attractions.

3 Los Angeles. Go for the glitz of the entertainment industry, but stay for the rich cultural attributes and myriad communities of people from different cultures.

4 The Central Coast. Three of the state's top stops—swanky Santa Barbara, Hearst Castle, and Big Sur—sit along the scenic 200-mi route.

5 Monterey Bay Area. Postcard-perfect Monterey, Victorian-flavor Pacific Grove, exclusive Carmel, and counterculture all share this stretch of California Coast. To the north, Santa Cruz boasts a boardwalk, a UC campus, ethnic clothing shops, and plenty of surfers.

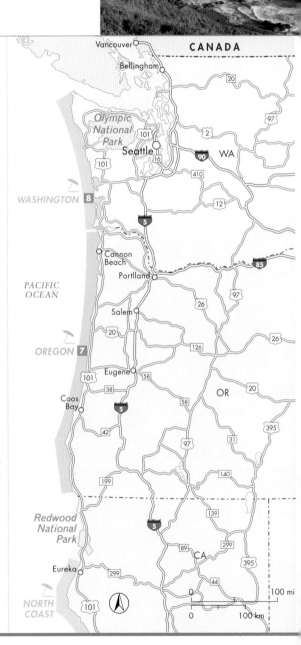

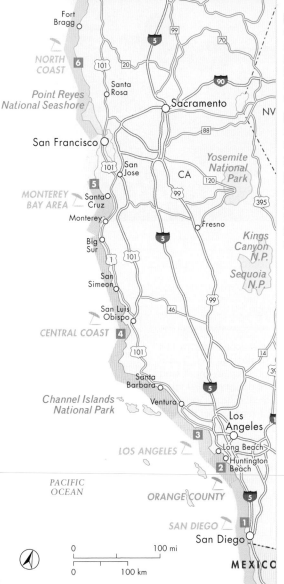

6 The North Coast. The star attractions here are the natural ones, from the secluded beaches and wave-battered bluffs of Point Reyes National Seashore to the towering redwood forests.

7 Oregon. Beautiful beaches line the 300-mi-long Oregon Coast, none of which is in private hands.

8 Washington. Mostly rocky with a few sandy beaches, Washington's coast is windswept and rugged but beautiful and beckons to beachcombers.

SAN DIEGO

San Diego's shore shimmers with crystalline Pacific waters rolling up to some of the prettiest stretches of sand on the West Coast, the most pristine of which are in La Jolla.

(this page, above) La Jolla Cove; (opposite page upper right) A jogger in Torrey Pines State Beach and Reserve; (opposite page lower left) Black's Beach

San Diego is a big California city—second only to Los Angeles in population—with a small-town feel. It also covers a lot of territory, roughly 400 square mi of land and sea. To the north and south of the city are 70 mi of beaches. Water temperatures in the Pacific are generally chilly, ranging from 55°F to 65°F from October through June, and 65°F to 75°F from July through September. And pollution, which has long been a problem near the Mexican border, is inching north and is generally worse near river mouths and storm drain outlets—especially within 72 hours of a rainstorm in the region. Finding a parking spot near the ocean can be hard in summer, but for the time being, unmetered parking is at all San Diego city beaches. Del Mar has a pay lot and metered street parking around the 15th Street beach.

HOTEL DEL CORONADO

One of San Diego's best-known sites, the hotel has been a National Historic Landmark since 1977. It has a colorful history, integrally connected with that of Coronado itself, making it worth a visit even if you don't stay here. Tours of the Del are available Tuesday at 10:30 and Friday to Sunday at 2 for $15 per person. Reservations are required through the Coronado Visitor Center.

2

CORONADO

Quiet **Silver Strand State Beach** is ideal for families; the water is relatively calm, lifeguards and rangers are on duty year-round, and there are places to rollerblade or ride bikes. With the famous Hotel Del Coronado as a backdrop, **Coronado Beach** is one of San Diego County's largest and most picturesque. It's perfect for sunbathing, people-watching, or Frisbee playing.

MISSION BAY

Mission Beach, San Diego's most popular beach, draws huge crowds on hot summer days, but is lively year-round. The 2-mi-long stretch extends from the north entrance of Mission Bay to **Pacific Beach**. A wide boardwalk paralleling the beach is popular with walkers, joggers, roller skaters, bladers, and bicyclists. Surfers, swimmers, and volleyball players congregate at the south end.

LA JOLLA

Wide and sandy, **Marine Street Beach** often teems with sunbathers, swimmers, walkers, and joggers. The water is known as a great spot for bodysurfing, although the waves break in extremely shallow water and you'll need to watch out for riptides. **La Jolla Cove** is one of the prettiest spots on the West Coast; a palm-lined park sits on top of cliffs formed by the incessant pounding of the waves. Divers, snorkelers, and kayakers can explore the underwater delights

of the San Diego–La Jolla Underwater Park Ecological Reserve. **La Jolla Shores** is one of San Diego's most popular beaches, with an incredible view of La Jolla Peninsula, a wide sandy beach, an adjoining grassy park, and the gentlest waves in San Diego. The powerful waves at **Black's Beach**, officially known as Torrey Pines City Park Beach, attract world-class surfers, and its relative isolation appeals to nudist nature lovers (although by law nudity is prohibited) as well as gays and lesbians.

DEL MAR

Torrey Pines State Beach and Reserve, one of San Diego's best beaches, encompasses 12,000 acres of bluffs and bird-filled marshes. A network of meandering trails leads to the sandy shoreline below. Along the way enjoy the rare Torrey pine trees, found only here and on Santa Rosa Island, offshore.

ENCINITAS

Palms and the golden lotus-flower domes of the nearby Self-Realization Center temple and ashram earned picturesque **Swami's** its name. Extreme low tides expose tide pools that harbor anemones, starfish, and other sea life. The beach is also a top surfing spot; the only access is by a long stairway leading down from cliff-top **Seaside Roadside Park**, where there's free parking.

ORANGE COUNTY

Few of the citrus groves that gave Orange County its name remain. This region south and east of Los Angeles is now ruled by tourism and high-tech business instead of farmers.

(this page above) Huntington Beach; (opposite page upper right) Dana Beach; (opposite page lower left) A surfer at Newport Beach

With its tropical flowers and palm trees, the stretch of coast between Seal Beach and San Clemente is often called the California Riviera. Exclusive Newport Beach, artsy Laguna, and the surf town of Huntington Beach are the stars, but lesser-known gems on the glistening coast—such as Corona del Mar—are also worth visiting. Running along the Orange County coastline is scenic Pacific Coast Highway (Highway 1, known locally as PCH). Older beachfront settlements, with their modest bungalow-style homes, are joined by posh new gated communities. The pricey land between Newport Beach and Laguna Beach is where Laker Kobe Bryant, novelist Dean Koontz, and a slew of Internet and finance moguls live. Though the coastline is rapidly being filled in, there are still a few stretches of beautiful, protected open land. And at many places along the way you can catch an idealized glimpse of surfers hitting the beach, boards under their arms.

SURFING GREATS

Many of the world's most famous surfers are represented on the **Surfing Walk of Fame** (✉ *Along Main St. and Pacific Coast Hwy., Huntington Beach*), including Robert August, the star of *Endless Summer,* Corky Carroll, a pioneer surfing promoter; and Mark Richard, winner of the most surfing championships. Super-surfers have been selected since 1994 by a committee representing the surfing industry worldwide.

HUNTINGTON BEACH

Once sleepy Huntington Beach has transformed itself into a resort destination. The town's appeal is its broad white-sand beaches with often-towering waves, complemented by a lively pier, shops, and restaurants on Main Street and luxury resort hotels. **Huntington City Beach** stretches north and south of the town's pier for 3 mi. **Huntington State Beach** is south of town, while **Bolsa Chica** is north of the city.

NEWPORT BEACH

This tony retreat for the über-wealthy has good beaches on **Balboa Peninsula**, where many jetties pave the way to ideal swimming areas. The most intense bodysurfing place in Orange County and arguably on the West Coast, known as the **Wedge**, is at the south end of the peninsula. Nearby outlet malls draw almost as many visitors as the beaches.

CORONA DEL MAR

A small jewel on the Pacific Coast, Corona del Mar (known by locals as "CDM") has exceptional beaches that some say resemble their majestic Northern California counterparts. **Corona del Mar State Beach** is actually made up of two beaches, Little Corona and Big Corona, separated by a cliff.

LAGUNA BEACH

While this artsy town is filled with fine art galleries, it also has 7 mi of beaches (a protected marine preserve) that are

among the loveliest in California. The **Main Beach Park**, at the end of Broadway at South Coast Highway, has a wooden boardwalk where you can watch people bodysurfing, playing sand volleyball, or scrambling around one of two half-basketball courts. **1,000 Steps Beach**, off South Coast Highway at 9th Street, is a hard-to-find locals' spot with great waves. **Woods Cove**, off South Coast Highway at Diamond Street, is especially quiet during the week. Big rock formations hide lurking crabs. Climbing the steps to leave, you can see a Tudor-style mansion that was once the home of Bette Davis.

DANA POINT

Dana Point's claim to fame is its small-boat marina tucked into a dramatic natural harbor and surrounded by high bluffs. At the south end of Dana Point, **Doheny State Beach** is one of Southern California's top surfing destinations. Divers and anglers hang out at the beach's western end (and at the fishing pier), and during low tide, the tide pools beckon both young and old. You'll also find five indoor tanks and an interpretive center devoted to the wildlife of the Doheny Marine Refuge. The beachfront campground here is one of the most popular in the state with 120 no-hookup sites.

LOS ANGELES

Getting some sand on the floor of your car is practically a requirement here, and the beach is an integral part of the Southern California lifestyle.

(this page above) Venice Beach boardwalk; (opposite page upper right) Sunset at the Santa Monica Pier; (opposite page lower left) Malibu Pier

From downtown, the easiest way to hit the coast is by taking the Santa Monica Freeway (I–10) due west. Once you reach the end of the freeway, I–10 runs into the famous Highway 1, leading you north to Malibu, with Zuma Beach at its northern edge, or south to Redondo Beach. Generally, the northernmost beaches are best for surfing, hiking, and fishing, and the wider and sandier southern beaches are better for tanning and relaxing. Almost all are great for swimming, but beware: pollution in Santa Monica Bay sometimes approaches dangerous levels, particularly after storms. Los Angeles County beaches (and state beaches operated by the county) have lifeguards on duty year-round, with expanded forces in summer. Public parking is usually available, though fees can be as much as $8; in some areas, it's possible to find free street and highway parking.

SURF CITY

Nothing captures the laid-back cool of California quite like surfing. Those wanting to sample the surf here should keep a few things in mind before getting wet. First, surfers can be notoriously territorial. Beginners should avoid Palos Verdes and Third Point, at the north end of Malibu Lagoon State Beach, where veterans rule the waves. Once in the water, be as polite and mellow as possible.

2

MALIBU

On the very edge of Ventura County, narrow **Leo Carrillo State Beach** is better for exploring than for sunning or swimming (watch that strong undertow!). Sequit Point, which divides the northwest and southeast halves of the beach, creates secret coves, sea tunnels, and boulders on which you can perch and fish. **Robert H. Meyer Memorial State Beach** is made up of three mini-beaches: El Pescador, La Piedra, and El Matador—all with the same spectacular view. "El Mat" has a series of caves, Piedra some nifty rock formations, and Pescador a secluded feel; but they're all picturesque and fairly private. **Zuma Beach Park,** 2 mi of white sand usually littered with tanning teenagers, has it all: from fishing and diving to swings for the kids to volleyball courts. Beachgoers looking for quiet or privacy should head elsewhere. **Malibu Lagoon State Beach/Surfrider Beach** offers steady 3- to 5-foot waves, making this beach, just west of Malibu Pier, a surfing paradise. The International Surfing Contest is held here in September—the surf's premium around that time.

PACIFIC PALISADES

Will Rogers State Beach clean, sandy, 3-mi beach, has a dozen volleyball nets, gymnastics equipment, and playground equipment for kids, and is an all-around favorite. The surf is gentle, perfect for swimmers and beginning surfers.

SANTA MONICA

Santa Monica State Beach the first beach you'll hit after the Santa Monica Freeway (I–10) runs into the PCH, and it's one of L.A.'s best known. Wide and sandy, Santa Monica is the place for sunning and socializing: be prepared for a mob scene on summer weekends, when parking becomes an expensive ordeal. Swimming is fine (with the usual post-storm pollution caveat); for surfing, go elsewhere.

VENICE

The surf and sand of **Venice City Beach** are fine, but the main attraction here is the boardwalk scene, which is a cosmos all its own—with fire-eating street performers, vendors hawking everything from cheap sunglasses and aromatherapy oils, and bicep'ed gym rats lifting weights at legendary Muscle Beach. Go on weekend afternoons for the best people-watching experience.

REDONDO BEACH

The **Redondo Beach** Pier marks the starting point of this wide, sandy, busy beach along a heavily developed shoreline community. Restaurants and shops flourish along the pier, excursion boats and privately owned crafts depart from launching ramps, and a reef formed by a sunken ship creates prime fishing and snorkeling conditions.

THE ULTIMATE ROAD TRIP

CALIFORNIA'S LEGENDARY HIGHWAY 1

by Cheryl Crabtree

One of the world's most scenic drives, California's State Route 1 (also known as Highway 1, the Pacific Coast Highway, the PCH) stretches along the edge of the state for nearly 660 miles, from Southern California's Dana Point to its northern terminus near Leggett, about 40 miles north of Fort Bragg. As you travel south to north, the water's edge transitions from long, sandy beaches and low-lying bluffs to towering dunes, craggy cliffs, and ancient redwood groves. The ocean changes as well; the relatively tame and surfable swells lapping the Southern California shore give way to the frigid, powerful waves crashing against weatherbeaten rocks in the north.

Ft. Bragg
Mendocino
SONOMA COUNTY
Point Reyes National Seashore
MARIN COUNTY
Marin Headlands
Sacramento
San Francisco
San Jose
17-Mile Drive
Monterey
Carmel
Big Sur
Fresno
Hearst San Simeon State Historical Monument
San Luis Obispo
Santa Barbara
Santa Monica
Los Angeles
Long Beach

HIGHWAY 1 TOP 10

- Santa Monica
- Santa Barbara
- Hearst San Simeon State Historical Monument
- Big Sur
- Carmel
- 17–Mile Drive
- Monterey
- San Francisco
- Marin Headlands
- Point Reyes National Seashore

(opposite) Highway 1 near Mill Creek, Big Sur

STARTING YOUR JOURNEY

You may decide to drive the road's entire 660-mile route, or bite off a smaller piece. In either case, a Highway 1 road trip allows you to experience California at your own pace, stopping when and where you wish. Hike a beachside trail, dig your toes in the sand, and search for creatures in the tidepools. Buy some artichokes and strawberries from a roadside farmstand. Talk to people along the way (you'll run into everyone from soul-searching meditators, farmers, and beatniks to city-slackers and working-class folks), and take lots of pictures. Don't rush—you could easily spend a lifetime discovering secret spots along this route.

To help you plan your trip, we've broken the road into three regions (Santa Monica to Carmel, Carmel to San Francisco, and San Francisco to Fort Bragg); each region is then broken up into smaller segments—many of which are suitable for a day's drive. If you're pressed for time, you can always tackle a section of Highway 1, and then head inland to U.S. 101 or I-5 to reach your next destination more quickly.

(top) Give yourself lots of extra time to pull off the road and enjoy the scenery, (opposite) Aerial of winding road Shoreline Highway on west coast with Pacific Ocean in California.

HIGHWAY 1 DRIVING

- Rent a convertible (You will not regret it).

- Begin the drive north from Santa Monica, where congestion and traffic delays pose less of a problem.

- Mind your manners on the freeway. Don't tailgate or glare at other drivers, and don't fly the finger.

- If you're prone to motion sickness, take the wheel yourself. Focusing on the landscape outside should help you feel less queasy.

- If you're afraid of heights, drive from south to north so you'll be on the mountain rather than the cliff side of the road.

WHAT'S IN A NAME?

Though it's often referred to as the Pacific Coast Highway (or PCH), sections of Highway 1 actually have different names. The southernmost section (Dana Point to Oxnard) is the Pacific Coast Highway. After that, the road becomes the Cabrillo Highway (Las Cruces to Lompoc), the Big Sur Coast Highway (San Luis Obispo County line to Monterey), the North Coast Scenic Byway (San Luis Obispo city limit to the Monterey County line), the Cabrillo Highway again (Santa Cruz County line to Half Moon Bay), and finally the Shoreline Highway (Marin City to Leggett). To make matters more confusing, smaller chunks of the road have additional honorary monikers.

Just follow the green triangular signs that say "California 1."

HIGHWAY 1: SANTA MONICA TO BIG SUR

Hearst Castle

THE PLAN

Distance: approx. 335 mi

Time: 3-5 days

Good Overnight Options: Malibu, Santa Barbara, Pismo Beach, San Luis Obispo, Cambria, Carmel

SANTA MONICA TO MALIBU (approx. 26 mi)

Highway 1 begins in Dana point, but it seems more appropriate to begin a PCH adventure in **Santa Monica.** Be sure to experience the beach culture, then balance the tacky pleasures of Santa Monica's amusement pier with a stylish dinner in a neighborhood restaurant.

MALIBU TO SANTA BARBARA (approx. 70 mi)

The PCH follows the curve of Santa Monica Bay all the way to **Malibu** and **Point Mugu,** near **Oxnard.** Chances are you'll experience *déjà vu* driving this 27-mile stretch: mountains on one side, ocean on the other, opulent homes perched on hillsides; you've seen this piece of coast countless times on TV and film. Be sure to walk out on the **Malibu Pier** for a great photo opp, then check out **Surfrider Beach,** with three famous points where perfect waves ignited a worldwide surfing rage in the 1960s.

After Malibu you'll drive through miles of protected, largely unpopulated coastline. Ride a wave at **Zuma Beach,** scout for offshore whales at **Point Dume State Preserve,** or hike the trails at **Point Mugu State Park.** After skirting Point Mugu, Highway 1 merges with U.S. 101 for about 70 mi before reaching **Santa Barbara.** A mini-tour of the city includes a real Mexican lunch at **La Super-Rica,** a visit to the magnificent **Spanish Mission Santa Barbara,** and a walk down hopping **State Street to Stearns Wharf.**

SANTA BARBARA TO SAN SIMEON (approx. 147 mi)

North of Santa Barbara, Highway 1 morphs into the Cabrillo Highway, separating from and then rejoining U.S. 101. The route winds through rolling vineyards and rangeland to **San Luis Obispo,** where any legit road trip

Santa Barbara

includes a photo stop at the wacky, pink **Madonna Inn.** Be sure to also climb the humungous dunes at **Guadalupe-Nipomo Dunes Preserve.**

In downtown San Luis Obispo, the **Mission San Luis Obispo de Tolosa** stands by a tree-shaded creek edged with shops and cafés. Highway 1 continues to **Morro Bay** and up the coast. About 15 mi north of Morro Bay, you'll reach the town of **Harmony** (population 18), a tiny burg with artists' studios, a wedding chapel, shops, and a winery. The road continues through **Cambria** to solitary **Hearst San Simeon State Historical Monument**—the art-filled pleasure palace at **San Simeon.** Just four miles north of the castle, elephant seals grunt and cavort at the **Piedras Blancas Elephant Seal Rookery,** just off the side of the road.

Santa Monica

Big Sur

TOP 5 PLACES TO LINGER

- Point Dume State Preserve
- Santa Barbara
- Hearst San Simeon State Historical Monument
- Big Sur/Julia Pfeiffer Burns State Park
- Carmel

SAN SIMEON TO CARMEL (approx. 92 mi)

Heading north, you'll drive through **Big Sur,** a place of ancient forests and rugged shoreline stretching 90 mi from San Simeon to **Carmel.** Much of Big Sur lies within several state parks and the 165,000-acre **Ventana Wilderness,** itself part of the **Los Padres National Forest.** This famously scenic stretch of the coastal drive, which twists up and down bluffs above the ocean, can last hours. Take your time.

At **Julia Pfeiffer Burns State Park** one easy but rewarding hike leads to an iconic waterfall off a beach-front cliff. When you reach lovely **Carmel,** stroll around the picture-perfect town's mission, galleries, and shops.

HIGHWAY 1: CARMEL TO SAN FRANCISCO

San Francisco

THE PLAN

Distance: approx. 123 mi

Time: 2-4 days

Good Overnight Options: Carmel, Monterey, Santa Cruz, Half Moon Bay, San Francisco

CARMEL TO MONTEREY (approx. 4 mi)

Between **Carmel** and **Monterey,** the Highway 1 cuts across the base of the Monterey Peninsula. Pony up the toll and take a brief detour to follow famous **17-Mile Drive,** which traverses a surf-pounded landscape of cypress trees, sea lions, gargantuan estates, and the world famous **Pebble Beach Golf Links.** Take your time here as well, and be sure to allow lots of time for pulling off to enjoy the gorgeous views.

If you have the time, spend a day checking out the sights in **Monterey,** especially the kelp forests and bat rays of the **Monterey Bay Aquarium** and the adobes and artifacts of **Monterey State Historic Park.**

MONTEREY TO SANTA CRUZ (approx. 42 mi)

From Monterey the highway rounds the gentle curve of Monterey Bay, passing through sand dunes and artichoke fields on its way to **Moss Landing** and the **Elkhorn Slough National Estuarine Marine Preserve.** Kayak or walk through the protected wetlands here, or board a pontoon safari boat—don't forget your binoculars. The historic seaside villages of **Aptos, Capitola,** and **Soquel,** just off the highway near the bay's midpoint, are ideal stopovers for beachcombing, antiquing, and hiking through redwoods. In boho **Santa Cruz,** just 7 mi north, walk along the **wharf,** ride the historic roller coaster on the **boardwalk,** and perch on the cliffs to watch surfers peel through tubes at **Steamers Lane.**

SANTA CRUZ TO SAN FRANCISCO (approx. 77 mi)

Highway 1 hugs the ocean's edge once again as it departs Santa Cruz and runs northward past a string of secluded beaches and small towns. Stop and stretch your legs in the tiny, artsy town

Davenport cliffs, Devenport

of **Davenport,** where you can wander through several galleries and enjoy sumptuous views from the bluffs. At **Año Nuevo State Reserve,** walk down to the dunes to view gargantuan elephant seals lounging on shore, then break for a meal or snack in **Pescadero** or **Half Moon Bay.**

FRIGID WATERS

If you're planning to jump in the ocean in Northern California, wear a wetsuit or prepare to shiver. Even in summer, the water temperatures warm up to just barely tolerable. The fog tends to burn off earlier in the day at relatively sheltered beaches near Monterey Bay's midpoint, near Aptos, Capitola and Santa Cruz. These beaches also tend to attract softer waves than those on the bay's outer edges.

Half Moon Bay

TOP 5 PLACES TO LINGER

- 17 Mile Drive
- Monterey
- Santa Cruz
- Año Nuevo State Reserve
- Half Moon Bay

From Half Moon Bay to **Daly City,** the road includes a number of shoulderless twists and turns that demand slower speeds and nerves of steel. Signs of urban development soon appear: mansions holding fast to Pacific cliffs and then, as the road veers slightly inland to merge with Skyline Boulevard, boxlike houses sprawling across **Daly City** and **South San Francisco.**

HIGHWAY 1: SAN FRANCISCO TO FORT BRAGG

Mendocino Coast Botanical Garden

THE PLAN

Distance: 177 mi

Time: 2-4 days

Good Overnight Options: San Francisco, Olema, Bodega Bay, Gualala, Mendocino, Fort Bragg

SAN FRANCISCO

The official Highway 1 heads straight through **San Francisco** along 19th Avenue through **Golden Gate Park** and the **Presidio** toward the **Golden Gate Bridge.** For a more scenic tour, watch for signs announcing exits for 35 North/Skyline Boulevard, then Ocean Beach/The Great Highway (past Lake Merced). The Great Highway follows the coast along the western border of San Francisco; you'll cruise past entrances to the **San Francisco Zoo, Golden Gate Park,** and the **Cliff House.** Hike out to **Point Lobos** or **Land's End** for awesome vistas, then drive through **Lincoln Park** and the **Palace of the Legion of**

Golden Gate Bridge

Honor and follow El Camino de Mar/Lincoln Boulevard all the way to the Golden Gate Bridge.

The best way to see San Francisco is on foot and public transportation. A **Union Square** stroll—complete with people-watching, window-shopping, and architecture-viewing—is a good first stop. In **Chinatown,** department stores give way to storefront temples, open-air markets, and delightful dim-sum shops. After lunch in one, catch a **Powell Street cable car** to the end of the line and get off to see the bay views and the antique arcade games at **Musée Mécanique** (the gem of otherwise mindless **Fisherman's Wharf**). For dinner and live music, try cosmopolitan **North Beach.**

SAN FRANCISCO TO OLEMA (approx. 37 mi)

Leaving the city the next day, your drive across the Golden Gate Bridge and a stop at a **Marin Headlands** overlook will yield memorable views (if fog hasn't socked in the bay). So will a hike in **Point Reyes National Seashore,** farther up Highway 1 (now called Shoreline Highway). On this wild swath of coast you'll likely be able to claim an unspoiled beach for yourself. You should expect

Point Reyes National Seashore

company, however, around the lighthouse at the tip of Point Reyes because year-round views—and seasonal elephant seal- and whale-watching—draw crowds. If you have time, poke around tiny **Olema,** which has some excellent restaurants, and **Inverness,** home to the famous Manka's Inverness Lodge.

OLEMA TO MENDOCINO (approx. 131 mi)

Passing only a few minuscule towns, this next stretch of Highway 1 showcases the northern coast in all its rugged glory. The reconstructed compound of eerily foreign buildings at **Fort Ross State Historic Park** recalls the era of Russian fur trading in California. Pull into **Gualala** for an espresso, a sandwich, and a little human contact before rolling onward. After another 50 mi of tranquil state beaches and parks

Point Reyes National Seashore

TOP 5 PLACES TO LINGER

- San Francisco
- Marin Headlands
- Point Reyes National Seashore
- Fort Ross State Historic Park
- Mendocino

you'll return to civilization in **Mendocino**.

MENDOCINO TO FORT BRAGG (approx. 9 mi)

Exploring Mendocino you may feel like you've fallen through a rabbit hole: the weather screams Northern California, but the 19th-century buildings—erected by homesick Yankee loggers—definitely say New England. Once you've browsed around the artsy shops, continue on to the **Mendocino Coast Botanical Gardens**; then travel back in time on the **Skunk Train**, which follows an old logging route from **Fort Bragg** deep into the redwood forest.

CALIFORNIA'S CENTRAL COAST

Balmy weather, glorious beaches, crystal-clear air, and serene landscapes have lured people to the Central Coast since prehistoric times. It's an ideal place to relax, slow down, and appreciate the good things in life.

(this page above) A beach near Santa Barbara; (opposite page upper right) Julia Pfeiffer Burns State Park, Big Sur; (opposite page lower left) Cliffs near Avila Beach

The Central Coast region begins about 60 mi north of Los Angeles, near the seaside city of Ventura. From there the coastline stretches north about 200 mi, winding through the small cities of Santa Barbara and San Luis Obispo, then north through the small towns of Morro Bay and Cambria to Carmel. The drive through this region, especially the section of Highway 1 from San Simeon to Big Sur, is one of the most scenic in the state. There's no doubt that Big Sur has some of the most dramatically beautiful beaches in all of California. But much of the Central Coast looks as wild and wonderful as it did centuries ago, and visitors will have myriad opportunities to kick back and revel in the casual California lifestyle. Surf, golf, kayak, hike, play tennis—or just hang out and enjoy the gorgeous scenery.

HEARST CASTLE

Hearst San Simeon State Historical Monument (more popularly known as "Hearst Castle") sits in solitary splendor atop La Cuesta Encantada (the Enchanted Hill) in San Simeon. Its buildings and gardens, designed by the architect Julia Morgan, spread over 127 acres that were the heart of newspaper magnate William Randolph Hearst's 250,000-acre ranch. It was given to California in 1958.

SANTA BARBARA

Santa Barbara's beaches don't have the big surf of the shoreline farther south, but they also don't have the crowds. The wide swath of sand at the east end of **Cabrillo Boulevard** on the harbor front is a great spot for people-watching. **East Beach** has sand volleyball courts, summertime lifeguard and sports competitions, and arts-and-crafts shows on Sunday and holidays. The usually gentle surf at **Arroyo Burro County Beach** makes it ideal for families with young children.

PISMO BEACH

About 20 mi of sandy shoreline begins at the town of **Pismo Beach**. The southern end of town runs along sand dunes, some of which are open to cars and off-road vehicles; sheltered by the dunes, a grove of eucalyptus trees attracts thousands of migrating monarch butterflies November through February. A long, broad beach fronts the center of town, where a municipal pier extends into the sea at the foot of shop-lined Pomeroy Street.

AVILA BEACH

Because the village of **Avila Beach** and the sandy, cove-front shoreline for which it's named face south into the Pacific Ocean, they get more sun and less fog than any other stretch of coast in the area. With its fortuitous climate and protected waters, Avila's public beach draws plenty of sunbathers and

families; weekends are very busy. The seaside promenade is lined with shops and hotels.

SOUTHERN BIG SUR

This especially rugged stretch of oceanfront is a rocky world of mountains, cliffs, and beaches. **Julia Pfeiffer Burns State Park** provides some fine hiking, from an easy ½-mi stroll with marvelous coastal views to a strenuous 6-mi trek through the redwoods. The big attraction here is an 80-foot waterfall that drops into the ocean.

CENTRAL BIG SUR

Through a hole in one of the gigantic boulders at secluded **Pfeiffer Beach**, you can watch the waves break first on the sea side and then on the beach side. Keep a sharp eye out for the unsigned road to the beach: it is the only ungated paved road branching west of Highway 1 between the post office and **Pfeiffer Big Sur State Park**. Among the many hiking trails at **Pfeiffer Big Sur State Park** is a short route through a redwood-filled valley that leads to a waterfall. You can double back or continue on the more difficult trail along the valley wall for views over miles of treetops to the sea. The Big Sur Station visitor center, off Highway 1, is less than ½ mi south of the park entrance.

THE MONTEREY BAY AREA

In the good life of Monterey Bay's coast-side towns, in the pleasures of its luxurious resorts, and in the vitality of its resplendent marine habitat, this piece of California shows off its natural appeal.

(this page above) Carmel Beach; (opposite page upper right) A boardwalk at Asilomar State Beach (opposite page lower left) Lovers Point Park, near Pacific Grove

North of Big Sur the coastline softens into lower bluffs, windswept dunes, pristine estuaries, and long, sandy beaches, bordering one of the world's most amazing marine environments—the Monterey Bay. On the Monterey Peninsula, at the southern end of the bay, are Carmel-by-the-Sea, Pacific Grove, and Monterey; Santa Cruz sits at the northern tip of the crescent. In between, Highway 1 cruises along the coastline, passing windswept beaches piled high with sand dunes. Along the route are wetlands, artichoke and strawberry fields, and workaday towns such as Castroville and Watsonville. Downtown Carmel-by-the-Sea and Monterey are walks through history. The bay itself is protected by the Monterey Bay National Marine Sanctuary, the nation's largest undersea canyon—bigger and deeper than the Grand Canyon. And of course, the backdrop of natural beauty is still everywhere to be seen.

WHALE-WATCHING

On their annual migration between the Bering Sea and Baja California, thousands of gray whales pass close by the Monterey Coast. They are sometimes visible through binoculars from shore, but a whale-watching cruise is the best way to get a close look at these magnificent mammals. The migration south takes place from December through March. January is prime viewing time.

CARMEL-BY-THE-SEA
Carmel-by-the-Sea's greatest attraction is its rugged coastline, with pine and cypress forests and countless inlets. **Carmel Beach**, an easy walk from downtown shops, has sparkling white sands and magnificent sunsets. **Carmel River State Beach** stretches for 106 acres along Carmel Bay and is adjacent to a bird sanctuary.

PACIFIC GROVE
The view of the coast is gorgeous from **Lovers Point Park**, on Ocean View Boulevard midway along the waterfront. The park's sheltered beach has a children's pool and picnic area, and the main lawn has a sand volleyball court and snack bar. **Asilomar State Beach**, 100 acres of beautiful coast, is on Sunset Drive between Point Pinos and the Del Monte Forest. The dunes, tidal pools, and pocket-size beaches form one of the region's richest areas for marine life. But the area may be best known for its annual pilgrimage of monarch butterflies, which still come from October through March.

APTOS
Backed by a redwood forest and facing the sea, downtown Aptos is a place of wooden walkways and false-fronted shops. Sandstone bluffs tower above **Seacliff State Beach**, a favorite of locals. You can fish off the pier, which leads out to a sunken World War I tanker ship.

CAPITOLA
The village of Capitola has been a seaside resort since the late 1800s, its walkable downtown jam-packed with casual eateries, surf shops, and ice-cream parlors. **New Brighton State Beach**, once the site of a Chinese fishing village, is now a popular surfing and camping spot. Its Pacific Migrations Visitor Center, opened in 2006, traces the history of immigrants who settled around Monterey Bay. New Brighton Beach connects with **Seacliff Beach**, and at low tide you can walk or run along this scenic stretch of sand for nearly 16 mi south.

SANTA CRUZ
Santa Cruz is less manicured than Carmel or Monterey. Long known for its surfing and its amusement-filled beach boardwalk, the town is a mix of grand Victorian-era homes and rinky-dink motels. Santa Cruz has been a seaside resort since the mid-19th century. Along one end of the broad, south-facing beach, the **Santa Cruz Beach** boardwalk celebrated its 100th anniversary in 2007. At the end of West Cliff Drive lies **Natural Bridges State Beach**, a stretch of soft sand edged with tide pools and sea-sculpted rock bridges. Surfers gather for spectacular waves and sunsets at **Pleasure Point**. **Steamer Lane**, near the lighthouse on West Cliff Drive, has a decent break. The area plays host to several competitions in summer.

CALIFORNIA'S NORTH COAST

The waters of the Pacific Ocean along the North Coast are fine for seals but not for people. When it comes to spectacular cliffs and seascapes, though, the North Coast beaches are second to none.

(this page above) A lighthouse at Point Reyes National Seashore; (opposite page upper right) The coast near Trinidad (opposite page lower left); Point Arena Lighthouse, near Mendocino

You can explore tidal pools, watch seabirds and sea lions, or dive for abalone—and you'll often have the beach all to yourself. South to north, Point Reyes National Seashore, the beaches in Manchester and Van Damme state parks, and the 10-mi strand in MacKerricher State Park are among the most notable. From any number of excellent observation points along the coast, you can watch gray whales during their annual winter migration season (mid-December to early April). In summer and fall you can see blue or humpback whales. Point Reyes Lighthouse, Gualala Point Regional Park, Point Arena Lighthouse, and Patrick's Point State Park are just a few of the places where you stand a good chance of spotting one of the giant sea creatures. Whale-watching cruises operate out of several towns, including Bodega Bay and Fort Bragg.

WHEN TO GO

The North Coast is a year-round destination. The migration of the Pacific gray whales is a wintertime phenomenon, which lasts roughly from mid-December to early April. Wildflowers follow the winter rain, as early as January in southern areas through June and July farther north. Summer is the high season for tourists, but spring, fall, and even winter are arguably better times to visit because everything is quieter.

POINT REYES NATIONAL SEASHORE

One of the Bay Area's most spectacular treasures and the only national seashore on the West Coast, the 66,500-acre **Point Reyes National Seashore** encompasses secluded beaches, rugged chaparral, and grasslands. **At Drakes Beach** the water is somewhat calm (often even swimmable), and there's a visitor center. Be sure to stop at the famous lighthouse.

GUALALA

This former lumber port on the Gualala River is the busiest town between Bodega Bay and Mendocino and has all the basic services plus a number of galleries and gift shops. **Gualala Point Regional Park**, 1 mi south of town, has a long, sandy beach, picnic areas and is an excellent whale-watching spot December through April.

POINT ARENA

Occupied by an odd mixture of long-time locals and long-haired surfers, this former timber town is partly New Age, partly rowdy—and always sleepy. For an outstanding view of the ocean and, in winter, migrating whales, take the marked road off Highway 1 north of town to the 115-foot Point Arena Lighthouse. The most notable beach is the one at **Manchester State Park**, 3 mi north of Point Arena, which has 5 mi of sandy, usually empty shoreline.

LITTLE RIVER

The town of Little River is not much more than a post office and a convenience store. Along its winding roads, though, you'll find numerous quiet inns with breathtaking ocean views. **Van Damme State Park** is best known for its beach and for being a prime abalone diving spot. The visitor center has displays on ocean life and Native American history.

FORT BRAGG

Three blocks west of Main Street in the commercial center of Mendocino County, a flat, dirt path leads to wild coastline where you can walk for miles in either direction along the bluffs. **Glass Beach** likely has more sea glass than you've ever seen in one place before. **MacKerricher State Park,** just north of Fort Bragg, includes 9 mi of sandy beach and several square miles of dunes. The headland is a good place for whale-watching from December to mid-April.

TRINIDAD

Trinidad, once a mining and whaling center, is now a quiet and genuinely charming community with enough sights and activities to entertain low-key visitors. Together, **Clam Beach County Park** and **Little River State Beach**, 6½ mi south of Trinidad, make a park that stretches from Trinidad to as far as one can see south. The sandy beach here is exceptionally wide and perfect for kids.

THE OREGON COAST

Oregon's coastline stretches south from Astoria to the California border, and while it's not a place you'd want to swim, the beaches here are among the most spectacular in the Pacific Northwest.

(this page above) Ecola State Park; (opposite page upper right) Oswald West State Park; (opposite page lower left) A forest near Cannon Beach

Oregon has 300 mi of white-sand beaches, not a grain of which is privately owned. U.S. 101, called Highway 101 by most Oregonians, parallels the coast along the length of the state. It winds past sea-tortured rocks, brooding headlands, hidden beaches, historic lighthouses, and tiny ports, with the gleaming gunmetal-gray Pacific Ocean always in view. With its seaside hamlets, outstanding fresh seafood eateries, and small hotels and resorts, the Oregon Coast epitomizes the finest in Pacific Northwest living. Among the coastal highlights are the 40-some-mi-long Oregon Dunes National Recreation Area near Florence, which offers more thrills than an amusement park. The drive along U.S. 101 between Port Orford and Brookings is one of the most scenic on the West Coast. Popular Cannon Beach will charm you with intimate hotels, gourmet restaurants, and the best coffee.

OREGON COAST AQUARIUM

The Oregon Coast Aquarium, a 4½-acre complex in Newport, has re-creations of offshore and near-shore Pacific marine habitats, all teeming with life: playful sea otters, comical puffins, fragile jellyfish, and even a 60-pound octopus. There's a hands-on interactive area for children and one of North America's largest seabird aviaries. A trio of tanks hold sharks, wolf eels, halibut, and other sea life.

SEASIDE

As a resort town Seaside has brushed off its former garish, arcade-filled reputation and now supports a bustling tourist trade, with hotels, condominiums, and restaurants surrounding a long beach. Just south of town, waves draw surfers to the **Cove**, a spot jealously guarded by locals. Eight miles south of Seaside, U.S. 101 passes the entrance to **Ecola State Park**, a playground of sea-sculpted rocks, sandy shoreline, green headlands, and panoramic views.

CANNON BEACH

Cannon Beach is a mellow and trendy place to enjoy art, wine, and fine dining and take in the sea air. One of the most charming hamlets on the coast, the town has beachfront homes and hotels, and a weathered-cedar downtown shopping district. Towering over the broad, sandy beach is Haystack Rock, a 235-foot-high monolith that is one of the most-photographed natural wonders on the Oregon Coast.

OSWALD WEST STATE PARK

Adventurous travelers will enjoy a sojourn at one of the best-kept secrets on the Pacific Coast, **Oswald West State Park**, at the base of Neahkahnie Mountain. An old-growth forest surrounds the 36 primitive campsites (reservations not accepted), and the spectacular beach contains caves and tidal pools.

FLORENCE

Florence's restored waterfront Old Town has restaurants, antiques stores, fish markets, and other diversions. But what really makes the town so appealing is its proximity to remarkable stretches of coastline. It is the gateway to the **Oregon Dunes National Recreation Area**, a 41-mi-long swath of undulating camel-color dunes, formed by eroded sandstone pushed up from the sea floor millions of years ago that are covered by forests, rivers, and lakes.

COOS BAY AREA

The best beaches in the Coos Bay Area are actually closer to Charleston. A placid semicircular lagoon protected from the sea by overlapping fingers of rock and surrounded by reefs, **Sunset Bay State Park** is one of the few places along the Oregon Coast where you can swim without worrying about the currents and undertows. Only the hardiest souls will want to brave the chilly water, however.

BANDON

Bandon is both a harbor town and a popular vacation spot. The town is famous for its cranberry products and its cheese factory, as well as its artists' colony, complete with galleries and shops. From the highway the 2-mi drive to reach **Bullards Beach State Park** passes through the Bandon Marsh, a prime bird-watching and picnicking area.

COASTAL WASHINGTON

While offering little of interest to swimmers, Washington's mostly windswept beaches are great if you like beachcombing, kayaking, and bird-watching; you'll find a few sandy shores, but most beaches are fairly rocky.

(this page above) Alki Beach, Seattle (opposite page upper right) Deception Pass, Whidby Island (opposite page lower left) Olympic National Park

The southwestern coast's long, surf-tossed sands are popular with hikers, kite flyers, bird-watchers, and surfers; in season, folks come here by the thousands to dig for tasty razor clams. The Olympic Peninsula's beaches are rocky, though there are a few sandy coves tucked between the headlands. The muddy shores of the Salish Sea are popular with clam diggers probing for the hard-shell mollusks. Sandy beaches are scarce, even in the San Juan Islands. More often than not, the glacier-cut rocks drop straight into the water. But tide pools teeming with sea slugs, crabs, anemones, and tiny fish hold a fascination all their own. Bird-watching is great along all of the shores. California gray whales migrate close to the beaches of the outer shore and frequently visit the sheltered waters of the Salish Sea. Sea kayaking is very popular, and most waterfront towns have kayak rentals.

FORKS

The former logging town of Forks has always been a small, quiet gateway town for Olympic National Park's Hoh River valley unit. Famous for getting more than 100 inches of rain per year, it's more popular now as the setting for the *Twilight* series of books and movies. The tree thought to be the world's largest cedar tree is just outside of town.

SEATTLE

In summer, cars inch along Alki Avenue, seeking a coveted parking space at 2½-mi **Alki Beach**, with its views of both the Seattle skyline and the Olympic Mountains. It's something of a California beach scene (except for the water temperature), with in-line skaters, joggers, and cyclists sharing the walkway and sun-loving singles playing volleyball and flirting. Leashed dogs are welcome on the trails of **Sand Point Magnuson Park**; a large off-leash area includes one of the few public beaches where pooches can swim.

OLYMPIC NATIONAL PARK

Miles of spectacular, rugged coastline dotted with tidal pools, sea stacks, and driftwood hem the edges of the Olympic Peninsula. The wild, pebble- and shell-strewn Pacific Coast teems with tide pools and clawed creatures. Crabs, sand dollars, anemones, starfish, and all sorts of shellfish are exposed at low tide, when flat beaches can stretch out for hundreds of yards. The most easily accessible sand-strolling spots are **Rialto, Ruby, First** and **Second** near Mora and La Push, and beaches **No. 2** and **No. 4** in the Kalaloch stretch.

WHIDBEY ISLAND

The best beaches are on the west side, where wooded and wildflower-bedecked bluffs drop steeply to sand or surf, which can cover the beaches at high tide and

can be rough on this exposed shore. **Maxwelton Beach**, with its sand, driftwood, and great views across Admiralty Inlet to the Olympic Mountains, is popular with the locals. **Possession Point** includes a park, a beach, and a boat launch. West of Coupeville, **Fort Ebey State Park** has a sandy spread; **Deception Pass State Park** has 19 mi of rocky shore and beaches 7 mi north of Oark Harbor.

THE SAN JUAN ISLANDS

The coastal waters of the Pacific Northwest, between mainland Washington and Vancouver Island, contain hundreds of islands; all are scenic and invite beachcombers and kayakers to explore them. **Odlin County Park** on Lopez Island has a mile of sandy shoreline—a rarity on the shores of the Salish Sea. **American Camp** on San Juan Island, has 6 mi of public beach on the southern end of the island. **San Juan County Park** has a wide gravel beachfront where orcas often frolic in summer, plus grassy lawns with picnic tables and a small campground.

SEQUIM

The **Dungeness Spit**, curving 5½ mi into the Straight of San Juan de Fuca, is the longest natural sand spit in the United States and a wild, beautiful section of shoreline. At high tide the thread of pebble-strewn whiteness might be only 50 feet wide, and it's completely covered when storms brew up turbulent waters.

Best Beaches in Hawai'i

WHAT'S WHERE

1 O'ahu. Honolulu and Waikīkī are here—and it's a great big lū'au. It's got hot restaurants and lively nightlife as well as gorgeous white-sand beaches, knife-edged mountain ranges, and cultural sites including Pearl Harbor.

2 Maui nō ka 'o. It means Maui is the best, the most, the tops. There's good reason for the superlatives. It's the most diversified Hawaiian island, perfect for families with divergent interests.

3 Hawai'i, the Big Island. It has two faces, watched over by snowcapped Mauna Kea and steaming Mauna Loa. The Kona side has parched, lava-strewn lowlands, and eastern Hilo is characterized by lush flower farms and waterfalls.

4 Kaua'i. This is the "Garden Isle," and it's where you'll find the lush, green folding sea cliffs of Nāpali Coast, the colorful and awesome Waimea Canyon, and more beaches per mile of coastline than any other Hawaiian island.

5 Moloka'i. It's the least changed, most laid-back of the Islands. Come here to experience riding a mule down a cliff to Kalaupapa Peninsula; the Kamakou Preserve, a 2,774-acre wildlife refuge; and plenty of peace and quiet.

6 Lāna'i. For years there was nothing here except for pineapples and red-dirt roads. Today it attracts the well-heeled in search of privacy, with a few upscale resorts, archery and shooting, four-wheel-drive excursions, and superb scuba diving.

PACIFIC OCEAN

Ka'iwi
Channel

MOLOKA'I

Kalaupapa
Hālawa
Kaunakakai

5

Kahului
Bay

Lahaina
Kahului
MAUI

Lāna'i City
Kīhei
Pu'u 'Ula'ula
10,023 ft

Hāna

6
Wailea

LĀNA'I
Kipahulu

KAHO'OLAWE

'Alenuihaha Channel

Hāwī

Honoka'a
Waimea

Mauna Kea
13,796 ft

KOHALA
COAST

Kailua-Kona

3
Hilo

Captain
Cook
Mauna Loa
13,677 ft
Pāhoa

HAWAI'I
(The Big Island)

KONA
COAST
Volcano

Ho'opuloa
Pahala

0   50 mi

0   50 km
Na'alehu

O'AHU

Tropical sun mixed with cooling trade winds and pristine waters make O'ahu's shores a literal heaven on Earth. But contrary to many assumptions, the island is not one big beach. There are miles and miles of coastline without a grain of sand, so you need to know where you are going to fully enjoy the Hawaiian experience.

(this page above) Waikīkī Beach, Honolulu; (opposite page upper right) Sailing in Waimea Bay; (opposite page lower left) Kailua Beach Park

Much of the island's southern and eastern coast is protected by inner reefs. The reefs provide still coastline water but not much as far as sand is concerned. However, where there are beaches on the South and East shores, they are mind-blowing. In West O'ahu and on the North Shore you can find the wide expanses of sand you would expect for enjoying the sunset. Sandy bottoms and protective reefs make the water an adventure in the winter months. Most visitors assume the seasons don't change a thing in the Islands, and they would be right—except for the waves, which are big on the South Shore in summer and placid in winter. It's exactly the opposite on the north side where winter storms bring in huge waves, but the ocean goes to glass come May and June.

OUTRIGGER CANOES

Outrigger canoes are a simple, cheap, but oft-overlooked way to have fun in Waikīkī. The long, funny-looking boats in front of Duke's Canoe Club allow you to get out on the water cheaply. At $10 for three rides, the price hasn't changed in a decade, and the beach boys negotiate you in and out of the break as they have been doing all their lives.

WAIKĪKĪ

The 2½-mi strand called **Waikīkī Beach** extends from Hilton Hawaiian Village on one end to Kapi'olani Park and Diamond Head on the other. Although it's one contiguous piece of beach, it's as varied as the people that inhabit the Islands. You can find every beach activity here without ever jumping in the rental car. **Duke Kahanamoku Beach** has the calmest waters, but **Fort DeRussy Beach Park** is one of the finest beaches on the south side of O'ahu.

WINDWARD O'AHU

Kailua Beach Park. A cobalt-blue sea and a wide continuous arc of powdery sand make Kailua Beach Park one of the island's best beaches, illustrated by the crowds of local families that spend their weekend days here. Kailua Beach has calm water, a line of palms and ironwoods that provide shade on the sand, and a huge park with picnic pavilions where you can escape the heat. This is the "it" spot if you're looking to try your hand at wind- or kiteboarding. ⊠ *Near Kailua town, turn right on Kailua Rd. at market, cross bridge, then turn left into beach parking lot.*

Makapu'u Beach. A magnificent beach protected by Makapu'u Point welcomes you to the windward side. Hang gliders circle above the beach, and the water is filled with body boarders. Just off the coast you can see Bird Island, a

sanctuary for aquatic fowl, jutting out of the blue. The currents can be heavy, so check with a lifeguard if you're unsure of safety. ⊠ *Across from Sea Life Park on Kalaniana'ole Hwy., 2 mi south of Waimānalo.*

NORTH SHORE

Waimea Bay. Made popular in that old Beach Boys song "Surfin' U.S.A.," Waimea Bay is a slice of big-wave heaven, home to king-size 25- to 30-foot winter waves. Summer is the time to swim and snorkel in the calm waters. The shore break is great for novice bodysurfers. Due to its popularity, the postage-stamp parking lot is quickly filled, but everyone parks along the side of the road and walks in. ⊠ *Across from Waimea Valley, 3 mi north of Hale'iwa on Kamehameha Hwy.*

White Plains. Concealed from the public eye for many years as part of the Barbers Point Naval Air Station, this beach is reminiscent of Waikīkī but without the condos and the crowds. It is a long, sloping beach with numerous surf breaks, but it is also mild enough at shore for older children to play freely. Expansive parking, great restroom facilities, and numerous tree-covered barbecue areas make it a great day-trip spot. ⊠ *Take the Makakilo exit off H1 west, turn left. Follow it into the base gates, turn left. Follow blue signs to the beach.*

MAUI

Of all the beaches in Hawai'i, Maui's are some of the most diverse. You can find pristine, palm-lined shores with clear and inviting waters, as well as rich red- and black-sand beaches, and craggy cliffs with surging waters.

(this page above) Surfer in Maui waters; (opposite page upper right) Nāpili Beach; (opposite page lower left) Wai'ānapanapa State Park

All of Maui's beaches are public—but that doesn't mean it's not possible to find a secluded cove. The South Shore and West Maui have the calmest, sunniest beaches. Hit the beach early, when the aquamarine waters are as accommodating as bathwater. In summer, afternoon winds can be a sandblasting force, which can chase even the most dedicated sun worshippers away. From November through May, the South and West beaches are also great spots to watch the humpback whales that spend winter and early spring in Maui's waters. Windward shores (the North Shore and East Maui) offer more adventurous beach-going. Beaches face the open ocean (rather than other islands) and tend to be rockier and more prone to powerful swells. This is particularly true in winter, when the North Shore becomes a playground for experienced big-wave riders and windsurfers.

> **GEAR UP!**
>
> Forget your beach gear? No need to fear. Look for Long's Drugs (in Kīhei and Kahului) or the ABC Stores (in Kā'napali, Lahaina, Kīhei, and more) for extra sunscreen, shades, towels, and umbrellas. If you want better deals and don't mind the drive into town, look for Kmart (✉ *424 Dairy Rd.*) or Walmart (✉ *101 Pakaula St.*) in Kahului. For more extensive gear, check out Sports Authority (✉ *270 Dairy Rd.*)in Kahului.

3

WEST MAUI

Kāʻanapali Beach. Stretching from the Sheraton Maui at its northernmost end to the Hyatt Regency Maui at its southern tip, Kāʻanapali Beach is lined with resorts, condominiums, restaurants, and shops. If you're looking for quiet and seclusion, this is not the beach for you. But if you want lots of action, lay out your towel here. The center section in front of Whalers Village is one of Maui's best people-watching spots: catamarans, windsurfers, and parasailers head out from here while the beautiful people take in the scenery. A cement pathway weaves along the length of this 3-mi-long beach. ⊠ *Follow any of 3 Kāʻanapali exits from Honoapiʻilani Hwy.*

Nāpili Beach. Surrounded by sleepy condos, this round bay is a turtle-filled pool lined with a sparkling white crescent of sand. Sunbathers love this beach, which is also a terrific sunset spot. The shore break is steep but gentle, so it's great for body boarding and bodysurfing. It's easy to keep an eye on kids here as the entire bay is visible from any point in the water. The beach is right outside the Nāpili Kai Beach Club, a few miles south of Kapalua. ⊠ *5900 Lower Honoapiʻilani Hwy.; look for Nāpili Pl. or Hui Dr.*

THE SOUTH SHORE

Mākena (Big Beach). Locals successfully fought to give Mākena—one of Hawaiʻi's

most breathtaking beaches—state-park protection. It's often mistakenly referred to as "Big Beach," but natives prefer its Hawaiian name, Oneloa. This stretch of deep-golden sand abutting sparkling aqua water is 3,000 feet long and 100 feet wide. It's never crowded, no matter how many cars cram into the lots. The water is fine for swimming, but use caution. ⚠ The shore drop-off is steep and swells can get deceptively big. Climb over Puʻu Ōlaʻi, the steep cinder cone near the first entrance, to discover "Little Beach"—clothing optional by popular practice, although this is technically illegal. ⊠ *Off Wailea Alanui Dr.*

EAST MAUI AND HĀNA

Waiʻānapanapa State Park. Small but rarely crowded, this beach will remain in your memory long after visiting. Fingers of white foam rush onto a black volcanic-pebble beach fringed with green beach vines and palms. Swimming here is both relaxing and invigorating: strong currents bump smooth stones up against your ankles while seabirds flit above a black, jagged sea arch draped with vines. ⊠ *Hāna Hwy. near MM 32.*

THE BIG ISLAND

Don't believe anyone who tells you that the Big Island lacks beaches. It's just one of the myths about Hawai'i's largest island that has no basis in fact.

(this page above) Kua Bay (opposite page upper right); Hāpuna Beach State Recreation Area; (opposite page lower left) Relaxing on the Kohala Coast

It's not so much that the Big Island has fewer beaches than the other islands, it's just that there's more island, so getting to the beaches can be slightly less convenient. That said, there are plenty of those perfect white-sand stretches you think of when you hear "Hawai'i," and the added bonus of black- and green-sand beaches, thanks to the age of the island and its active volcanoes. The bulk of the island's beaches are on the northwest part of the island, along the Kohala Coast. Black-sand beaches and green-sand beaches are in the southern region, along the coast nearest the volcano. On the eastern side of the island, beaches tend to be of the rocky-coast–surging-surf variety, but there are still a few worth visiting, and this is where the Hawaiian shoreline is at its most picturesque.

GREEN SAND

Tired of the same old gold-, white-, or black-sand beach? You'll need good hiking shoes or sneakers at the very least to get to olive-green crescent Papakōlea Beach, one of the most unusual beaches on the island. The greenish tint is caused by an accumulation of olivine crystals that form in volcanic eruptions. Unfortunately, it's a 2-mi (two-hour) hike to get here.

3

KOHALA COAST

'Anaeho'omalu Beach (A-Bay). This expansive beach of golden sand mixed with black lava grains fronts the Waikoloa Beach Marriott and is perfect for swimming, windsurfing, snorkeling, and diving. It's along a well-protected bay, so even when surf is rough on the rest of the island, it's fairly calm here. A walking trail follows the coastline to the Hilton Waikoloa Village next door, passing by tide pools and ponds. Footwear is recommended for the trail. ✉ *Follow Waikoloa Beach Dr. to Kings' Shops, then turn left; parking lot and beach right-of-way south of Waikoloa Beach Marriott.*

Hāpuna Beach State Recreation Area. By any measurement, this is one fine beach. And with ample parking you don't have to get here at dawn. The beach itself is a long (½-mi), white, perfect crescent, one of the Big Island's largest. The turquoise water is very calm in summer, with just enough rolling waves to make bodysurfing or boogie boarding fun. There's some excellent snorkeling around the jagged rocks that border the beach on either side, but a strong current means it's only for experienced swimmers. ✉ *Hwy. 19, near MM 69, at Hāpuna Beach Prince Hotel.*

Kauna'oa Beach (Mauna Kea Beach). Hands-down one of the most beautiful beaches on the island, Kauna'oa is a long white crescent of sand. The beach,

which fronts the Mauna Kea Beach Hotel, slopes very gradually. It's a great place for snorkeling. When conditions permit, there is good body- and board surfing also. Currents can be strong, and powerful winter waves can be dangerous, so be careful. ✉ *Off Hwy. 19; entry through gate to Mauna Kea Beach Resort.*

Kua Bay. Remoteness does have its merits at this lovely beach, the northernmost beach in the stretch of coast that comprises Kekaha Kai State Park. At one time you had to hike over a few miles of unmarked, rocky trail to get here. Now, a newly paved road leads to Kua Bay, which is one of the most beautiful bays you will ever see—the water is crystal clear, deep aquamarine, and peaceful in summer. ✉ *Hwy. 19 north of MM 88.*

SOUTH KONA AND KA'Ū

Punalu'u Beach Park (Black Sand Beach). Endangered Hawaiian green sea turtles nest in the black sand of this beautiful and easily accessible beach. You can see them feeding on the seaweed along the surf break or napping on the sand. You can even swim with them. However, strong shoreward currents make being in the water here a hazard. ✉ *Hwy. 11, 27 mi south of Hawai'i Volcanoes National Park.*

KAUA'I

With more sandy beaches per mile of coastline than any other Hawaiian island, Kaua'i could be nicknamed the Sandy Island just as easily as it's called the Garden Island.

(this page above and opposite page upper right) Polihale State Park; (opposite page lower left) Hā'ena Beach Park, North Shore

Totaling more than 50 mi, Kaua'i's beaches make up 44% of the island's shoreline—almost twice that of O'ahu, second on this list. It is, of course, because of Kaua'i's age as the eldest sibling of the inhabited Hawaiian Islands, allowing more time for water and wind erosion to break down rock and coral into sand. But not all Kaua'i's beaches are the same. Generally speaking, surf kicks up on the North Shore in winter and the South Shore in summer, although summer's southern swells aren't nearly as frequent or big as the northern winter swells that attract those surfers. Kaua'i's longest and widest beaches are found on the North Shore and West Side and are popular with beachgoers, although during winter's rains, everyone heads to the dry West Side. The East Side beaches tend to be narrower and have onshore winds less popular with sunbathers, yet fishers abound. Smaller coves are characteristic of the South Shore and attract all kinds of water lovers year-round, including monk seals.

SPOTTING SEALS

When strolling on one of Kaua'i's lovely beaches, don't be surprised if you find yourself in the rare company of Hawaiian monk seals, one of the rarest of sea mammals. They're fond of hauling out on the beach for a long snooze in the sun, particularly after a night of gorging on fish. They need this time to rest and digest, safe from predators. If you're lucky enough to see a monk seal, keep your distance and let it be.

3

THE NORTH SHORE

Hā'ena Beach Park (Tunnels Beach). The wide bay here—named Mākua and commonly known as Tunnels—is bordered by two large reef systems creating favorable waves for surfing during peak winter conditions. In July and August, waters at this same beach are as calm as a lake, usually, and snorkelers enjoy the variety of fish life found in a hook-shape reef made up of underwater lava tubes, on the east end of the bay. ⊠ *Near end of Rte. 560, across from lava-tube sea caves, after crossing stream.*

Hanalei Bay Beach Park. This 2-mi, crescent-shaped beach surrounds a spacious bay that is quintessential Hawai'i. But the sight of the mountains, ribboned with waterfalls, will also take your breath away. In winter, the surf is tremendous, but in summer the bay is transformed—calm waters lap the beach, sailboats moor in the bay, and outrigger-canoe paddlers ply the sea. ⊠ *In Hanalei, turn makai (toward the coast) at Aku Rd. and drive 1 block to Weli Weli Rd. Parking areas are on makai side of Weli Weli Rd.*

THE EAST SIDE

Lydgate State Park. This is hands-down the best family beach park on Kaua'i. The waters off the beach are protected by a hand-built breakwater creating two boulder-enclosed saltwater pools for safe swimming and snorkeling just

about year-round. It's also a busy beach, especially on afternoons and weekends. ⊠ *Just south of Wailua River, turn makai off Rte. 56 onto Lehu Dr. and left onto Nalu Rd.*

THE SOUTH SHORE

Māhā'ulepū Beach. This 2-mi stretch of coast with its sand dunes, limestone hills, sinkholes, and caves is unlike any other on Kaua'i. The evidence indicates that Hawaiians lived in this area as early as AD 700. There are three beach areas with bits of sandy-bottom swimming; however, we think the best way to experience Māhā'ulepū is simply to roam, especially at sunrise. ⊠ *Continue on Po'ipū Rd. past Hyatt (it turns into a dirt road) to T-intersection and turn makai.*

THE WEST SIDE

Polihale State Park. The longest stretch of beach in Hawai'i starts in Kekaha and ends about 15 mi away at the start of the Nāpali Coast. In addition to being long, this beach is 300 feet wide in places and backed by sand dunes 50 to 100 feet tall. Polihale is a remote beach accessed via a 5-mi cane-haul road (four-wheel drive preferred but not required) at the end of Route 50 in Kekaha. ⊠ *Drive to end of Rte. 50 and continue on dirt road.*

NĀPALI COAST: EMERALD QUEEN OF KAUAʻI

If you're coming to Kauaʻi, Nāpali ("cliffs" in Hawaiian) is a major must-see. More than 5 million years old, these sea cliffs rise thousands of feet above the Pacific, and every shade of green is represented in the vegetation that blankets their lush peaks and folds. At their base, there are caves, secluded beaches, and waterfalls to explore.

The big question is how to explore this gorgeous stretch of coastline. You can't drive to it, through it, or around it. You can't see Nāpali from a scenic lookout. You can't even take a mule ride to it. The only way to experience its magic is from the sky, the ocean, or the trail.

FROM THE SKY

If you've booked a helicopter tour of Nāpali, you might start wondering what you've gotten yourself into on the way to the airport. Will it feel like being on a small airplane? Will there be turbulence? Will it be worth all the money you just plunked down?

Your concerns will be assuaged on the helipad, once you see the faces of those who have just returned from their journey: Everyone looks totally blissed out. And now it's your turn.

Climb on board, strap on your headphones, and the next thing you know the helicopter gently lifts up, hovers for a moment, and floats away like a spider on the wind—no roaring engines, no rumbling down a runway. If you've chosen a flight with music, you'll feel as if you're inside your very own IMAX movie.

Pinch yourself if you must, because this is the real thing. Your pilot shares history, legend, and lore. If you miss something, speak up: pilots love to show off their island knowledge. You may snap a few pictures (not too many or you'll miss the eyes-on experience!), nudge a friend or spouse, and point at a whale breeching in the ocean, but mostly you stare, mouth agape. There is simply no other way to take in the immensity and greatness of Nāpali but from the air.

Helicopter flight over Nāpali Coast

GOOD TO KNOW

Helicopter companies depart from the north, east, and west shores. Our advice? Choose your departure location based on its proximity to where you're staying.

If you want more adventure—and air—choose one of the helicopter companies that flies with the doors off.

Some companies offer flights without music. Know the experience you want ahead of time. Some even sell a DVD of your flight, so you don't have to worry about taking pictures.

Wintertime rain grounds some flights; plan your trip early in your stay in case the flight gets rescheduled.

IS THIS FOR ME?

Taking a helicopter trip is the most expensive way to see Nāpali—as much as $280 for an hour-long tour.

Claustrophobic? Choose a boat tour or hike. It's a tight squeeze in the helicopter, especially in one of the middle seats.

Short on time? Taking a helicopter tour is a great way to see the island.

WHAT YOU MIGHT SEE

■ Nu'alolo Kai (an ancient Hawaiian fishing village) with its fringed reef

■ The 300-foot Hanakāpī'ai Falls

■ A massive sea arch formed in the rock by erosion

■ The 11-mile Kalalau Trail threading its way along the coast

■ The amazing striations of a'a and pāhoehoe lava flows that helped push Kaua'i above the sea

FROM THE OCEAN

Nāpali from the ocean is two treats in one: spend a good part of the day on (or in) the water, and gaze up at majestic green sea cliffs rising thousands of feet above your head.

There are three ways to see it: a mellow pleasure-cruise catamaran allows you to kick back and sip a mai tai; an adventurous raft (Zodiac) tour will take you inside sea caves under waterfalls, and give you the option of snorkeling; and a daylong outing in a kayak is a real workout, but then you can say you paddled 16 miles of coastline.

Any way you travel, you'll breathe ocean air, feel spray on your face, and see pods of spinner dolphins, green sea turtles, flying fish, and, if you're lucky, a rare Hawaiian monk seal.

Nāpali stretches from Ke'e Beach in the north to Polihale beach on the West Side. If your departure point is Ke'e, your journey will start in the lush Hanakāpī'ai Valley. Within a few minutes, you'll see caves and waterfalls galore. About halfway down the coast just after the Kalalau Trail ends, you'll come to an immense arch—formed where the sea eroded the less dense basaltic rock—and a thundering 50-foot waterfall. And as the island curves near Nu'alolo State Park, you'll begin to notice less vegetation and more rocky outcroppings.

(left and top right) Kayaking on Nāpali Coast
(bottom right) Dolphin on Nāpali Coast

GOOD TO KNOW

If you want to snorkel, choose a morning rather than an afternoon tour—preferably during a summer visit—when seas are calmer.

If you're on a budget, choose a non-snorkeling tour.

If you want to see whales, take any tour, but be sure to plan your vacation for December through March.

If you're staying on the North Shore or East Side, embark from the North Shore. If you're staying on the South Shore, it might not be worth your time to drive to the north, so head to the West Side.

IS THIS FOR ME?

Boat tours are several hours long, so if you have only a short time on Kaua'i, a helicopter tour is a better alternative.

Even on a small boat, you won't get the individual attention and exclusivity of a helicopter tour.

Prone to seasickness? A large boat can be surprisingly rocky, so be prepared.

WHAT YOU MIGHT SEE

■ Hawai'i's state fish—the humuhumunukunukuapuaa—otherwise known as the Christmas wrasse

■ Waiahuakua Sea Cave, with a waterfall coming through its roof

■ Tons of marine life, including dolphins, green sea turtles, flying fish, and humpback whales, especially in February and March

■ Waterfalls—especially if your trip is after a heavy rain

FROM THE TRAIL

If you want to be one with Nāpali—feeling the soft red earth beneath your feet, picnicking on the beaches, and touching the lush vegetation—hiking the Kalalau Trail is the way to do it.

Most people hike only the first 2 miles of the 11-mile trail and turn around on Hanakāpī'ai Trail. This 4-mile round-trip hike takes three to four hours. It starts at sea level and doesn't waste any time gaining elevation. (Take heart—the uphill lasts only a mile and tops out at 400 feet; then it's downhill all the way.) At the half-mile point, the trail curves west and the folds of Nāpali Coast unfurl.

Along the way you might share the trail with feral goats and wild pigs. Some of the vegetation is native; much is introduced.

After the 1-mile mark the trail begins its drop into Hanakāpī'ai. You'll pass a couple of streams of water trickling across the trail, and maybe some banana, ginger, the native uluhe fern, and the Hawaiian ti plant. Finally the trail swings around the eastern ridge of Hanakāpī'ai for your first glimpse of the valley and then switchbacks down the mountain. You'll have to boulder-hop across the stream to reach the beach. If you like, you can take a 4-mile, round-trip fairly strenuous side trip from this point to the gorgeous Hanakāpī'ai Falls.

(left) Awaawapuhi mountain biker on razor-edge ridge
(top right) Feral goats in Kalalau Valley
(bottom right) Nāpali Coast

GOOD TO KNOW

Wear comfortable, amphibious shoes. Unless your feet require extra support, wear a self-bailing sort of shoe (for stream crossings) that doesn't mind mud. Don't wear heavy, waterproof hiking boots.

During winter the trail is often muddy, so be extra careful; sometimes it's completely inaccessible.

Don't hike after heavy rain—flash floods are common.

If you plan to hike the entire 11-mile trail (most people do the shorter hike described at left) you'll need a permit to go past Hanakāpī'ai.

IS THIS FOR ME?

Of all the ways to see Nāpali (with the exception of kayaking the coast), this is the most active. You need to be in decent shape to hit the trail.

If you're vacationing in winter, this hike might not be an option due to flooding—whereas you can take a helicopter or boat trip year-round.

WHAT YOU MIGHT SEE

■ Big dramatic surf right below your feet

■ Amazing vistas of the cool blue Pacific

■ The spectacular Hanakāpī'ai Falls; if you have a permit don't miss Hanakoa Falls, less than ½ mile off the trail

■ Wildlife, including goats and pigs

■ Zany-looking ōhi'a trees, with aerial roots and long, skinny serrated leaves known as hala. Early Hawaiians used them to make mats, baskets, and canoe sails.

MOLOKA'I

Moloka'i's unique geography gives the island plenty of drama and spectacle along the shorelines but not so many places for seaside basking and bathing.

(this page above and opposite page upper right) Pāpōhaku Beach; (opposite page lower left) The cliffs of the Kalaupapa Peninsula

The long North Shore is virtually inaccessible and has no beaches. And much of the South Shore is enclosed by a huge reef that blunts the action of the waves. Within this reef you can find a thin strip of sand, but the water here is flat, shallow, and at times clouded with silt, better suited to wading, pole fishing, kayaking, or learning how to windsurf than swimming or snorkeling. The big, fat, sandy beaches lie along the west end. These stretches of west-end sand are generally unpopulated, but the sea can be treacherous so never swim here alone. At the east end, where the road hugs the sinuous shoreline, you encounter a number of pocket-size beaches in rocky coves, good for snorkeling, but there also dangerous currents. The island's east-end road ends at Hālawa Valley with its unique double bay, which is not recommended for swimming.

HAWAI'I'S FIRST SAINT

A long-revered figure on Moloka'i and in Hawai'i, Father Damien, who cared for the desperate patients at Kalaupapa Leper Colony, was elevated to sainthood in 2009, garnering worldwide attention. Plans call for a small museum and bookstore in his honor in Kaunakakai, and the refurbishment of the three churches in the Catholic parish.

3

WEST MOLOKA'I

Kapukahehu Bay. Locals like to surf just out from this bay in a break called Dixie's or Dixie Maru. The sandy protected cove is usually completely deserted on weekdays but can fill up when the surf is up. The water in the cove is clear and shallow with plenty of well-worn rocky areas. These conditions make for excellent snorkeling, swimming, and boogie boarding on calm days. ⊠ *Drive about 3½ mi south of Pāpōhaku Beach to end of Kaluako'i Rd.; beach-access sign points to parking.*

Fodor's Choice ★ **Pāpōhaku Beach.** One of the most sensational beaches in Hawai'i, Pāpōhaku is a 3-mi-long strip of light golden sand, the longest of its kind on the island. Sadly, there is a dangerous undertow except on exceptionally calm summer days. But there's so much sand here that Honolulu once purchased barge loads in order to replenish Waīkīkī Beach. A shady beach park just inland is the site of the Ka Hula Piko Festival of Hawaiian Music and Dance, held each year in May. The park is also a great sunset-facing spot for a rustic afternoon barbecue. ⊠ *Kaluako'i Rd.; 2 mi south of Kaluako'i Hotel and Golf Club (now closed).*

CENTRAL MOLOKA'I

One Ali'i Beach Park. Clear, close views of Maui and Lāna'i across the Pailolo Channel dominate One Ali'i Beach Park (*One* is pronounced *o-nay*, not *won*), the only well-maintained beach park on the island's south-central shore. Moloka'i folks gather here for family reunions and community celebrations; the park's tightly trimmed expanse of lawn could almost accommodate the entire island population. Swimming within the reef is perfectly safe, but don't expect to catch any waves. Nearby is the restored One Ali'i fishpond. ⊠ *Rte. 450, east of Hotel Moloka'i.*

EAST MOLOKA'I

Waialua Beach Park. This arched strip of golden sand, a roadside pull-off near MM 20, also goes by the name Twenty Mile Beach. The water here, protected by the flanks of the little bay, is often so clear and shallow (sometimes too shallow) that even from land you can watch fish swimming among the coral heads. Watch out for traffic when you enter the highway. ■TIP➜ This is the most popular snorkeling spot on the island, a pleasant place to stop on the drive around the east end. ⊠ *Drive east on Rte. 450 to MM 20.*

SNORKELING IN HAWAI'I

The waters surrounding the Hawaiian Islands are filled with life—from giant manta rays cruising off the Big Island's Kona Coast to humpback whales giving birth in Maui's Māʻalaea Bay. Dip your head beneath the surface to experience a spectacularly colorful world: pairs of milletseed butterflyfish dart back and forth, red-lipped parrotfish snack on coral algae, and spotted eagle rays flap past like silent spaceships. Sea turtles bask at the surface while tiny wrasses give them the equivalent of a shave and a haircut. The water quality is typically outstanding; many sites afford 30-foot-plus visibility. On snorkel cruises, you can often stare from the boat rail right down to the bottom.

Certainly few destinations are as accommodating to every level of snorkeler as Hawai'i. Beginners can tromp in from sandy beaches while more advanced divers descend to shipwrecks, reefs, craters, and sea arches just offshore. Because of Hawai'i's extreme isolation, the island chain has fewer fish species than Fiji or the Caribbean—but many of the fish that are here exist nowhere else. The Hawaiian waters are home to the highest percentage of endemic fish in the world.

The key to enjoying the underwater world is slowing down. Look carefully. Listen. You might hear the strange crackling sound of shrimp tunneling through coral, or you may hear whales singing to one another during winter. A shy octopus may drift along the ocean's floor beneath you. If you're hooked, pick up a waterproof fishkey from Long's Drugs. You can brag later that you've looked the Hawaiian turkeyfish in the eye.

(opposite and top) South Shore Kihei, Maui.

Picasso Triggerfish	Milletseed Butterflyfish*	Yellow Tang
Moorish Idol	Hawaiian Whitespotted Toby*	Saddleback Wrasse*
Red-lipped Parrotfish	Hawaiian Turkeyfish*	Zebra Moray Eel
Stocky Hawkfish	Green Sea Turtle (Honu)	Spotted Eagle Ray

*endemic to Hawai'i

POLYNESIA'S FIRST CELESTIAL NAVIGATORS: HONU

Honu is the Hawaiian name for two native sea turtles, the hawksbill and the green sea turtle. Little is known about these dinosaur-age marine reptiles, though snorkelers regularly see them foraging for *limu* (seaweed) and the occasional jellyfish in Hawaiian waters. Most female honu nest in the uninhabited Northwestern Hawaiian Islands, but a few sociable ladies nest on Maui and Big Island beaches. Scientists suspect that they navigate the seas via magnetism—sensing the earth's poles. Amazingly, they will journey up to 800 miles to nest—it's believed that they return to their own birth sites. After about 60 days of incubation, nestlings emerge from the sand at night and find their way back to the sea by the light of the stars.

LĀNA'I

With no traffic or traffic lights and miles of open space, Lāna'i seems lost in time, and that can be a good thing. Sparsely populated, it is the smallest inhabited Hawaiian island and has just 3,500 residents.

Lāna'i offers miles of secluded white-sand beaches on its windward side, plus the moderately developed Hulopo'e Beach, which is adjacent to the Four Seasons Resort Lāna'i at Mānele Bay. This more developed beach side of the island is where it's happening: swimming, picnicking, off-island excursions, and boating are all concentrated in this accessible area. Hulopo'e is easily reached by car or hotel shuttle bus; to reach the windward beaches you need a four-wheel-drive vehicle. If you do head out to explore the wilder regions of the island, know that road conditions can change overnight and become impassable due to rain in the uplands. Reef, rocks, and coral make swimming on the windward side problematic, but it's fun to splash around in the shallow water. Expect debris on the windward beaches due to the Pacific convergence ocean currents. Driving on the beach itself is illegal.

(this page above and opposite page lower left) Hulopo'e Beach; (opposite page upper right) Shipwreck Beach

THE GHOSTS OF LĀNA'I

Lāna'i has a reputation for being haunted (at one time by "cannibal spirits") and evidence abounds: a mysterious purple *lehua* (an evergreen tree that normally produces red flowers) at Keahialoa; the crying of a ghost chicken at Kamoa; Pohaku O, a rock that calls at twilight; and remote spots where cars mysteriously stall, and lights are seen at night.

3

HULOPO'E BEACH

A short stroll from the Four Seasons Resort, **Hulopo'e Beach** is considered one of the best beaches in Hawai'i. The sparkling crescent beckons with calm waters safe for swimming almost year-round, great snorkeling reefs, tide pools, and, sometimes, spinner dolphins. A shady, grassy beach park is perfect for picnics. If the shore break is pounding, or if you see surfers riding big waves, stay out of the water. In the afternoons, watch Lāna'i High School students race outrigger canoes just off-shore. ⊠ *From Lāna'i City turn left on Hwy. 440 (Mānele Rd.) and go 9 mi south to bottom of hill; turn right.*

LŌPĀ BEACH

A popular surfing spot for locals, **Lōpā Beach** is also an ancient fishpond. With majestic views of West Maui and Kaho'olawe, this remote, white-sand beach is a great place for a picnic. ⚠ Don't let the sight of surfers fool you: the channel's currents are too strong for swimming. ⊠ *East side of Lāna'i; take Hwy. 440 (Keōmuku Hwy.) to its eastern terminus, then turn right on dirt road and continue south for 7 mi.*

POLIHUA BEACH

The often-deserted Polihua Beach gets a star for beauty with its long wide stretch of white sand and clear views of Moloka'i. However, the dirt road to get here can be bad with deep sandy

places (when it rains it's impassable), and frequent high winds whip up sand and waves. ■TIP➔ In addition, strong currents and a sudden drop in the ocean floor make swimming dangerous. On the more positive side, the northern end of the beach ends at a rocky lava cliff with some interesting tide pools. Polihua is named after the sea turtles that lay their eggs in the sand. Curiously, wild bees sometimes gather around cars that stop here. ⊠ *Windward Lāna'i, 11 mi north of Lāna'i City. Turn right on marked dirt road past Garden of the Gods.*

SHIPWRECK BEACH

Beachcombers come to the fairly accessible **Shipwreck Beach** for shells and washed-up treasures; photographers for great shots of Moloka'i, just across the 9-mi-wide Kalohi Channel; and walkers for the long stretch of sand. Kaiolohia, its Hawaiian name, is a favorite local diving spot. ■TIP➔ An offshore reef and rocks in the water mean that it's not for swimmers, though you can play in the shallow water on the shoreline. ⊠ *North Shore, take Hwy. 440 (Keōmuku Hwy.) to its eastern terminus, then turn left on dirt road and continue north for 3 mi.*

Best Beaches on the East Coast

WHAT'S WHERE

1 Maine. Few will want to brave the cold Maine waters for swimming, but beach-combers and kayakers will be pleased with the pristine conditions at many of the state's beaches.

2 Cape Cod. Typically divided into regions—the Upper, Mid, Lower, and Outer—Cape Cod is a place of many moods.

3 Martha's Vineyard. The Vineyard lies 5 mi off the Cape's southwest tip. The Down-Island towns are the most popular and most populated. But much of what makes this island special is found in its rural Up-Island reaches where dirt roads lead past crystalline ponds, cranberry bogs, and conservation lands.

4 Nantucket. Nantucket, or "Far Away Island" in the Wampanoag tongue, is some 25 mi south of Hyannis. Ferries dock in pretty Nantucket Town, where tourism services are concentrated. The rest of the island is mostly residential (trophy houses abound), and nearly all roads terminate in tiny beach communities.

5 New York. Long Island has some of the East Coast's best beaches, most of which are on long barrier islands on the South Shore.

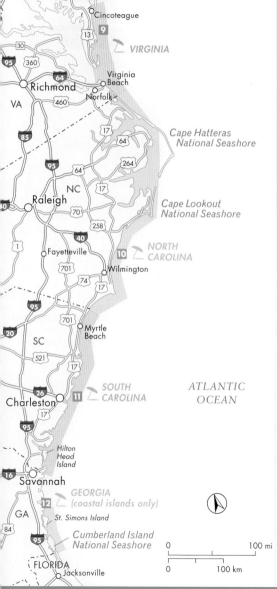

6 New Jersey. The New Jersey coastline has several unique beach communities as well as soft, sandy beaches to enjoy.

7 Delaware. Though a small state, Delaware has some 25 mi of popular beachfront that draws vacationers from around the immediate region.

8 Maryland. With only one major resort, Ocean City, Maryland's eastern shore is otherwise know for pristine beauty and shell fishing.

9 Virginia. Virginia Beach has long been a popular summertime vacation destination, but pristine Chincoteague Island is also bustling.

10 North Carolina. The state has more than 300 mi of coastline, much of it protected by a system of barrier islands that are as beautiful as they are fragile.

11 South Carolina. Myrtle Beach is one of the biggest draws along the Carolina coast, while Hilton Head and Edisto islands are more low-key. Golf is as big a draw to the region as the many beautiful beaches.

12 Georgia. Georgia's coastal islands (at least those that have been developed as vacation destinations) were once the province of the rich and mighty.

4

MAINE

Families love Maine's unspoiled beaches and safe inlets dotting the shoreline. Since the water is cold, these beaches are as popular with beachcombers, hikers, and kayakers as well as swimmers.

(this page above) Old Orchard Beach; (opposite page upper right) Kennebunk Beach; (opposite page lower left) Wells Beach

The Maine Coast is several places in one. Portland may be Maine's largest metropolitan area, but south of Portland, Ogunquit, Kennebunkport, Old Orchard Beach, and other resort towns predominate along a reasonably smooth shoreline, and this coastal region between Kittery to just outside Portland is Maine's most-visited region. Maine's southernmost coastal towns—Kittery, the Yorks, Ogunquit, the Kennebunks, and the Old Orchard Beach Area—reveal a few of the stunning faces of the state's coast, from the miles and miles of inviting sandy beaches to the beautifully kept historic towns and carnival-like attractions. There is something for every taste, whether you seek solitude in a kayak or prefer being caught up in the infectious spirit of fellow vacationers. There are very few sandy beaches north of Portland, so the state's best beaches are in a relatively compact area. Look for the season to begin in earnest on July 4.

KITTERY OUTLETS

Known as the "Gateway to Maine," Kittery has come to more recent light as a major shopping destination thanks to its complex of factory outlets. Flanked on either side of U.S. 1 are more than 120 stores in three major outlet centers (the Tanger Outlet Center, Kittery Premium Outlets, and the Kittery Outlets); the stores attract hordes of shoppers year-round.

YORK

Just a few miles from the village proper, **York Harbor** opens up to the water and offers many places to linger and explore. The harbor is busy with boats of all kinds, while the harbor beach is a good stretch of sand for swimming. **York Beach**, about 6 mi farther north, is a real family destination, devoid of all things staid and stuffy. Just beyond the sands of **Short Sand Beach** are a host of amusements, from bowling to indoor minigolf and the Fun-O-Rama arcade.

OGUNQUIT

A resort village in the 1880s, stylish **Ogunquit** gained fame as an artists' colony. Today it has become a mini Provincetown, with a gay population that swells in summer. For a scenic drive, take Shore Road through downtown toward the 100-foot Bald Head Cliff; you'll be treated to views up and down the coast.

WELLS

Lacking any kind of noticeable village center, Wells could be easily overlooked as nothing more than a commercial stretch on U.S. 1 between Ogunquit and the Kennebunks. But look more closely—this is a place where people come to enjoy some of the best beaches on the coast. Nearly 7 mi of sand stretch along the boundaries of Wells, where beach-going is a prime occupation. The

major beaches are **Crescent Beach, Wells Beach,** and **Drakes Island Beach**.

KENNEBUNK

Kennebunk is a classic small New England town, with an inviting shopping district, steepled churches, and fine examples of 18th- and 19th-century brick and clapboard homes. **Kennebunk** Beach has three parts: **Gooch's Beach, Mother's Beach,** and **Kennebunk Beach.** Beach Road, with its cottages and old Victorian boardinghouses, runs right behind them. Gooch's and Kennebunk attract teenagers; **Mother's Beach,** which has a small playground and tidal puddles for splashing, is popular with families. Three-mile-long **Goose Rocks**, a few minutes' drive north of town off Route 9, has plenty of shallow pools for exploring and a good long stretch of smooth sand; it's a favorite of families with small children.

OLD ORCHARD BEACH

Back in the late 19th century **Old Orchard Beach** was a classic, upscale, place-to-be-seen resort area. Although a good bit of this aristocratic hue has dulled in more recent times, Old Orchard Beach remains a good place for those looking for entertainment by the sea. The center of the action is a 7-mi strip of sand beach and its accompanying amusement park. Despite the summertime crowds and fried-food odors, the atmosphere can be captivating.

MAINE'S LIGHTHOUSES
GUARDIANS OF THE COAST   By John Blodgett

Perched high on rocky ledges, on the tips of wayward islands, and sometimes seemingly on the ocean itself are the more than five dozen lighthouses standing watch along Maine's craggy and ship-busting coastline.

Marshall Point Light

LIGHTING THE WAY: A BIT OF HISTORY

Portland Head Light

Most lighthouses were built in the first half of the 19th century to protect the vessels from running aground at night or when the shoreline was shrouded in fog. Along with the mournful siren of the foghorn and maritime lore, these practical structures have come to symbolize Maine throughout the world.

SHIPWRECKS AND SAFETY

These alluring sentinels of the eastern seaboard today have more form than function, but that certainly was not always the case. Safety was a strong motivating factor in the erection of the lighthouses. Commerce also played a critical role. For example, in 1791 Portland Head Light was completed, partially as a response to local merchants' concerns about the rocky entrance to Portland Harbor and the varying depths of the shipping channel, but approval wasn't given until a terrible accident in 1787 in which a 90-ton sloop wrecked. Beginning in 1790, the federal government was the owner of these towers of light, with the U.S. Lighthouse Service (later the U.S. Coast Guard) managing them.

Some lighthouses in Maine were built in a much-needed venue, but the points and islands upon which they sat eventually eroded into the ocean. This meant that over the years many lighthouses had to be rebuilt or replaced.

LIGHTHOUSES TODAY

In modern times, many of the structures still serve a purpose. Technological advances, such as GPS and radar, augment a ship's navigation through the choppy waters, but they don't replace a lighthouse or its foghorns. The numerous channel-marking buoys still in existence also are testament to the old tried-and-true methods.

Of the 61 lighthouses along this far northeastern state, 55 are still working, alerting ships (and even small aircraft) of the shoreline's rocky edge. Towns, historical organizations, the National Park Service, and a few private individuals own the decommissioned lights.

KEEPERS OF THE LIGHT

Some keepers also used bells and sirens, like this Fog Signal Station on Manana Island in 1898.

Pemaquid Point's fourth-order Fresnel lens

LIFE OF A LIGHTKEEPER

One thing that has changed with the modern era is the disappearance of the lighthouse keeper. In the 20th century, lighthouses began the conversion from oil-based lighting to electricity. A few decades later, the U.S. Coast Guard switched to automation, phasing out the need for an on-site keeper.

While the keepers of tradition were no longer needed, the traditions of these stalwart, 24/7 employees live on through museum exhibits and retellings of Maine's maritime history, legends, and lore. The tales of a lighthouse keeper's life are the stuff romance novels are made of: adventure, rugged but lonely men, and a beautiful setting along an unpredictable coastline.

The lighthouse keepers of yesterday probably didn't see their own lives so romantically. Their daily narrative was one of hard work and, in some cases, exceptional solitude. A keeper's primary job was to ensure that the lamp was illuminated all day, every day. This meant that oil (whale oil or coal oil) had to be carried about and wicks trimmed on a regular basis. When fog shrouded the coast, they sounded the solemn horn to pierce through the damp darkness that hid their light. Their quarters were generally small and often attached to the light tower itself. The remote locations of the lights added to the isolation a keeper felt, especially before the advent of radio and telephone, let alone the Internet. Though some brought families with them, the keepers tended to be men who lived alone.

THE LIGHTS 101

Over the years, Fresnel (fray-NELL) lenses were developed in different shapes and sizes so that ship captains could distinguish one lighthouse from another. Invented by Frenchman Augustin Fresnel in the early 19th century, the lens design allows for a greater transmission of light perfectly suited for lighthouse use. Knowing which lighthouse they were near helped captains know which danger was present, such as a submerged ledge or shallow channel. Some lights, such as those at Seguin Island Light, are fixed and don't flash. Other lights are colored red.

DID YOU KNOW?

A lighthouse's personality shines through its flash pattern. For example, Bass Harbor Light (pictured) blinks red every four seconds. Some lights, such as Seguin Island Light, are fixed and don't flash.

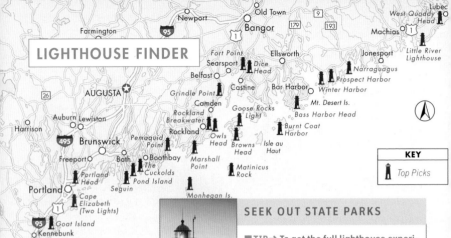

LIGHTHOUSE FINDER

Lubec
West Quoddy Head
Old Town
Newport
Bangor
Machias
Little River Lighthouse
Farmington
95
179
193
Jonesport
Fort Point
Ellsworth
Narraguagus
Searsport
Dice Head
Prospect Harbor
Belfast
Winter Harbor
AUGUSTA
Castine
Bar Harbor
Grindle Point
Mt. Desert Is.
26
Camden
Goose Rocks Light
Bass Harbor Head
Auburn Lewiston
Rockland Breakwater
Burnt Coat Harbor
Harrison
Rockland
Owls Head
Isle au Haut
495
Brunswick
Pemaquid Point
Browns Head
Freeport
Bath
Boothbay
Marshall Point
Matinicus Rock
Portland Head
The Cuckolds
Pond Island
Seguin
Portland
Cape Elizabeth (Two Lights)
Monhegan Is.
1
95
Goat Island
Kennebunk
Kennebunkport
Ogunquit
York
Cape Neddick (Nubble Light)
Whaleback
Kittery
Portsmouth

KEY

🏠 Top Picks

West Quoddy Head

SEEK OUT STATE PARKS

■ **TIP →** To get the full lighthouse experience your best bet is to visit one that is part of a state park. These are generally well kept and tend to allow up-close approach, though typically only outside. While you're at the parks you can picnic or stroll on the trails. Wildlife is often abundant in and near the water; you might spot sea birds and even whales in certain locations (try West Quoddy Head, Portland Head, or Two Lights).

VISITING MAINE'S LIGHTHOUSES

As you travel along the Maine Coast, you won't see lighthouses by watching your odometer—there were no rules about the spacing of lighthouses. The decision as to where to place a lighthouse was a balance between a region's geography and its commercial prosperity and maritime traffic.

Lighthouses line the shore from as far south as York to the country's easternmost tip at Lubec. Accessibility varies according to location and other factors. A handful are so remote as to be outright impossible to reach (except perhaps by kayaking and rock climbing). Some don't allow visitors according to Coast Guard policies, though you can enjoy them through the zoom lens of a camera. Others you can walk right up to and, occasionally, even climb to the top. Lighthouse enthusiasts and preservation groups restore and maintain many of them. All told, approximately 30 lighthouses allow some sort of public access.

MUSEUMS, TOURS, AND MORE

Most keeper's quarters are closed to the public, but some of the homes have been converted to museums, full of intriguing exhibits on lighthouses, the famous Fresnel lenses used in them, and artifacts of Maine maritime life in general. Talk to the librarians at the **Maine Maritime Museum** in Bath (⊕ *www.mainemaritimemuseum.org*) or sign up for one of the museum's daily lighthouse cruises to pass by no fewer than ten on the Lighthouse Lovers Cruise. In Rockland, the **Maine Lighthouse Museum** (⊕ *www.mainelighthousemuseum.com*) has the country's largest display of Fresnel lenses. The museum also displays keepers' memorabilia, foghorns, brassware, and more.

For more information, check out the lighthouse page at Maine's official tourism site: ⊕ *www.visitmaine.com/attractions/sightseeing_tours/lighthouse*.

SLEEPING LIGHT: STAYING OVERNIGHT

Goose Rock, where you can play lighthouse keeper for a week.

Want to stay overnight in a lighthouse? There are several options to do so. ■ TIP→ Book lighthouse lodgings as far in advance as possible, up to one year ahead.

Our top pick is **Pemaquid Point Light** (*Newcastle Square Vacation Rentals* ☎ *207/563–6500*) because it has one of the most dramatic settings on the Maine coast. Four miles south of **New Harbor,** the second floor of the lighthouse keeper's house is rented out on a weekly basis early May through mid-November to support upkeep of the grounds. When you aren't enjoying the interior, head outdoors: the covered front porch has a rocking-chair view of the ocean. The one-bedroom, one-bath rental sleeps up to a family of four.

Situated smack dab in the middle of a major maritime thoroughfare between two Penobscot Bay islands, **Goose Rocks Light** (☎ *207/867–4747*) offers lodging for the adventuresome—the 51-foot cast-iron lighthouse is completely surrounded by water. Getting there requires a ferry ride from Rockland to nearby

North Haven, a ten-minute ride by motorboat, and then a climb up an iron-rung ladder from the pitching boat—all based on high tide and winds, of course. There's room for up to eight people. It's a bit more cushy experience than it was for the original keepers: there's a flat-screen TV with DVD player and a selection of music and videos for entertainment. In addition, a hammock hangs on the small deck that encircles the operational light; it's a great place from which to watch the majestic windjammers and the fishing fleet pass by.

Little River Lighthouse (☎ *207/259–3833*), along the far northeastern reaches of the coast in **Cutler,** has three rooms available for rent from July through September. You're responsible for food and beverages, linens, towels, and other personal items (don't forget the bug spray), but kitchen and other basics are provided. The lighthouse operators will provide a boat ride to the island upon which the lighthouse sits.

TOP LIGHTHOUSES TO VISIT

BASS HARBOR LIGHT

One Maine lighthouse familiar to many because it is the subject of countless photographs is Bass Harbor Light, at the southern end of **Mount Desert Island.** It is a short drive from Acadia National Park and the town of Bar Harbor. The station grounds are open year-round, but the former keeper's house is now a private home for a Coast Guard family. This lighthouse is so close to the water it seems as if a blustery wind could tip it over the rocks right into the North Atlantic. ■TIP→ To photograph Bass Harbor, get up close, or walk a short trail for a horizontal shot of the lighthouse and its outbuildings. Also use a tripod or stand firm in the salted wind.

Bass Harbor

CAPE ELIZABETH LIGHT

Two Lights State Park, as the name suggests, is home to two lighthouses. Both of these **Cape Elizabeth** structures were built in 1828, the first twin lighthouses to be erected on the Maine coast. The western light was converted into a private residence in 1924; the eastern light still projects its automated cylinder of light 17 mi out to sea, from a height of 129 feet, and is the subject of Edward Hopper's *Lighthouse at Two Lights* (1929). The grounds immediately surrounding the building and the lighthouse itself are closed to the public, but the structure is easily viewed and photographed from the nearby parking lot. Explore the tidal pools for the small snails known as periwinkles. ■TIP→ If it's foggy, don't stand too close to the foghorn, and in season (late March through late October) be sure to eat a lobster roll at the Lobster Shack Restaurant—but do not feed the seagulls; you will be publicly chastised on the restaurant's loudspeaker if you do.

Cape Elizabeth

CAPE NEDDICK LIGHT

More commonly known as Nubble Light for the small-ish offshore expanse of rock it rests upon, Cape Neddick Light sits a few hundred feet off **York Beach.** With such a precarious location, its grounds are inaccessible to visitors, but close enough to be exceptionally photogenic, especially during the Christmas season when the Town of York hangs Christmas lights and wreaths from the lighthouse and its surrounding buildings (Santa Claus makes an appearance via lobster boat at the annual lighting celebration). You also can view it from Sohier Park. Notice that it emits a red light.

Cape Neddick

MONHEGAN ISLAND LIGHT

Only the adventuresome and the artistic see this light, because **Monhegan Island**, known both for its fishing and artistic communities, is accessible by a 90-minute ferry ride. To reach the lighthouse, you have an additional half-mile walk uphill from the ferry dock. But it's well worth the effort, especially if you enjoy island life—it's nothing but the rugged North Atlantic out here. The light was automated back in 1959, and since the early 1960s the former keeper's quarters has been home to the Monhegan Museum, which has exhibits about the island more so than the lighthouse. The tower itself is closed to the public. ■TIP→ If you've made it this far, stay a quiet night at one of a handful of lodging options on the island, lulled to sleep by muffled waves and the distance from the mainland.

Monhegan Island

PORTLAND HEAD LIGHT

The subject of Edward Hopper's painting *Portland Head-Light* (1927) and one of Maine's most photographed lighthouses (and its oldest), the famous Portland Head Light was completed in January 1791. Its first keeper, Revolutionary War veteran Captain Joseph Greenleaf, was appointed by George Washington. At the edge of Fort Williams Park, in **Cape Elizabeth**, the towering white stone lighthouse stands 101 feet above the sea. The United States Coast Guard operates it and it is not open for tours. However the adjacent keeper's dwelling, built in 1891, is now a museum, where you can inspect various lenses used in lighthouses. Visitors can also explore the numerous trails within the park, as well as its grassy areas, popular for having picnics, kite flying, and watching ships from around the globe enter Portland Harbor.

Portland Head

WEST QUODDY HEAD LIGHT

Originally built in 1808 by mandate of President Thomas Jefferson, West Quoddy Head Light sits in **Lubec** on the easternmost tip of land in the mainland United States—so far east that at certain times of the year it's the first object in the country to be touched by the rising sun's rays. The 49-foot-high lighthouse, now famously painted with distinctive red and white candy stripes, is part of 541-acre Quoddy Head State Park, which has some of the state's best wildlife watching, including humpback, minke, and finback whales. Learn more in the lightkeeper's house-turned-visitor center. You also can climb the 50 steps to the top of the tower.

West Quoddy Head

CAPE COD

Even if you haven't visited Cape Cod, you can likely—and accurately—imagine it. Continually shaped by ocean currents, this windswept land of sandy beaches and dunes has compelling natural beauty.

(this page above) Sandy Neck Beach; Barnstable (opposite page upper right); Race Point Beach, Provincetown (opposite page lower left); Coast Guard Beach, Eastham

Separated from the Massachusetts mainland by the 17½-mi Cape Cod canal—at 480 feet, the world's widest sea-level canal—and linked to it by two heavily trafficked bridges, the Cape is likened in shape to an outstretched arm bent at the elbow, its Provincetown fist turned back toward the mainland. Traditionalists contend that Nauset Light, Coast Guard, Marconi, and Race Point, all set within the Cape Cod National Seashore, are the quintessential beaches. It's hard to argue with that assessment. Combining serious surf, sweeping expanses of sand, magnificent dunes, and mesmerizing views, the four biggies do offer the greatest wow factor. Nevertheless, each of us defines the "perfect" beach differently, and there are many more to choose from. Cape Cod alone has more than 150—enough to keep the most inveterate beachcomber busy all year long. So whatever your taste, there is one to fit your criteria.

CAPE SEAFOOD

If you are what you eat, then most Cape Codders would be a clam...or maybe a lobster roll. It should go without saying that a land named for a type of fish would abound with opportunities to sample tasty seafood, and the region does not disappoint. Five specialties predominate: fried clams, lobster rolls, New England clam chowder, plump scallops, and oysters (especially on the half-shell).

4

FALMOUTH

Old Silver Beach is a long, beautiful crescent of soft white sand in North Falmouth bordered by the Sea Crest Resort at one end. It's especially good for small children because a sandbar keeps it shallow at the southern end and creates tidal pools full of crabs and minnows.

BARNSTABLE

Hovering above Barnstable Harbor and the 4,000-acre **Great Salt Marsh, Sandy Neck Beach** stretches some 6 mi across a peninsula that ends at **Sandy Neck Light.** It is one of the Cape's most beautiful—dunes, sand, and sea spread endlessly east, west, and north. The lighthouse, standing a few feet from the eroding shoreline at the tip of the neck, has been out of commission since 1952.

ORLEANS

The town-managed **Nauset Beach**—not to be confused with Nauset Light Beach on the National Seashore—is a 10-mi sweep of sandy ocean beach with low dunes and large waves good for bodysurfing or board surfing. **Skaket Beach** on Cape Cod Bay is a sandy stretch with calm, warm water good for children, plus restrooms, lifeguards, and a snack bar.

EASTHAM

Nauset Light Beach, adjacent to **Coast Guard Beach**, continues the National Seashore landscape of long, sandy beach backed by tall dunes and grass. It

has showers and lifeguards in summer, but as with other National Seashore beaches, there's no food concession. In this centuries-old area even a fun-in-the-sun day can double as a history lesson. At Eastham's popular **First Encounter Beach**, a bronze plaque marks the spot where Myles Standish and his Mayflower buddies first encountered Native Americans in 1620.

CHATHAM

The 2,500-acre Monomoy Islands (now **Monomoy National Wildlife Refuge**), a fragile 9-mi-long barrier-beach area south of Chatham that is accessible only by boat, is a haven for bird-watchers and an important stop along the North Atlantic Flyway for migratory waterfowl and shorebirds—peak migration times are May and late July.

WELLFLEET

Cahoon Hollow Beach has lifeguards, restrooms, and a restaurant and music club on the sand. This beach tends to attract younger and slightly rowdier crowds; it's a big Sunday-afternoon party place.

PROVINCETOWN

Race Point Beach, one of the Cape Cod National Seashore beaches in Provincetown, has a wide swath of sand stretching far off into the distance around the point and Coast Guard station. Because of its position facing north, the beach gets sun all day long.

MARTHA'S VINEYARD

Far less developed than Cape Cod—thanks to a few local conservation organizations—yet more cosmopolitan than neighboring Nantucket, Martha's Vineyard is an island with a double life: busy and frenetic in summer, quiet and convivial off-season.

(this page above) Wasque Beach, Chappaquiddick Island; (opposite page upper right) Moshup Beach, Aquinnah; (opposite page lower left) Lambert's Cove Beach

Beaches on the North Shore, facing Vineyard Sound, have more-gentle waters, and they're also often slightly less chilly, so they are perfect for swimmers and for families. The Vineyard's South Shore—from the Aquinnah Cliffs to Katama—is said to be among the longest continuous uninterrupted stretches of white-sand beach from Georgia to Maine. The surf, which crashes in refreshingly chilly waves, is a great place for bodysurfing. Public beaches are split between beaches with free parking—such as the Joseph A. Sylvia State Beach—and several where parking fees are collected—such as Moshup Beach in Aquinnah. Private beaches are reserved for permanent and summer residents, who must obtain parking or resident stickers from the appropriate town hall.

NAVIGATING

The island is roughly triangular, with maximum distances of about 20 mi east to west and 10 mi north to south. The west end of the Vineyard, known as Up-Island—from the nautical expression of going "up" in degrees of longitude as you sail west—is more rural and wild than the eastern Down-Island end, comprising Vineyard Haven, Oak Bluffs, and Edgartown.

VINEYARD HAVEN

Owen Park Beach is just steps away from the ferry terminal in Vineyard Haven, making it a great spot to catch some last rays before heading home. **Tisbury Town Beach** is a public beach next to the Vineyard Haven Yacht Club.

OAK BLUFFS

Eastville Beach is a small beach where children can swim in the calm waters and dive off the pilings under the drawbridge. **Joseph A. Sylvia State Beach** is a 2-mi-long sandy beach with a view of Cape Cod across Nantucket Sound. Food vendors and calm, warm waters make this a popular spot for families. **Oak Bluffs Town Beach** is a crowded, narrow stretch of calm water on Nantucket Sound, with snack stands, lifeguards, roadside parking, and restrooms at the steamship office. One section has been nicknamed **Inkwell Beach** by the generations of African-Americans who summer on the Vineyard and have been enjoying this stretch for more than a century.

EDGARTOWN

South Beach, also called Katama Beach, is the island's largest and most popular. A 3-mi ribbon of sand on the Atlantic, it sustains strong surf and occasional dangerous riptides, so check with the lifeguards before swimming.

CHAPPAQUIDDICK ISLAND

One mile southeast of Edgartown, this makes for a pleasant day trip or bike

ride on a sunny day. **East Beach,** one of the area's best beaches, is accessible by car from Dike Road. There's a $3 fee to enter the beach. **Wasque Beach,** at the Wasque Reservation, is an uncrowded ½-mi sandy beach with a parking lot and restrooms. The surf and currents are sometimes strong.

WEST TISBURY

Lambert's Cove Beach, one of the island's prettiest, has fine sand and clear water. The Vineyard Sound–side beach has calm waters good for children and views of the Elizabeth Islands. In season it's restricted to residents and those staying in West Tisbury.

CHILMARK

Lucy Vincent Beach, on the South Shore, is one of the island's most beautiful. The wide strand of fine sand is backed by high clay bluffs facing the Atlantic surf. Keep walking to the left (east, or Down-Island) to reach the unofficial nude beach. In season, Lucy Vincent is restricted to town residents and visitors with passes.

AQUINNAH

Moshup Beach is, according to the Land Bank, "probably the most glamorous" of its holdings, because the beach provides access to the awesome Aquinnah Cliffs. The best views of the cliffs and up to the lighthouse are from a 25-plus-minute walk via boardwalk and beach.

NANTUCKET

Essentially Nantucket is *all* beach—a boomerang-shape sand spit measuring 3½ by 14 mi at its widest points with about 80 mi of sandy shoreline, all of it open, as a matter of local pride, to absolutely everyone.

(this page above) Surfside Beach, South Shore; (opposite page upper right and lower left) Madaket Beach, West End

Whereas elsewhere along the New England Coast private interests have carved prime beachfront into exclusive enclaves, Nantucketers are resolved that the beaches should remain accessible to the general public. A half dozen or so town-supervised beaches have amenities such as snack bars and lifeguard stations. The rest are the purview of solitary strollers. From Nantucket Town, Madaket Road proceeds 6 mi west to Madaket Beach. Milestone Road, accessed from a rotary at the end of Orange Street off Main Street, is a straight, 8-mi shot to the easternmost town of Sconset (formally, Siasconset). To find your way to the South Shore beaches or among the hillocks of Polpis—Altar Rock is the island's highest point, at a mere 100 feet—you'll want to use a map. A bike may be the ideal form of transportation.

CAPE TOURS

Cape Cod Potato Chips Factory (✉ *Independence Dr. to 100 Breed's Hill Rd., off Rte. 132* ⊕ *www.capecodchips.com*) offers a free tour of the factory and free samples on weekdays. The **Cape Cod Central Railroad** (⊕ *www.capetrain.com*) offers two-hour, 42-mi narrated rail tours from Hyannis to the Cape Cod Canal ($21) from late May through October; trains generally run daily.

4

NANTUCKET TOWN

A calm area by the harbor, **Children's Beach** (off Harbor View Way) is an easy walk north from the center of town and a perfect spot for small children. The beach has a grassy park with benches, a playground, lifeguards, a café, picnic tables, showers, and restrooms.

NORTHWEST OF NANTUCKET TOWN

Dionis Beach, 3 mi west of town, is, at its entrance, a narrow strip of sand that turns into a wider, more private strand with high dunes and fewer children. The beach has a rocky bottom and calm, rolling waters; there are lifeguards on duty and restrooms. A short bike- or shuttle-bus ride from town, **Jetties Beach** is a most popular family beach because of its calm surf, lifeguards, bathhouse, restrooms, and snack bar.

WEST END

Madaket Beach is reached by shuttle bus from Nantucket Town or the Madaket Bike Path (5 mi from Upper Main Street) and has lifeguards, but no restrooms. It's known for challenging surf (beware the rip currents) and unbeatable sunsets.

SOUTH SHORE

Surfside Beach, accessible via the Surfside Bike Path (3 mi) or shuttle bus, is the island's most popular surf beach, with lifeguards, restrooms, a snack bar, and a wide strand of sand. It pulls in college students as well as families and is great for kite flying and surf casting. **Cisco**

Beach has heavy surf and lifeguards but no food or restrooms. It's not easy to get to or from Nantucket Town, though: it's 4 mi from town, and there are no bike trails to it, so you'll have to ride in the road, walk, drive, or take a taxi. Also, the dunes are severely eroded, so getting down onto the beach can be difficult. Still, the waves make it a popular spot for body- and board surfers.

WAUWINET

A trip to an unpopulated spit of sand, comprising three cooperatively managed wildlife refuges, is a great way to spend a day relaxing or pursuing a favorite activity, such as bird-watching or fishing. **Coatue**, the strip of sand enclosing Nantucket Harbor, is open for many kinds of recreation including shell fishing (permit required). **Coskata's beaches**, dunes, salt marshes, and stands of oak and cedar attract seabirds, particularly during spring and fall migration. Because of dangerous currents and riptides and the lack of lifeguards, swimming is strongly discouraged in the refuges, especially within 200 yards of the 70-foot stone tower of Great Point Light. Those currents, at the same time, are fascinating to watch at the Great Point tide rip. Seals and fishermen alike benefit from the unique feeding ground that it creates.

A WHALE OF A TALE

by Steve Larese

WHALING IN NEW ENGLAND TIMELINE

mid-1600s	America enters whaling industry
1690	Nantucket enters whaling industry
1820	*Essex* ship sunk by sperm whale
1840s	American whaling peaked
1851	*Moby-Dick* published
1927	The last U.S. whaler sails from New Bedford
1970s	Cape Cod whale-watching trips begin
1986	Ban on whaling by the International Whaling Commission
1992	Stellwagen Bank National Marine Sanctuary established

Cameras have replaced harpoons in the waters north of Cape Cod. While you can learn about New England's whaling history and perhaps see whales in the distance from shore, a whale-watching excursion is the best way to connect with these magnificent creatures—who may be just as curious about you as you are about them.

Once relentlessly hunted around the world by New Englanders, whales today are celebrated as intelligent, friendly, and curious creatures. Whales are still important to the region's economy and culture, but now in the form of ecotourism. Easily accessible from several ports in Massachusetts, the 842-square-mi Stellwagen Bank National Marine Sanctuary attracts finback, humpback, minke, and right whales who feed and frolic here twice a year during their migration. The same conditions that made the Stellwagen Bank area of the mouth of Massachusetts Bay a good hunting ground make it a good viewing area. Temperature, currents, and nutrients combine to produce plankton, krill, and fish to feed marine mammals.

(opposite) Whaling museum custodian and a sperm whale jaw in the 1930s. (top) Hunted to near extinction, humpbacks today number about 80,000, and are found in oceans worldwide.

ON LAND: MARINE AND MARITIME MUSEUMS

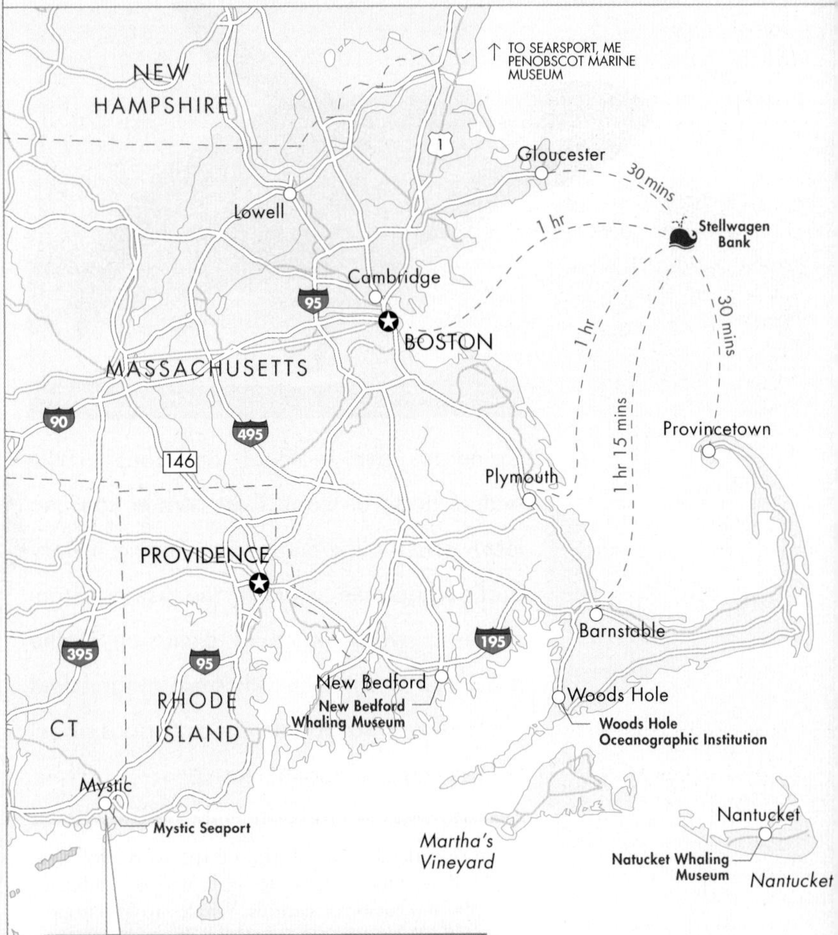

TO SEARSPORT, ME
PENOBSCOT MARINE
MUSEUM

NEW
HAMPSHIRE

Gloucester

30 mins

Lowell

1 hr

Stellwagen
Bank

Cambridge

95

BOSTON

30 mins

MASSACHUSETTS

1 hr

90

495

Provincetown

146

1 hr 15 mins

Plymouth

PROVIDENCE

195

Barnstable

395

RHODE

95

New Bedford

Woods Hole

CT

ISLAND

New Bedford
Whaling Museum

Woods Hole
Oceanographic Institution

Mystic

Nantucket

Mystic Seaport

Martha's
Vineyard

Natucket Whaling
Museum

Nantucket

0   20 miles

0   20 km

Whaling ships, like the *Charles W. Morgan* at Mystic Seaport, hunted whales for their baleen and oil.

Even landlubbers can learn about whales and whaling at these top New England institutions.

Nantucket Whaling Museum. This former whale-processing center and candle factory was converted into a museum in 1929. See art made by sailors, including masterful scrimshaw—intricate nautical scenes carved into whale bone or teeth and filled in with ink (⊠ *Nantucket, Massachusetts* ⊕ *www.nha.org*).

★ **New Bedford Whaling Museum.** More than 200,000 artifacts are collected here, from ships' logbooks to harpoons. A must-see is the 89-foot, half-scale model of the 1826 whaling ship *Lagoda* (⊠ *New Bedford, Massachusetts* ⊕ *www.whalingmuseum.org*).

Woods Hole Oceanographic Institution. The Ocean Science Exhibit Center at this famous Cape Cod research facility highlights deep-sea exploration. An interactive exhibit examines the importance of sound to cetaceans, or marine mammals (⊠ *Woods Hole, Massachusetts* ⊕ *www.whoi.edu*).

★ **Mystic Seaport.** Actors portray life in a 19th-century seafaring village at this 37-acre living-history museum. Don't miss the 1841 *Charles W. Morgan*, the world's only surviving wooden whaling ship (⊠ *Mystic, Connecticut* ⊕ *www.mysticseaport.org*).

Penobscot Marine Museum. Maine's seafaring history and mostly shore-whaling industry is detailed inside seven historic buildings (⊠ *Searsport, Maine* ⊕ *www.penobscotbayhistory.org*).

Nantucket Whaling Museum

New Bedford Whaling Museum

THE GREAT WHITE WHALE

Herman Melville based his 1851 classic *Moby-Dick: or, The Whale* on the true story of the *Essex*, which was sunk in 1821 by huge whale; an albino sperm whale called Mocha Dick; and his time aboard the whaling ship *Acushnet*.

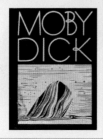

Mystic Seaport

AT SEA: WHALE-WATCHING TOURS

COMMON NORTH ATLANTIC SPECIES

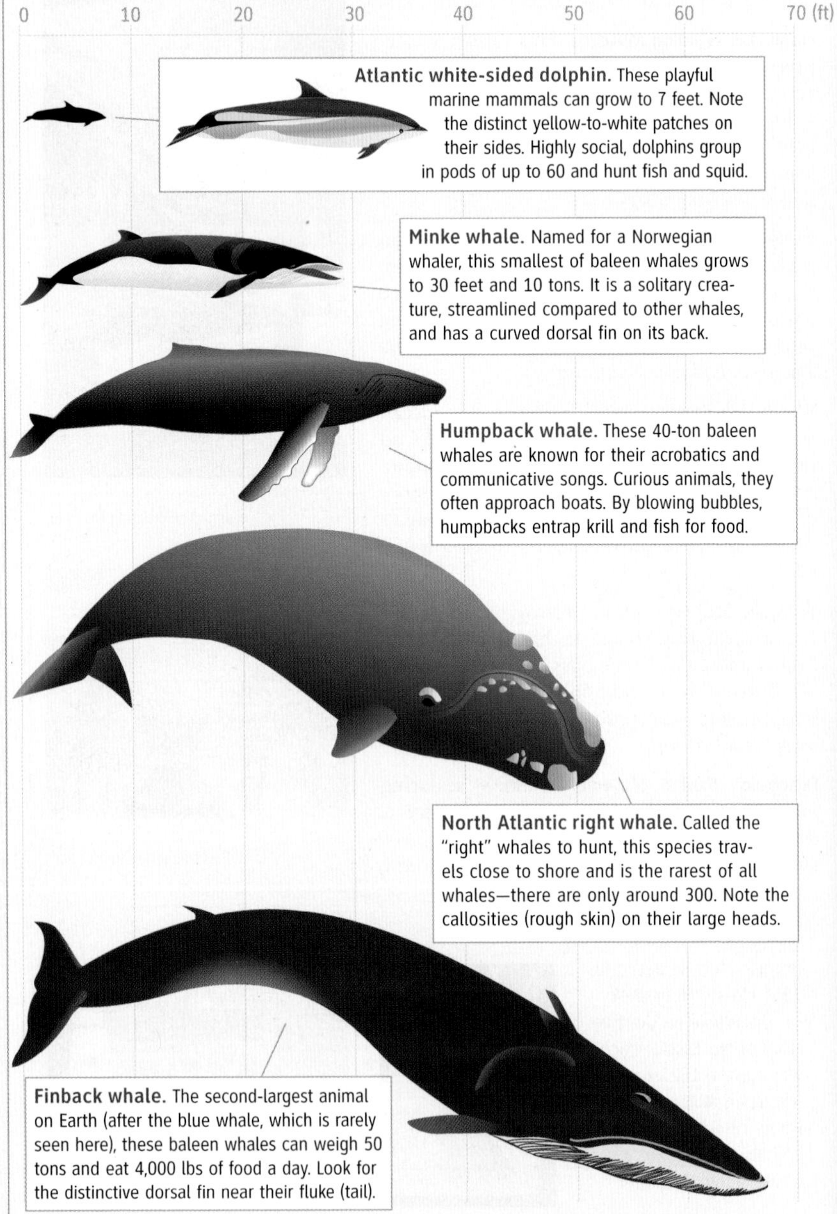

0   10   20   30   40   50   60   70 (ft)

Atlantic white-sided dolphin. These playful marine mammals can grow to 7 feet. Note the distinct yellow-to-white patches on their sides. Highly social, dolphins group in pods of up to 60 and hunt fish and squid.

Minke whale. Named for a Norwegian whaler, this smallest of baleen whales grows to 30 feet and 10 tons. It is a solitary creature, streamlined compared to other whales, and has a curved dorsal fin on its back.

Humpback whale. These 40-ton baleen whales are known for their acrobatics and communicative songs. Curious animals, they often approach boats. By blowing bubbles, humpbacks entrap krill and fish for food.

North Atlantic right whale. Called the "right" whales to hunt, this species travels close to shore and is the rarest of all whales—there are only around 300. Note the callosities (rough skin) on their large heads.

Finback whale. The second-largest animal on Earth (after the blue whale, which is rarely seen here), these baleen whales can weigh 50 tons and eat 4,000 lbs of food a day. Look for the distinctive dorsal fin near their fluke (tail).

SEAWORTHY TRIP TIPS

When to Go: Tours operate April through October; May through September are the most active months in the Stellwagen Bank area.

Ports of Departure: Boats leave from Barnstable and Provincetown on Cape Cod, and Plymouth, Boston, and Gloucester, cutting across the Cape Cod bay to the Stellwagen area. Book tours at least a day ahead. Hyannis Whale Watcher in Barnstable, the Dolphin Fleet, Alpha Whale Watch and Captain John's Whale Watch in Provincetown, and the New England Aquarium, Beantown Whale Watch and Boston Harbor Cruises in Boston are just a few of your options.

Cost: Around $40. Check company Web sites for coupons.

What to Expect: All companies abide by guidelines so as not to harass whales. Tours last 3 to 4 hours and almost always encounter whales; if not, vouchers are often given for another tour. Passengers are encouraged to watch the horizon for water spouts, which indicate a surfaced whale clearing its blowhole to breathe air. Upon spotting an animal, the boat slows and approaches the whale to a safe distance; often, whales will approach an idling boat and even swim underneath it.

What to Bring: Plastic bags protect binoculars and cameras from damp spray. Most boats have a concession stand, but pack bottled water and snacks. ■ TIP ➔ Kids (and adults) will appreciate games or other items to pass the time in between whale sightings.

What to Wear: Wear rubber-soled footwear for slick decks. A waterproof outer layer and layers of clothing will help in varied conditions, as will sunscreen, sunglasses, and a hat that can be secured.

Hyannis Whale Watcher Cruises, Cape Cod Bay

Most boats have cabins where you can warm up and get out of the wind.

Comforting Advice: Small seat cushions like those used at sporting events may be appreciated. Consider taking motion-sickness medication before setting out. Ginger candy and acupressure wristbands can also help. If you feel queasy, get some fresh air and focus your eyes on a stable feature on the shore or horizon.

Photo Hints: Use a fast shutter speed, or sport mode, to avoid blurry photographs. Most whales will be a distance from the boat; have a telephoto lens ready. To avoid shutter delay on your point-and-shoot camera, lock the focus at infinity so you don't miss that breaching whale shot.

DID YOU KNOW?

Most boats have a naturalist aboard to discuss the whales and their environment. Many companies contribute to population studies by reporting the individual whales they spot. Whale tails, called flukes, are distinct and used like fingerprints for identification.

NEW YORK

At 1,377 square mi, Long Island is the largest island on the East Coast, as well as the most varied, shifting from suburban sprawl to verdant farmland and fruit-laden vineyards punctuated by historic seaside villages.

(this page above) Fire Island; (opposite page upper right) Sag Harbor; (opposite page lower left) Montauk Lighthouse

Clean white-sand beaches are Long Island's main attraction for most visitors, whether their idea of beach fun is lounging on the warm sand, watching the sun drop slowly into the water, swimming or surfing in the rolling waves, or just strolling along the shore and breathing the fresh salt air. The pounding surf and endless horizons make the South Shore unforgettable. For serious waves, head to the magnificent South Shore beaches like Jones Beach and Robert Moses, as well as Fire Island. The seashore tends to get crowded on summer weekends, but as you move out east, the crowds thin—especially all the way out in Montauk. Most Hamptons beaches are open only to residents, but lodging properties usually have beach passes for their guests. Fronting Long Island Sound, the beaches on the North Shore are tame in comparison. The shores also are rocky.

WINERIES

The white-sand beaches of the North Fork encircle a broad, central agricultural belt that, it turns out, has near-perfect conditions for ripening European grape varieties like merlot and chardonnay. Now that the quality of Long Island wines rivals that of the world's top labels, the North Fork draws serious wine lovers and sightseeing fun seekers alike.

LONG BEACH

Eleven miles east of Long Beach, the 6½ mi of white sand at **Jones Beach State Park** is one of the best known and most popular of Long Island's beaches, loaded with facilities and a popular boardwalk. **Ocean Beach Park** stretches for 5 mi on the barrier island's south side.

FIRE ISLAND

Fire Island is basically a long stretch of pristine beach. Most of the 32-mi-long barrier island belongs to the **Fire Island National Seashore**. Vehicles aren't allowed on most of the island, which is accessible by ferry, private boat, and water taxi, although you can drive to **Robert Moses State Park** and **Smith Point County Park**, on opposite ends of the island. The island is home to a string of small communities.

SHELTER ISLAND

Reachable only by boat (there's regular ferry service), the 11½-square-mi island offers at least a partial escape from the summer traffic-and-crowd snarls of the Hamptons. **Crescent Beach**, a long sandy strip across the street from the trendy **Sunset Beach** restaurant is especially popular at sunset. Shallow, sandy **Wades Beach** is the island's south side.

WESTHAMPTON

The 296-acre **Cupsogue Beach County Park** on Moriches Inlet has a 1-mi stretch of white-sand beach. A secret spot for

locals and surfers, **Lashley Beach** is a pristine white-sand beach.

SOUTHAMPTON

For a fee, you can stretch out on the sand of **Cooper's Beach**, studying the sea in one direction and historic mansions—including Calvin Klein's massive manse (the one with the turrets)—in the other.

SAG HARBOR

A walk or bike ride from the village center, long, sandy **Havens Beach** has calm waters for swimming, a swing set and playing field, and public restrooms. But a parking permit is required.

AMAGANSETT

Atlantic Avenue Beach is convenient to the center of Amagansett, and there are food concessions, making it possible to stay all day. An East Hampton parking permit is required on weekends and holidays, but not during the week.

MONTAUK

The spectacular undeveloped beaches and parks attract surfers and hikers, and the waters are superb for fishing. On Block Island sound, **Gin Beach** (east of the jetty) has calm water and sparkling clean sand—perfect for families with little ones. You can watch the boats go in and out of the harbor all day. Sandy, clean **Kirk Park Beach** is a protected ocean beach with a picnic area across the street; public restrooms are in the parking lot.

NEW JERSEY

From bird sanctuaries and historic forts in the north to Victorian estates in the south and working-class party towns and casinos in between, the 127-mi Jersey Shore surprisingly caters to all types of travelers.

(this page above) Seaside Heights; (opposite page upper right) Sandy Hook; (opposite page lower left) Asbury Park

The Jersey Shore has worked hard to upgrade its tarnished image from the 1980s. Implementation of beach-use fees and gentrification projects have revitalized the coastline, refurbished the boardwalks, lighthouses, and piers while reinventing the beach-carnival atmosphere. Although it has been the bastion of pride for Garden State residents for generations, the Jersey Shore's charm has been experienced by few outside neighboring states. Today's Jersey Shore combines nature, upscale eateries, and history with funnel cakes, fireworks, and Bruce Springsteen's legacy. The most unspoiled beaches and downy sands are found at the Shore's extremes. In particular, Cape May shines as its crown jewel, a flawlessly preserved Victorian beach resort that meets the calm waters of the Atlantic. The boardwalk in Atlantic City provides a little glitz, now featuring more luxe options as an East Coast Vegas after a multi-billion-dollar face-lift.

MTV'S *JERSEY SHORE*

The wildly popular MTV show follows the summer antics of eight young Italian-Americans in notoriously tawdry Seaside Heights. Endless hours in tanning beds, cheesy hairdos, incomprehensible Jersey accents, and deliciously entertaining trash-talking have ironically become the Shore's biggest marketing machine, much to the chagrin of recently revitalized neighboring towns.

GUNNISON BEACH

The only legal nude beach on the Shore is at **Sandy Hook**. With picture-perfect views of Brooklyn and impressive remnants of Ft. Hancock and Gunnison Battery, the pure quartz of **Gunnison Beach** is enjoyed by both the nude and clothed.

ASBURY PARK

Asbury Park has recently experienced a renaissance and has begun redeveloping the areas surrounding its great, wide beaches and famous boardwalk. Marketing to an upscale clientele, this beach community is known for a variety of fine dining options and tame nightclubs and live music venues.

SPRING LAKE

Known as the "Irish Riviera," **Spring Lake**, a wealthy beach community, promotes its old-fashioned family beaches and surroundings, including two pavilions with public pools. It's a classic Jersey Shore family town, home of locally famous Jean Louise Candies.

POINT PLEASANT BEACH

Family fun meets spring break here, with packed beaches, beachside volleyball courts, and decent nightlife. **Point Pleasant Beach** offers all of what one expects in New Jersey: arcades, psychics, boardwalk fries, amusement rides, and saltwater taffy. Jenkinson's Boardwalk is a family favorite.

SEASIDE HEIGHTS

The underage flock to this working-class party town, which specializes in summer house rentals. **Seaside Heights Beach** is a showcase of debauchery and nightclub mayhem, peppered with families that were here before the town ran amuck with youth gone wild. There is a popular fishing pier, cheesy arcades, and teens with blindingly orange tans.

ATLANTIC CITY

A poor choice for families but a fun option for couples or singles, **Atlantic City** hardly showcases the region's finest waters or sands, but it offers the excitement of world-class shopping, gambling, and partying. The partially overhauled oceanfront boardwalk still lacks attractions for the kids, but it's a boisterous playground for adults.

CAPE MAY

With more than 600 wooden Victorian houses, the postcard-perfect town is a true destination experience. With a laid-back flare and a focus on the beautiful surroundings, it's an ideal location for soaking up the sun, gazing at the turquoise waters, and picnicking with the family. **Sunset Beach** at Cape May Point is a worthwhile destination for the quaint swimming cove and the remains of the WWI warship the *Atlantis,* and for venturing 2 mi farther south to Cape May Lighthouse.

DELAWARE

The First State offers nearly a 25-mi stretch of pristine, sandy beaches along its southern coast. They are the perfect complement to exploring the surrounding small towns and the tax-free shopping opportunities.

(this page above) A view of Herring Point from Lewes Beach; (opposite page upper right) Bethany Beach; (opposite page lower left) Rehoboth Beach

Originally founded as Christian seaside resorts, the small towns along Delaware's southern coastline swell during the summer season with a different type of modern missionary. The thousands of visitors that flock to the beaches—mostly from the surrounding area—come seeking the area's famed "slower, lower" pace. The main season runs from Memorial Day weekend through Labor Day, and water temperatures are warmest in late July and August. The communities of Lewes, Rehoboth, Dewey, and Bethany run north–south, sandwiched between the shore and Route 1, the state's main highway. Interspersed are state parks including Cape Henlopen, accessed north of Rehoboth; Delaware Seashore, located between Dewey and Bethany; and Fenwick Island, located south of Bethany. Each of these parks provides lifeguard patrols during season and modern bathhouses, which offer convenient showers and changing rooms.

TAX-FREE

While prices traditionally run higher at restaurants and retail stories in areas that depend on seasonal sales, the price you see in Delaware is the price you pay. The state is free of all sales taxes, which adds to its appeal (even for the non-beachgoers). Along Route 1, Lewes to Rehoboth, are three large outlet centers with name-brand stores.

LEWES BEACH

Lewes Beach sits at the end of the main street and offers a small oasis of soft sand and calm waters. It is part of a protected natural harbor that sits at the mouth of the Delaware Bay. As residential and commercial growth has brought more people, the beach remains relatively uncrowded and relaxed. There is a metered parking lot adjacent to beach for easy access. A ferry offers daily car and passenger service to Cape May, New Jersey. Here you can boat and fish, and a 6-mi bike trail connects Lewes to Rehoboth and weaves through coastal wetlands, providing sweeping views of the ocean and Cape Henlopen's Great Dune and historic World War II observation towers.

REHOBOTH BEACH

The largest of the Delaware beaches, **Rehoboth Beach** provides all the charm expected from a seaside resort town, including a 1-mi boardwalk lined with souvenir shops, restaurants, and take-out joints (a slice of Grotto's Pizza has been a tradition for half a century), arcade games, and even a small amusement park. It is one of the best areas in the Mid-Atlantic for watching dolphins, which can be spotted just offshore nearly all summer. On major holiday weekends there is barely any unoccupied sand to be found; on July Fourth, thousands gather on the beach and boardwalk to watch fireworks launched over the

ocean. The wide beach is well guarded, and there are multiple public restrooms. At the far south end of the boardwalk is a section, fondly referred to as "Poodle Beach," that is popular with the gay and lesbian community. There are a few large oceanfront hotels and many other options for accommodations, including B&Bs and guesthouses.

DEWEY BEACH

Dewey Beach is consistently ranked as one of the top party beaches in the United States. Visitors here typically spend their days lounging on the beach and their nights enjoying themselves in the town's bars and nightclubs or hosting large (and sometimes rowdy) house parties. There are a few small hotels, but most of the accommodations are house and condo rentals. In recent years, it has become a popular destination for kitesurfing.

BETHANY BEACH

Bethany Beach has traditionally attracted families who own second homes (which are often rented out to visitors) in the area and are seeking a serene beach setting. A small quaint boardwalk, which rarely gets crowded, lines the public beach and includes special wheelchair-access ramps. Many sections of the beach adjacent to the boardwalk are private. The nightlife is very low-key.

MARYLAND

To understand the Eastern Shore, look to the bay. The Chesapeake is 195 mi long and the nation's largest estuary (a semi-enclosed body of water with free connection to the open sea).

(this page above) Wild ponies on Assateague Island; (opposite page upper right) Ocean City; (opposite page lower left) Elk Neck State Park

The Eastern Shore's first permanent English settlement—indeed, the first in Maryland and one of the earliest along the Atlantic—took root on Kent Island, now Queen Anne's County, in 1631. The region's long heritage is recorded in architecture and on paper and canvas, and many Eastern Shore families have been here for many generations. A visit to Maryland's Eastern Shore might consist of exploring hospitable communities and historic sites, strolling through wildlife parks and refuges, pausing at a few of the myriad shops, dining at third-generation-owned waterfront restaurants, and overnighting at inns and bed-and-breakfasts. One of the region's most popular summertime destinations is Ocean City, which clings to a narrow barrier island off the southeastern edge of Maryland's Eastern Shore. Its ocean-side culture differs dramatically from that of the Chesapeake, lacking as it does the early-American aura that pervades the rest of the peninsula.

MARYLAND'S BOUNTY

Oysters—and the Chesapeake's renowned blue crab—are still harvested by a diminishing number of watermen, their fleets of skipjacks—small, flat-bottom boats sometimes powered by modified automobile engines that seem to skim over the surface of the water—concentrated in locales such as Crisfield and Kent Narrows as well as Smith and Tangier islands.

NORTH EAST

About 6 mi south of the town of North East, **Elk Neck State Park** juts into the headwaters of the Chesapeake Bay to its west, with the Elk River flowing along its eastern flank. You can drive almost the length of the peninsula and then walk about a mile through pleasant woodlands to the cliffs on its tip. Elk Neck is a prime location for picnicking as well as for fishing and swimming.

OCEAN CITY

Stretching some 10 mi along a narrow barrier island off Maryland's Atlantic Coast, **Ocean City** draws crowds to its broad, sandy beaches and the innumerable activities and amenities that cling to them, as well as to the quiet bay side. O.C.'s renowned and brilliantly maintained 3-mi-long boardwalk reaches northward as far as 27th Street, nothing but sand to one side, everything else— hotels and eateries and shops—crowding every available square inch lining the other. While it's a little less hectic toward O.C.'s northern end, beaches can still be crowded.

ASSATEAGUE ISLAND

The Assateague Island National Seashore, established in 1962, occupies the northern two-thirds of a 37-mi-long barrier island, encompassing a small portion operated as **Assateague State Park**. Although most famous for the small, shaggy, wild horses (adamantly

4

called "ponies" by the public) that roam freely along the beaches and roads, this stunning island is also worth getting to know for its wildland, wildlife (including the beautiful sika deer), and for simply enjoying a pristine ocean-side environment. In summer the seashore's mild surf is where you can find shorebirds tracing the lapping waves back down the beach. Swimming, biking, hiking, surf fishing, picnicking, and camping are all available on the island. The visitor center at the entrance to the park has aquariums and exhibits about the seashore's fauna, including the famous ponies.

CRISFIELD

In William W. Warner's study of the Chesapeake Bay, *Beautiful Swimmers*, Crisfield was described as a "town built upon oyster shells, millions of tons of it. A town created by and for the blue crab, Cradle of the Chesapeake seafood industries, where everything was tried first." **Janes Island State Park**, nearly surrounded by the waters of the Chesapeake Bay and its inlets, has two distinct areas: a developed mainland section with cabins and camping areas (April through October) a minute's drive from Crisfield, and a portion accessible only by boat. Miles of isolated shorelines and marsh areas beckon those who enjoy the peacefulness of nature.

VIRGINIA

Perhaps no other region in Virginia contains more variety and options for the traveler than its southeastern coastline, both for its historic significance and opportunities for recreation.

(this page above) Surfing at Virginia Beach; (opposite page upper right) Norfolk waterfront; (opposite page lower left) Chincoteague Island

This entire Hampton Roads Area, known as the Tidewater, is land where water in rivers and streams is affected by tides. The channel where the James, Elizabeth, and Nansemond rivers meet is surrounded by both small and larger towns that include the historic settlements of Hampton and Portsmouth, and today's cities Newport News and Norfolk. Linked to the Hampton Roads Area by the unusual Chesapeake Bay Bridge-Tunnel is Virginia's "other coastline," the quiet, largely untrafficked Eastern Shore. The cities in southeast Virginia take on different roles depending on their proximity to the Chesapeake Bay and the rivers that empty into it. Hampton contains the world's largest naval base, and enormous shipbuilding yards are in Norfolk and Newport News. The area is also committed to recreation and tourism: there are many resort hotels, a bustling beachfront, and boardwalk attractions. Virginia Beach, which in the 1950s claimed to have the world's longest public beach, has a showy boardwalk.

FT. MONROE

The channel between Chesapeake Bay and Hampton Roads is the "mouth" of Hampton Roads. On the north side of this passage is Hampton's Ft. Monroe, built in stages between 1819 and 1834. The largest stone fort in the country, it's also the only one still in operation to be enclosed by a moat. It remained a Union stronghold in Confederate territory throughout the Civil War.

CHINCOTEAGUE

Chincoteague (pronounced *shin'*-coh-teeg) exudes a pleasant aura of seclusion. Small, but bustling, with affordable eateries and myriad shops, it is eminently walkable. Within a few minutes' drive or an easy bike ride, relatively uncrowded beaches stretch northward for some 10 mi. Small inns and B&Bs abound. Virginia's Chincoteague National Wildlife Refuge occupies the southern third of Assateague Island, directly off **Chincoteague Island.** (The northern two-thirds, part of Maryland, comprise the Assateague Island National Seashore.) The famed Chincoteague ponies occupy a section of the refuge isolated from the public. Swimming, surf fishing, picnicking, and camping are all available on the island.

CAPE CHARLES

Established in the early 1880s as a railroad-ferry junction, **Cape Charles** has quieted down considerably after its heyday, but in the past few years its very isolation has begun to attraction people from farther and farther away. The town holds one of the largest concentrations of late-Victorian and turn-of-the-20th-century buildings in the region. Clean, uncrowded public beaches beckon, as do a marina, renowned golf courses, and the Eastern Shore of Virginia National Wildlife Refuge.

VIRGINIA BEACH

The heart of **Virginia Beach**—a stretch of the Atlantic shore from Cape Henry south to Rudee Inlet—has been a popular summertime destination for years. With 6 mi of public beach, high-rises, amusements, and a busy 40-block boardwalk, Virginia's most populated city is now a place for communion with nature. The boardwalk and Atlantic Avenue have an oceanfront park; an old-fashioned fishing pier with shops, a restaurant, and a bar; and a 3-mi bike trail. The farther north you go, the more beach you find in proportion to bars, T-shirt parlors, and video arcades. Most activities and events in town are oriented to families. A wide variety of water sports are available, including diving, kayaking, and fishing from several local outfitters.

NORFOLK

Although it has no beaches, Norfolk is a worthwhile side trip for those visiting Virginia Beach, especially if they want a small dose of history to go with their beach trip. Like many other old Southern towns, Norfolk has undergone a renaissance, one that's especially visible in the charming shops and cafés in the historic village of Ghent. There's plenty to see in this old navy town. Nauticus, the waterfront maritime science museum, is a popular family attraction, and the vast Norfolk Naval Station is worth a visit as well.

NORTH CAROLINA

North Carolina's Outer Banks stretch from the Virginia state line south to Cape Lookout. Think of the OBX (a shorthand used on popular bumper stickers) as a series of stepping stones in the Atlantic Ocean.

(this page above) Wrightsville Beach; (opposite page upper right) Nags Head; (opposite page lower left) Jockey's Ridge State Park

THE WRIGHT BROTHERS

A 60-foot granite monument that resembles the tail of an airplane stands as a tribute to Wilbur and Orville Wright. The two bicycle mechanics from Ohio took to the air south of Kitty Hawk on December 17, 1903. You can see a replica of the *Flyer* and stand on the spot where it made four takeoffs and landings, the longest flight a distance of 852 feet.

The state's 300-plus mi of coastline are fronted by a continuous series of fragile barrier islands. Broad rivers lead inland from the sounds, along which port cities have grown. Lighthouses, dunes, and vacation homes (often built by out-of-staters) dot the water's edge. There are battle sites from the American Revolution and the Civil War, elegant golf links, and kitschy putt-putt courses. Aquariums, fishing charters, and museum outreach programs put you up close and personal with the seashore critters. The coast is generally divided into three broad sections that include islands, shoreline, and coastal plains: the Outer Banks (Corolla south through Ocracoke, including Roanoke Island), the Crystal Coast (Core and Bogue Banks, Beaufort, Morehead City), and the greater Cape Fear region (Wrightsville Beach through the Brunswick County islands, including Wilmington).

NAGS HEAD

Nags Head has 11 mi of beach with 40 public access points from Route 12. **Jockey's Ridge State Park** has 426 acres that encompass the tallest sand dune on the East Coast (about 80 to 100 feet). Walk along the 384-foot boardwalk from the visitor center to the edge of the dune. **Coquina Beach**, in the Cape Hatteras National Seashore, is considered by locals to be the loveliest beach in the Outer Banks. The wide-beam ribs of the shipwreck *Laura Barnes* rest in the dunes here.

CAPE LOOKOUT NATIONAL SEASHORE

Extending for 55 mi from Portsmouth Island to Shackleford Banks, **Cape Lookout National Seashore** includes 28,400 acres of uninhabited land and marsh. The remote, sandy islands are linked to the mainland by private ferries. Loggerhead sea turtles, which have been placed on the federal list of threatened and endangered species, nest here. To the south, wild ponies roam Shackleford Banks. The Cape Lookout visitor center is on Harkers Island at the end of U.S. 70 East near a private ferry terminal.

MOREHEAD CITY

The quiet commercial waterfront at Morehead City is dotted with restaurants and shops that have put new life in its old buildings; it's a major charter fishing center. Outside the city, you can fish, swim, picnic, and hike at **Fort Macon**

State Park. Route 58 passes through all the beach communities on Bogue Banks, a barrier island across Bogue Sound from Morehead City. There are a number of popular family beaches, including **Atlantic Beach** and **Emerald Isle**. Points of public access along the shoreline are marked by orange-and-blue signs.

WRIGHTSVILLE BEACH

Wrightsville Beach is a quiet, upscale place. Many houses have been in the same families for generations. Increasingly, however, they're being razed in favor of striking contemporary homes. The beaches are havens for serious sunning, swimming, surfing, and surf fishing, and the beach patrol is vigilant about keeping ATVs, glass containers, alcohol, pets, and bonfires off the sands. In summer, parking can be a problem if you don't arrive early.

KURE BEACH

Kure Beach contains Fort Fisher State Historic Site and one of North Carolina's three aquariums. In some places twisted live oaks still grow behind the dunes. The community has miles of beaches; public access points are marked by orange-and-blue signs. A stroll down the boardwalk in **Carolina Beach** is the romantic cap to an evening. Carolina Beach's popularity with young partiers once earned it the nickname "Pleasure Island," but an influx of affluent families is changing the demographics.

SOUTH CAROLINA

From Myrtle Beach and the Grand Strand in the north to Hilton Head in the south, the South Carolina Coast beckons with beautiful beaches and golf. Whether you like your vacation busy or laid-back there's something for everyone here.

(this page above) Hilton Head; (opposite page upper right) Edisto Island; (opposite page lower left) Myrtle Beach

The lively, family-oriented Grand Strand is one of the eastern seaboard's mega–vacation centers. The main attraction, of course, is the broad, beckoning beach— 60 mi of white sand, stretching from the North Carolina border south to Georgetown, with Myrtle Beach at the hub. Most of the sand is packed hard, so that at low tide you can explore for miles on a bicycle. But the state has other beaches on several sea islands, most notably Hilton Head, a half-tame, half-wild island that is home to more than 25 world-class golf courses, not to mention beautiful beaches. But some of the smaller islands, including St. Simon's, Hunting, and Edisto (which has the best shelling beaches in South Carolina), also have beautiful and unspoiled beaches.

GOLF

If you are looking to combine a beach trip with some golf, the Myrtle Beach Area is the place to go. Some 120 golf courses at all skill levels meander through pine forests, dunes, and marshes. The Arrowhead Course in the Briarcliffe Area offers holes and vistas along the Intracoastal Waterway. Many of the region's golf courses have championship lay-outs; most are public.

MYRTLE BEACH

You shouldn't have too much trouble getting to a spot of sand in **Myrtle Beach**. There are nearly 150 public beach-access points in the city, all marked with signs. Most are located off Ocean Boulevard and have parking and "shower towers" for cleaning up. For a more out-of-the-way experience, head south of Myrtle Beach to the relatively calm **Myrtle Beach State Park**. There you can swim in the ocean, hike on a nature trail, and fish in the surf or from a pier.

CHARLESTON AREA BEACHES

Trees, palmettos, and other natural foliage cover the interior, and there's a river that winds through **Folly Beach County Park**. The beach is 12 mi southwest of Charleston. You can play beach volleyball or rent a raft at the 600-foot-long beach in the **Isle of Palms County Park**. The public **Kiawah Beachwalker Park**, about 28 mi southwest of Charleston, has 500 feet of deep beach.

ST. HELENA ISLAND

Nine miles southeast of Beaufort via U.S. 21, **St. Helena Island** is the site of the Penn Center Historic District. Established in the middle of the Civil War, Penn Center was the South's first school for freed slaves. This island is both residential and commercial, with nice beaches, cooling ocean breezes, and a great deal of natural beauty.

HUNTING ISLAND

Secluded **Hunting Island State Park** has about 3 mi of public beaches—some dramatically and beautifully eroding. It harbors 5,000 acres of rare maritime forests. Nonetheless, the light sands decorated with driftwood and the raw, subtropical vegetation are breathtaking. Stroll the 1,300-foot-long fishing pier, among the longest on the East Coast, or you can go fishing or crabbing.

EDISTO ISLAND

Edisto Beach State Park covers 1,255 acres and includes marshland and tidal rivers, a 1½-mi-long beachfront, towering palmettos, and a lush maritime forest with a 3½-mi trail running through it. The park has the best shelling on public property in the Lowcountry.

HILTON HEAD

There are four public entrances to **Hilton Head**'s 12 mi of ocean beach. The two main parking spots are off U.S. 278 at Coligny Circle in the South End, near the Holiday Inn, and on Folly Field Road, Mid-Island. Both have changing facilities. South of Folly Field Road, Mid-Island along U.S. 278, Bradley Beach Road and Singleton Road lead to beaches where parking space is limited. ■TIP→ Put your towels, shoes, and other earthly possessions way up on the sand. Tides here can fluctuate as much as 7 feet.

GEORGIA

Some of Georgia's coastal islands are developed and easily accessible, while others are remote and completely pristine. They all offer natural beauty, beaches, and a slower pace of life.

(this page above) St. Simons Island; (opposite page upper right) Jekyll Island; (opposite page lower left) Horses on Cumberland Island

Georgia's coastal isles are a string of lush barrier islands meandering down the Atlantic Coast from Savannah to the Florida border. Notable for their subtropical beauty and abundant wildlife, the isles also strike a unique balance between some of the wealthiest communities in the country and some of the most jealously protected preserves found anywhere. Until recently, large segments of the coast were in private hands, and as a result much of the region remains as it was when the first Europeans set eyes on it 450 years ago. The marshes, wetlands, and waterways teem with birds and other wildlife, and they're ideal for exploring by kayak or canoe. Though the islands have long been a favorite getaway of the rich and famous, they no longer cater only to the well-heeled. There's mounting pressure to develop these wilderness shores and make them even more accessible.

HORSES OF CUMBERLAND

Cumberland Island is about as far removed from civilization as you can get, accessible only by ferry. The island's forests are inhabited by some 200 feral horses. The animals are descendants of horses that were abandoned by the Spanish in the 1500s, and seeing the majesty of these horses running wild across the shore makes the effort of getting here worthwhile.

SAPELO ISLAND

Sapelo Island is reachable only by ferry. It is home to the Geechee, direct descendants of African slaves who speak a creole of English and various African languages. This rapidly dwindling community maintains many traditional African practices, including the making of sweetgrass baskets and the use of herbal medicines made from recipes passed down for generations. It's also a nearly pristine barrier island with miles of undeveloped beaches and abundant wildlife.

ST. SIMONS ISLAND

St. Simons Island may be the Golden Isles' most developed vacation destination: here you can swim and sun, golf, hike, fish, ride horseback, tour historic sites, and feast on local seafood at more than 50 restaurants. Despite the development, the island has managed to maintain some of its charmingly slow-paced Southern atmosphere.

LITTLE ST. SIMONS ISLAND

Little St. Simons Island is 15 minutes by boat from St. Simons, but in character it's a world apart. The entire island is a privately owned resort; there are no telephones and no TVs. There are 7 mi of undisturbed beaches, where you can swim in the mild surf, fish from the dock, or seine for shrimp and crab in the marshes.

JEKYLL ISLAND

Jekyll Island, a resort for the rich and famous from the Gilded Age, is now much more inviting. A water park, picnic grounds, and facilities for golf, tennis, fishing, biking, and jogging are all open to the public. One side of the island is lined by nearly 10 mi of hard-packed Atlantic beaches; the other by picturesque salt marshes. Egrets, pelicans, herons, and sandpipers skim the gentle surf. The island's clean, public beaches are free and open year-round. Bathhouses with restrooms, changing areas, and showers are open at regular intervals along the beach.

CUMBERLAND ISLAND

Cumberland, the largest of Georgia's coastal isles, is a nearly unspoiled 18-mi spit of land off the coast of St. Marys. Largely undeveloped, its pristine beaches are a place where wild horses roam free. Though the **Cumberland Island National Seashore** is open to the public, the only public access to the island is via the *Cumberland Queen,* a reservations-only, 146-passenger ferry based near the National Park Service Information Center at St. Marys. From the Park Service docks at the island's south end, you can follow wooded nature trails, swim and sun on 18 mi of undeveloped beaches, go fishing and bird-watching, and view the ruins of Thomas Carnegie's great estate, Dungeness.

4

Best Beaches in Florida and the Gulf Coast

WHAT'S WHERE

1 Panhandle. Southern gentility and redneck rambunctiousness make the Panhandle a colorful place—but it's the green Gulf waters and sugar-white sands that keep devotees coming back for more.

2 Northeast Florida. Though time rewinds in historic St. Augustine, it's on fast-forward in Daytona Beach and the Space Coast, where horse-drawn carriages are replaced by race cars and rocket ships.

3 Tampa Bay Area. Tampa's Busch Gardens and Ybor City are only part of the area's appeal. Culture vultures flock to St. Petersburg and Sarasota for concerts and museums, while eco-adventurers veer north to the Nature Coast.

4 Lower Gulf Coast. Blessed with beaches, this was the last bit of coast to be settled. But as Naples's manicured golf greens and Fort Myers's mansion-cum-museums prove, it is far from uncivilized.

5 Palm Beach and the Treasure Coast. This area scores points for diversity. Palm Beach and environs are famous for golden sand and glitzy residents, whereas the Treasure Coast has unspoiled natural delights.

6 Fort Lauderdale and Broward County. The "Suds and Sun Capital of the Universe"

has grown up. The beaches that first drew college kids are now complemented by luxe lodging and entertainment options.

7 Miami and Miami Beach. Art deco buildings and balmy beaches set the scene. Vacations here are as much about lifestyle as locale, so prepare for power shopping, club hopping, and decadent dining.

8 Florida Keys. This slender string of landfalls, linked by a 110-mi highway, marks the southern edge of the continental United States. It's nirvana for anglers, divers, book lovers, and Jimmy Buffet wannabes.

9 Alabama. The beaches here are not high on many visitors' radar, but these sandy beaches rival anything Florida has to offer.

10 Mississippi. Better known for Biloxi's casinos and honky-tonk atmosphere, the Mississippi Coast still has some lovely beaches on its barrier islands.

11 Texas. Stretching from Galveston to South Padre Island, the beaches along Texas's coast are wide, sandy, and (except during spring break) fairly quiet.

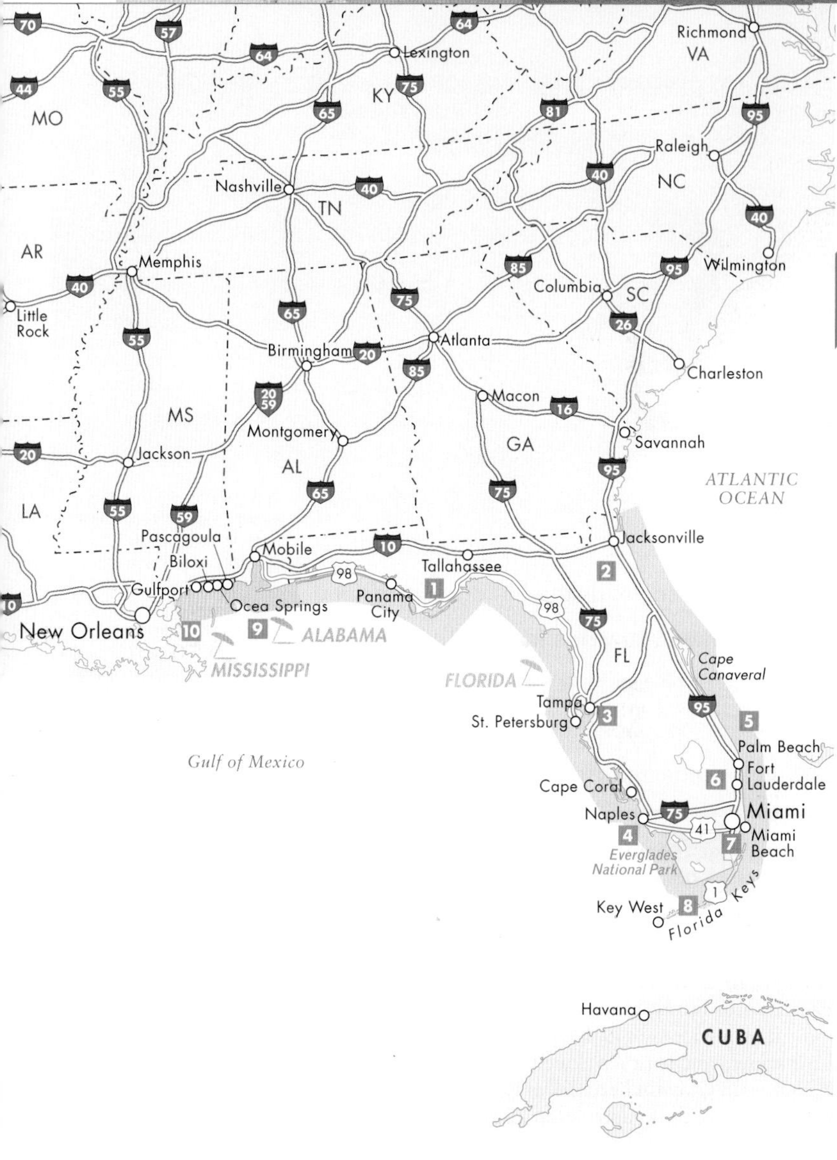

Map

- 70
- 57
- 64 Lexington
- KY
- 75
- 64
- 44
- 55
- 65
- 81
- Richmond
- VA
- 95
- MO
- AR
- 40
- Nashville
- TN
- 40
- 40
- Raleigh
- NC
- 40
- Wilmington
- Little Rock
- Memphis
- 65
- 75
- 85
- 95
- Columbia SC
- 55
- Birmingham
- 20
- Atlanta
- 26
- Charleston
- MS
- 20 59
- Montgomery
- AL
- Macon
- 16
- GA
- Savannah
- 20
- Jackson
- 55
- 59
- 65
- 75
- 95
- ATLANTIC OCEAN
- LA
- Pascagoula
- Biloxi
- Mobile
- 10
- Jacksonville
- 0
- Gulfport
- 98
- Tallahassee
- Ocea Springs
- 9
- Panama City
- 1
- 2
- New Orleans
- 10
- ALABAMA
- 98
- 75
- MISSISSIPPI
- FLORIDA
- FL
- Cape Canaveral
- Tampa
- 3
- St. Petersburg
- 95
- 5
- Gulf of Mexico
- Palm Beach
- Cape Coral
- 6
- Fort Lauderdale
- Naples
- 4
- 75
- Miami
- 41
- Everglades National Park
- 7
- Miami Beach
- Key West
- 8
- 1
- Florida Keys
- Havana
- CUBA

THE PANHANDLE

Not every stretch of Florida coastline features great beaches; some have rough sands, others may find you contending with rocks, mud, and stingrays when you wade in. What's appealing about the Panhandle—especially the Emerald Coast—are beaches that are marked by soft, powdery sands and clear, clean water.

(this page above) Pensacola Beach; (opposite page upper right) Panama City Beach pier; (opposite page lower left) Surfing at Pensacola Beach

WHEN TO GO

The Panhandle beaches are best visited in the summer months. In late summer and fall, jellyfish can be a problem. Florida's Gulf Coast beaches also have to occasionally endure annoying red-tide algae that can make breathing difficult and cause itchy eyes. For current status on red tide in the area, go to ⊕ *research. myfwc.com*, the home page for Florida's Fish and Wildlife Research Institute.

Nineteen beach communities cluster along Route 30A, which breaks off U.S. 98 south of Sandestin and runs along the water for more than 17 mi before rejoining with U.S. 98. Here, sugar-white, quartz-crystal sands and emerald-green waters make for some of the finest stretches of sand and sea in the country. Known as the Beaches of South Walton, many of these beaches are little more than a wide spot in the road, and all are among the least known and least developed in the Gulf Coast Area, even though Grayton Beach, near Route 283, is regularly ranked among the country's top 20 beaches.

PENSACOLA

Here you get miles of perfect beach and a convenient location, fringed by a commercial district and just over the bridge from Pensacola itself. Even though it was smacked by Hurricane Ivan and some homes will never be rebuilt, it's part of the **Gulf Island National Seashore,** and the stretch around **Santa Rosa Island** to the west and **Opal Beach** to the east gives you plenty of room to roam. It's a nice balance that blends privacy and accessibility, as well as passive lounging and active beach recreation. The sand is white and soft, and water adventures include scuba diving (explore the sunken USS *Oriskany*), fishing (the Pensacola Fishing Pier is 1,471 feet long!), kayaking, sailing, wave-running, surfing, and swimming. The water temperatures are in the 80s in summer and in the 60s in winter. For shopping, there's the **Quietwater Beach** Boardwalk.

GRAYTON BEACH

This area will take you back to Old Florida where there are no condos, no strip malls, and no beach concessions. Instead, **Grayton Beach** is a state park that has preserved the area and its sea oats and miles of walking trails for a laid-back time in the outdoors. The park has even added cabins (sans telephones and televisions), so you can experience Florida's Gulf Coast in its natural state. There are big dunes, ample bird-watching and wildlife viewing, and on-the-water activities like canoeing, fishing, sailing, and swimming. It may be too slow paced for kids.

PANAMA CITY

If your visit to the Panhandle is based purely on beach access and activities, then **Panama City Beach** is where you want to be. Granted, Front Beach Road can get crowded, but parallel roads can move you up and down the coast fairly swiftly. Then again, once you check into your condo or hotel you may never need to hit the road. Instead, plant yourself by the pool, which is usually no more than a few feet away from the Gulf waters—reached by stepping over the softest and whitest sands in the state. Paradise. A popular family retreat most times, families tend to steer clear during spring break, when it gets a bit crazy, but arrive in droves in summer. For a peaceful excursion, arrive in winter. You won't be able to swim, but the views are still splendid.

NORTHEAST FLORIDA

(this page above and opposite page upper right) Daytona Beach; (opposite page lower left) Cocoa Beach

Northeastern Florida's primary draw is its beaches. Hugging the coast are long, slender barrier islands whose entire eastern sides make up a broad band of spectacular sand. Except in the most populated areas, development has been modest, and beaches are lined with funky, appealing little towns.

These towns range from Jacksonville and its environs to historic St. Augustine and Daytona Beach to the surfer's paradise of Cocoa Beach. Also in Northeast Florida is Amelia Island and Fernandina Beach, an idyllic playland amid Victorian buildings and natural surroundings, where wildlife viewing and water sports are key.

Separated from the mainland by the Intracoastal Waterway, Jacksonville's main beaches run along the barrier island that includes the laid-back towns of Jacksonville Beach, Neptune Beach, Atlantic Beach, and Ponte Vedra Beach.

QUIETER BEACHES

Small and scenic, Paradise Beach is a 1,600-foot stretch of sand that is part of a 10-acre park north of Indialantic, about 20 mi south of Cocoa Beach on Route A1A. It has showers, restrooms, picnic tables, a refreshment stand, and lifeguards in summer. Meanwhile, Satellite Beach, about 15 mi south of Cocoa Beach on Route A1A, is popular for family vacations because of the slow pace and lack of crowds.

AMELIA ISLAND/FERNANDINA BEACH

Far from the madness of some of the popular spring break beaches, the shores of **Amelia Island** puts you close to nature: observe sea turtles nesting, go horseback riding along the side, and fish for tarpon, kingfish, and amberjack. Access the beach on Fletcher Avenue.

DAYTONA

Daytona Beach, the World's Most Famous Beach is fronted with a mixture of tall condos and apartments, hotels, low-rise motels, and flashy nightclubs. Although the hurricanes of 2004 and 2005 caused hundreds of millions of dollars in damage to the Daytona Area, most commercial properties and many smaller family-owned properties have since reopened. Traffic can get backed up, as driving on the sand is allowed (be careful, because cars can, and do, get stuck); areas marked no-car zones are less frenetic and more family-friendly.

COCOA BEACH

As home to Ron Jon Surf Shop (the world's largest surf shop) and the Cocoa Beach Surf Company (the world's largest surf complex), and the birthplace of eight-time world surfing champion Kelly Slater, it's only fitting that **Cocoa Beach** be dubbed "Surfing Capital of the East Coast." Grommets looking to follow in his aqua shoes should head to the beach at 3rd Street North (renamed "Slater Way" in his honor), where he learned

the basics, then head to the East Coast Surfing Hall of Fame and Museum (located inside the Cocoa Beach Surf Company on Atlantic Avenue) for inspiration. Stretching far over the Atlantic, the Cocoa Beach Pier is an everyday gathering spot as well as a beachside grandstand for space-shuttle launches. There are several souvenir shops, bars, and restaurants, as well as a bait-and-tackle shop. It costs $3 to park here, and another $1 for access to the fishing part of the pier that dangles 800 feet out into the Atlantic.

JACKSONVILLE

The northernmost of Jacksonville's beaches, **Atlantic Beach** is more subdued but a favorite with local surfers. Adjacent Neptune Beach is largely residential and draws bicyclists and in-line skaters who cruise up and down 1st Street. Just south is **Jacksonville Beach**, which has a decidedly more active shoreline, with volleyballs and Frisbees buzzing through the air and portable radios blaring everything from Kanye West to Van Halen. With multimillion-dollar homes stretching for miles, **Ponte Vedra** is the most difficult beach to access but makes for a lovely drive down Route A1A. Lifeguards are on duty on the more populated stretches of the beaches from 10 to 6 in summer.

TAMPA BAY

Tampa Bay gets rave reviews for having some of the state's best beaches. The allure includes warm water from spring through fall, gentle waves (when there are any at all), good shelling, and usually smaller crowds than oceanfront beaches. These are great places to go for romantic walks, or enjoy spectacular sunsets.

(this page above) Caladesi Island State Park; (opposite page upper right) Siesta Beach; (opposite page lower left) Clearwater Beach

Tampa Bay Area beaches include Madeira Beach (called Mad Beach by locals), where you can see dolphins at play, and North Redington Beach, once a vacationing spot for Marilyn Monroe and Joe DiMaggio. In Sarasota County, beaches range from artsy Siesta Key to the mansion-affronted Casey Key. Farther south, Venice beaches are good for shelling, but they're most known for their wealth of sharks' teeth and fossils, washed up from the ancient shark burial grounds just offshore. To learn more, contact **Tampa Bay Beaches Chamber of Commerce** (✉ *6990 Gulf Blvd., St. Pete Beach* ☎ *800/944–1847* ⊕ *www.tampabaybeaches.com*) or **Sarasota Convention & Visitors Bureau** (✉ *701 N. Tamiami Trail [U.S. 41], Sarasota* ☎ *800/522–9799* ⊕ *www.sarasotafl.org*).

WHEN TO GO

Tampa Bay Area beaches can be very crowded in summer, when families flock here, as well as in winter, when snowbirds land to escape the cold in their home states. Arguably, the best times to visit are early fall and late spring, when there are fewer people and milder temperatures. But occasional red tides, caused by an algae, can make swimming unsafe.

BEACH AT SOUTH LIDO PARK

At the southern tip of Sarasota's Island, at 2201 Ben Franklin Drive in Lido Key, **South Lido Park** has one of the best beaches in the region, but note that there are no lifeguards. The sugar-sand beach offers little for shell collectors, but try your luck at fishing, take a dip in the Gulf, or picnic as the sun sets through the Australian pines into the water. Facilities include nature trails, canoe and kayak trails, restrooms, and picnic grounds.

CALADESI ISLAND STATE PARK

The beach at **Caladesi**, accessible by ferry from Honeymoon Island State Recreation Area, offers three reasons to visit: pure white beaches, beautiful sunsets, and, by Florida standards, relative seclusion. Oh, we left out the fact that this is an excellent spot for bird-watching.

CLEARWATER BEACH

You will find crowds on weekends and during spring break, which are a turnoff for some. **Clearwater Beach**, a sun worshippers' shrine off State Road 60, is the west coast's best muscle beach. Expect to see tanned bods draped with minimal bikinis and Speedos, plenty of hot cars, and sunsets nearly as grand as at Caladesi.

PASS-A-GRILLE BEACH

Located where Tampa Bay meets the Gulf of Mexico in southern Pinellas County, long-popular **Pass-a-Grille Beach**

is wide and still dotted with small dunes and sea oats, two throwbacks that are rapidly vanishing in Florida. Pass-a-Grille (also called St. Pete Beach) tends to be crowded on weekends and during summer and spring break.

SIESTA BEACH

This 40-acre park at 948 Beach Road in Siesta Key, Sarasota, has nature trails, a concession stand, fields for soccer and softball, picnic facilities, a playground, restrooms, a fitness trail, and tennis and volleyball courts. **Siesta Beach** has fine, powdery quartz sand that squeaks under your feet, very much like the sand along the state's northwestern coast. It has been ranked as one of the country's top beaches.

TURTLE BEACH

Only 14 acres, this beach-park at 8918 Midnight Pass Road in Siesta Key, Sarasota, is popular with families and is more secluded than most Gulf beaches. **Turtle Beach** doesn't have the soft sand of **Siesta Beach**, but it does have boat ramps, a canoe and kayak launch, bay and Gulf fishing, picnic facilities, restrooms, and a volleyball court.

LOWER GULF COAST

Gorgeous, long, white-sand beaches fringe the Lower Gulf Coast and barrier islands. Known ultimately for their great shelling and kid-friendly waves, the beaches here range from the natural, undeveloped sands of Sanibel Island to the manicured parks of Naples.

(this page above) Shelling on Sanibel Island; (opposite page upper right) A pier on Sanibel; (opposite page lower left) Kayaking at Sanibel

Sanibel Island holds the highest reputation for seashells on the seashore in these parts due to the east–west torque at its south end. Shelling is best at low tide and after a storm has washed shells ashore. Remember, collecting live shells is illegal on Sanibel Island and in all state parks, so look only for uninhabited specimens. Other local laws limit the taking of live shells to two per person per species per day.

All of the beaches charge for parking; some are resident-only designated and require a car sticker. (Many of the latter you can walk or ride a bike to if you're looking for quiet and seclusion. For the utmost in getaway-ness, rent a boat and hit the bridgeless islands of Don Pedro, Cayo Costa, North Captiva, and Keewaydin.)

SEASHELLING

Veteran shell-seekers go out before the sun rises so they can be the first on the beach after a storm or night of high tides. (Storms and cold fronts bring in the best catches.) Most shellers use a bag for collecting, but before packing your shells for transport, wash them thoroughly to remove sand and debris. Sanibel shops sell books and supplies for identifying your finds and turning them into craft projects.

BAREFOOT BEACH PRESERVE

Although it's not easy to reach—the drive from Bonita Beach Road along Lely Beach Road to the Collier County treasure **Barefoot Beach Preserve** takes you through a speed-bump-mined development—it's worth the inconvenience if you're looking for a natural encounter along with your beach play. Past the speed bumps, gopher tortoises crossing the road will slow you down. Beachgoers come for shells, canoeing, and exploring nature off the beach.

BOWMAN'S BEACH

Long, wide **Bowman's Beach**, on Sanibel's northwest end, is the island's most secluded strand. Walk the length of the beach and leave humanity behind, finding some of the area's greatest concentrations of shells along the way. In fact, while most beaches in Sanibel and Captiva are worthy hunting grounds for shell devotees, Bowman's tops them all. This is because Bowman's is the hardest to reach, most spread-out, and least populated of the island's many beaches. You might even score one of the island's most coveted shells, the Junonia. The sunsets at the north end are spectacular.

DELNOR-WIGGINS PASS STATE PARK

Its placement across the pass from **Barefoot Beach** and a preserved bay backdrop make **Delnor-Wiggins Pass State Park** in north Naples popular with both fishermen and nature lovers. Rangers conduct

birding and sea turtle programs at different times of year. Beach buffs adore its stretch of sand immune from the high-rise rash to the south. Picnic facilities and an observation tower add to the family fun-ness of the park.

LOVERS KEY STATE PARK

Among Florida's most-visited parks, **Lovers Key State Park**, on a barrier island south of Fort Myers Beach, on Route 865, is a natural haven. Birds flock to its estuary, kayakers paddle through, and a gazebo on the beach sees many a wedding. The island got its name, legend has it, before it was accessible by car, when only lovers dared venture.

LOWDERMILK PARK

Looking for pure fun with your beach day, hold the nature lessons? That's what prettily landscaped **Lowdermilk Park** in Naples is all about. Families appreciate the grassy lawn, playground, volleyball nets, picnic facilities, shallow waters, playful waves, and food concession at this beach on Gulf Shore Boulevard at Banyan Boulevard.

TURNER BEACH

Turner Beach, a patch of undulating sand on the southern tip of Captiva, is a good spot for catching the setting sun. Due to the strong currents here it's much better for surfing than swimming.

GONE FISHIN

by Gary McKechnie

My favorite uncle has a passion for fishing.

It was one I didn't really understand—I'm more of a motorcycle guy, not a fishing pole–toting one. But one day he piqued my curiosity by telling me that fishing has many of the same enticements as motorcycling. Come again? He beautifully described the peaceful process of it all—how the serenity and solitude of the sport wash away concerns about work and tune him into the wonder of nature, just like being on a bike (minus the helmet and curvy highways).

I took the bait, and early one morning a few weeks later, my Uncle Bud and I headed out in a boat to a secluded cove on the St. Johns River near DeLand. We'd brought our rods, line, bait, and tackle—plus hot chocolate and a few things to eat. We didn't need much else. We dropped in our lines and sat silently, watching the fog hover over the water.

There was a peaceful stillness as we waited (and waited) for the fish to bite. There were turtles sunning themselves on logs and herons perched in the trees. We waited for hours for just a little nibble. I can't even recall now if we caught anything, but it didn't matter. My uncle was right: it was a relaxing way to spend a Florida morning.

(opposite) Fisherman holding big tuna, (top) Family fishing on boat.

REEL TIME

Florida is recognized as the "Fishing Capital of the World" as well as the "Bass Capital of the World." It's also home to some of the nation's most popular crappie tournaments.

Florida and fishing have a bond that goes back to thousands of years before Christ, when Paleo-Indians living along Florida's rivers and coasts were harvesting the waters just as readily as they were harvesting the land. Jump ahead to the 20th century and along came amateur anglers like Babe Ruth, Clark Gable, and Gary Cooper vacationing at central Florida fishing camps in pursuit of bream, bluegill, and largemouth bass, while Ernest Hemingway was scouring the waters off Key West in hopes of snagging marlin, tarpon, and snapper. Florida was, and is, a sportsman's paradise.

A variety of fish and plentiful waterways—7,800 lakes and 1,700 rivers and creeks, not to mention the gulf and the ocean—are just two reasons why Florida is the nation's favorite fishing spot. And let's not forget the frost-free attributes: unlike their northern counterparts, Florida anglers have yet to

When he wasn't writing, Ernest Hemingway loved to fish in the Florida Keys. He's shown here in Key West in 1928.

drill through several feet of ice just to go fishing in the wintertime. Plus, a well-established infrastructure for fishing—numerous bait and tackle shops, boat rentals, sporting goods stores, public piers, and charters—makes it easy for experts and first-time fishermen to get started. For Floridians and the visitors hooked on the sport here, fishing in the Sunshine State is a sport of sheer ease and simplicity.

An afternoon on the waters of Charlotte County in southwest Florida.

CASTING WIDE

The same way Florida is home to rocket scientists and beach bums, it's home to a diverse variety of fishing methods. What kind will work for you depends on where you want to go and what you want to catch.

From the Panhandle south to the Everglades, fishing is as easy as finding a quiet spot on the bank or heading out on freshwater lakes, tranquil ponds, spring-fed rivers, and placid inlets and lagoons.

Perhaps the biggest catches are found offshore—in the Atlantic Ocean, Florida Straits, or the Gulf of Mexico. For saltwater fishing, you can join a charter, be it a private one for small groups or a large party one; head out along the long jetties or public piers that jut into the ocean; or toss your line from the shore into the surf (known as surf casting). Some attempt a tricky, yet effective form of fishing called net casting: tossing a circular net weighted around its perimeter; the flattened net hits the surface and drives fish into the center of the circle.

Surf casting on Juno Beach, about 20 mi north of Palm Beach.

FRESHWATER FISHING VS. SALTWATER FISHING

FRESH WATER
With about 8,000 lakes to choose from, it's hard to pick the leading contenders, but a handful rise to the top: Lake George, Lake Tarpon, Lake Weohyakapka, Lake Istokpoga, Lake Okeechobee, Crescent Lake, Lake Kissimmee, Lake George, and Lake Talquin. Florida's most popular freshwater game fish is the largemouth bass. Freshwater fishermen are also checking rivers and streams for other popular catches, such as spotted bass, white bass, Suwannee bass, striped bass, black crappie, bluegill, redear sunfish, and channel catfish.

SALT WATER
The seas are filled with some of the most challenging (and tasty) gamefish in America. From piers, jetties, private boats, and charter excursions, fishermen search for bonefish, tarpon, snook, redfish, grouper, permit, spotted sea trout, sailfish, cobia, bluefish, snapper, sea bass, dolphin (the short, squat fish, not Flipper), and sheepshead.

Tarpon

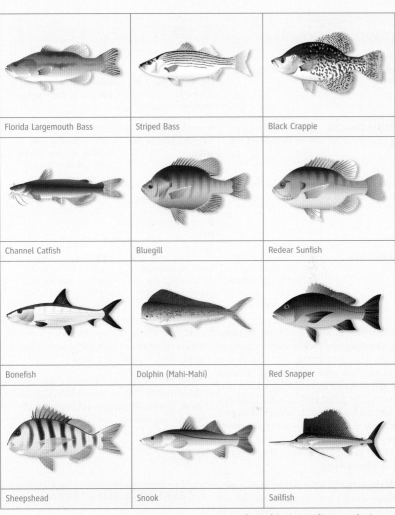

Florida Largemouth Bass

Striped Bass

Black Crappie

Channel Catfish

Bluegill

Redear Sunfish

Bonefish

Dolphin (Mahi-Mahi)

Red Snapper

Sheepshead

Snook

Sailfish

(top six) freshwater, (bottom six) saltwater

HERE'S THE CATCH

The type of fish you're after will depend on whether you fish in Florida's lake, streams, and rivers, or head out to sea. The Panhandle has an abundance of red snapper, while Lake Okeechobee is the place for bass fishing—although the largemouth bass is found throughout the state (they're easiest to catch in early spring, when they're in shallower waters). If you're looking for a good charter, Destin has the largest charter-boat fishing fleet in the nation. In the Florida Keys, you can fish by walking out in the very shallow water for hundreds of yards with the water only up to your knees; the fish you might reel in this way include bonefish, tarpon, and permit.

CHARTING THE WATERS

TYPE OF TRIP	COST	PROS	CONS
LARGE PARTY BOAT	$40/person for 4 hrs.	The captain's fishing license covers all passengers; you keep whatever you catch.	Not much privacy or solitude: boats can hold as many as 35 passengers.
PRIVATE CHARTER	Roughly $1,200 for up to six people for 9 hrs.	More personal attention and more time on the water.	Higher cost ($200 per person instead of $40); tradition says you split the catch with the captain.
GUIDED TRIP FOR INLAND WATERS	Around $200–$360 for one or two people for 6 hrs.	Helpful if your time is limited and you want to make sure you go where the fish are biting.	Can be expensive and may not be as exciting as deep-sea fishing.
GOING SOLO	Cost for gear (rod, line, bait, and tackle) and license ($30-$100 depending on where you fish and if you need gear).	Privacy, flexibility, your time and destination are up to you; you can get fishing tips from your fellow anglers.	If you require a boat, you need to pay for and operate it yourself, plus pay for gear and a fishing license.

With a little hunting (by calling marinas, visiting bait and tackle stores, asking at town visitor centers), you can find a fishing guide who will lead you to some of the best spots on Florida's lakes and rivers. The guide provides the boat and gear, and his license should cover all passengers. A guide is not generally necessary for freshwater fishing, but if you're new to the sport, it might be a worthwhile investment.

On the other hand, if you're looking for fishing guides who can get you into the deep water for tarpon, redfish, snook, snapper, and dolphin, your best bet is to hang out at the marinas along the Florida coast and decide whether price or privacy is more important. If it's price, choose one of the larger party boats. If you'd prefer some privacy and the privilege of creating an exclusive passenger list, then sign up for a private charter. The average charter runs about nine hours, but some companies offer overnight and extended trips, too. Gear is provided in both charter-boat methods, and charters also offer the service of cleaning your catch. All guided trips encourage tipping the crew.

Most people new to the sport choose to do saltwater fishing via a charter party boat. The main reasons are expert guidance, convenience, and cost. Plus, fishing with others can be fun. Charter trips depart from marinas throughout Florida.

CREATING A FLOAT PLAN

If you're fishing in a boat on your own, let someone know where you're headed by providing a float plan, which should include where you're leaving from, a description of the boat you're on, how many are in the boat with you, what survival gear and radio equipment you have onboard, your cell phone number, and when you expect to return. If you don't return as expected, your friend can call the Coast Guard to search for you. Also be sure to have enough life jackets for everyone on board.

RULES AND REGULATIONS

To fish anywhere in (or off the coast of) Florida, you need a license, and there are separate licenses for freshwater fishing and saltwater fishing.

For non-residents, either type of fishing license cost $47 for the annual license, $30 for the 7-day one, or $17 for a 3-day license. Permits/tags are needed for catching snook ($2), crawfish ($2), and tarpon ($51.50). License and permit costs help generate funds for the Florida Fish and Wildlife Conservation Commission, which reinvests the fees into ensuring healthy habitats to sustain fish and wildlife populations, to improve access to fishing spots, and to help ensure public safety.

You can purchase your license and permits at county tax collectors' offices as well as wherever you buy your bait and tackle, such as Florida marinas, specialty stores, and sporting goods shops. You can also buy it online at ⊕ www.myfwc. com/license and have it mailed to you; a surcharge is added to online orders.

If you're on a charter, you don't need to get a license. The captain's fishing license covers all passengers. Also, some piers have their own saltwater fishing licenses that cover you when you're fishing off them for recreational purposes—if you're pier fishing, ask the personnel at the tackle shop if the pier is covered.

RESOURCES

For the latest regulations on gear, daily limits, minimum sizes and seasons for certain fish, and other fishing requirements, consult the **Florida Fish and Wildlife Conservation Commission** (☎ 888/347–4356 ⊕ www.myfwc.com).

WEB RESOURCES
Download the excellent, and free, Florida Fishing PDF at www.visitflorida.com/ planning/guide. Other good sites:
www.floridafishinglakes.net
www.fishingcapital.com
www.floridasportsman.com
www.floridamarine.org

PALM BEACH AND TREASURE COAST

While not as white and fine as the shores on Florida's west coast, the beaches here provide good stomping grounds for hikers, well-guarded waters for swimmers, decent waves for surfers, and plenty of opportunities for sand-castle building and shell collecting.

(this page above) A lifeguard hut on Juno Beach; (opposite page upper right) John D. MacArthur State Park; (opposite page lower left) Delray Beach

Miles of sandy shoreline can be found here beside gorgeous blue-green waters you won't find farther north. The average year-round water temperature is 74°F, much warmer than Southern California beaches that average a comparatively chilly 62°F.

Humans aren't alone in finding the shores inviting. Migratory birds flock to the beaches, too, as do sea turtles, which come between May and August to lay their eggs in the sand. Locally organized watches take small groups out at night to observe mother turtles as they waddle onto shore, dig holes with their flippers, and deposit their golf-ball-size eggs into the sand. Hatchlings emerge about 45 days later.

WHEN TO GO

The water is warm, clear, and sparkling all year long, but the best time to get in is between December and March. The shorelines are often more crowded, but you don't have to worry about jellyfish or sea lice when you take a dip. Sea lice can cause welts, blisters, and rashes. The crowds thin out during summer and fall months, which is inviting, but jellyfish and sea lice can be a problem then.

DELRAY

If you're looking for a place to see and be seen, head for **Delray Beach**'s wide expanse of sand, which stretches 2 mi, half of it supervised by lifeguards. Reefs off the coast are popular with divers, as is a sunken Spanish galleon less than ½ mi offshore from the Seagate Club on the south end of the beach. **Pros:** good for swimmers and sunbathers; bars and restaurants across the street; cabanas and catamarans available for rent. **Cons:** often a long walk to the public restrooms.

JOHN D. MACARTHUR STATE PARK

If getting far from the madding crowd is your goal, **John D. MacArthur State Park** on the north end of Singer Island is a good choice. You will find a great place for snorkeling, kayaking, bird-watching, and fishing. Part of the beach was once dedicated to topless bathers, but that is no longer the case. **Pros:** guides to local flora and fauna are available; a good place to spot sea turtles. **Cons:** beach is a long walk from the parking lot.

JUNO BEACH

Juno Beach sports a 990-foot pier and a bait shop for those who like to spend their morning fishing. But the shoreline itself is a favorite for families with kids who drag along sand toys, build castles, and hunt for shells. **Pros:** concession stand and a bait shop. **Cons:** beach isn't as wide as others.

RED REEF PARK

Looking for a great place to snorkel? **Red Reef Park** in Boca Raton is just the ticket, and it doesn't matter if you're a beginner or a pro. The reef is only about 50 feet offshore. Expect to see tropical fish and maybe even a manatee or two. **Pros:** the park's showers and bathrooms are kept clean and there's a playground for kids. **Cons:** if you go at low tide, you're not going to see as many tropical fish.

STUART BEACH

When the waves robustly roll in at **Stuart Beach**, the surfers are rolling in, too. Beginning surfers are especially keen on Stuart Beach because of its ever-vigilant lifeguards, while pros to the sport like the challenges the choppy waters here bring. Beachgoers with kids like the snack bar known for its chicken fingers, and those who like a side of museum musing with their day in the sun can view an impressive collection of antique cars at a museum just steps from the beach. **Pros:** parking is easy to find and there are three boardwalks for easy access to the beach. **Cons:** sand and surf can be rocky.

FORT LAUDERDALE AND BROWARD COUNTY

A wave-capped, 20-mi shoreline with wide ribbons of golden sand for beachcombing and sunbathing remains the anchor draw for Fort Lauderdale and Broward County.

(this page above) Fort Lauderdale restaurants; (opposite page upper right) High-rise condos in Fort Lauderdale; (opposite page lower left) Children on Fort Lauderdale Beach

Fort Lauderdale isn't just for spring breakers. In fact, ever since investors have been pouring money into the waterfront scene there, beginning in the '90s, the beach is luring a more upscale clientele. That being said, it still has great people-watching and opportunities for partying.

Beyond the city, Broward County's beachfront extends for miles without interruption, although the character of communities along the shoreline varies. In Hallandale, in the south, the beach is backed by towering condominiums, and tee times and nightlife venues beckon during the day and after dark, respectively. Meanwhile Deerfield Beach in the north is the place for active families, while nearby Pompano Beach particularly attracts anglers. Many places elsewhere in the region—blessedly, for purists—there's virtually nothing but sand and turquoise waters.

SAFETY TIPS

In Fort Lauderdale, double red flags mean water is closed to the public, often because of lightning or sharks; a lone red flag means strong currents; purple signals men-of-war or jellyfish; green means calm conditions. In Hollywood, orange signals rip currents with easterly onshore winds; blue warns of marine life like jellyfish; red means hazardous; green signals good conditions.

FORT LAUDERDALE BEACH

Alone among Florida's major beach-front communities, **Fort Lauderdale Beach** remains gloriously open and uncluttered. A wave theme unifies the setting on the Fort Lauderdale beachfront—from the low, white, wave-shape wall between the beach and beachfront promenade to the widened and bricked inner promenade in front of shops, restaurants, and hotels. Walkways line both sides of the beach roadway, and traffic has been trimmed to two gently curving northbound lanes, where in-line skaters skim past slow-moving cars. On the beach side, a low masonry wall doubles as an extended bench, separating sand from the promenade. The beach is most crowded between Las Olas and Sunrise boulevards.

HOLLYWOOD'S BROADWALK

The name might be Hollywood, but there's nothing hip or chic about **Hollywood North Beach Park**, which sits at the north end of Hollywood, **Florida's Broadwalk**'s north end (Route A1A and Sheridan Street). And that's a good thing. It's just a laid-back, old-fashioned place for enjoying the sun, sand, and sea. Also, no high-rises overpower the scene here. Parking is $5. The main part of the Broadwalk is quite a bit more fashionable and has spiffy features like pedestrian pavers, a concrete bike path, a crushed-shell jogging path, an 18-inch decorative wall separating the actual Broadwalk from the sand, and places to shower off the sand. Fido fans take note: dog beaches in the area are making a comeback; the year-round **Dog Beach of Hollywood** is right along with them.

LAUDERDALE-BY-THE-SEA

The small village of **Lauderdale-by-the-Sea** packs a big punch for beach-going pleasure. Especially popular with divers and snorkelers, this laid-back stretch of sand provides great access to lovely coral reefs. When you're not down in the waters, look up and you'll likely see a pelican flying by. The gentle trade winds make this a place to go for utter relaxation without all the hubbub of the Fort Lauderdale party scene. The place livens up on weekends with live entertainment on Friday nights, but it's still a small-town, easygoing feel where parents feel comfortable taking their kids.

POMPANO BEACH

As route A1A enters this town directly north of Lauderdale-by-the-Sea, the high-rise scene resumes. Sportfishing is big in **Pompano Beach**, as its name implies, but there's more to beachside attractions than the popular Fisherman's Wharf. Behind a low coral-rock wall, Alsdorf Park (also called the 14th Street boat ramp) extends north and south of the wharf along the road and beach.

5

MIAMI AND MIAMI BEACH

Almost every side street in Miami Beach dead-ends at the ocean. Sandy shores also stretch along the southern side of the Rickenbacker Causeway to Key Biscayne, where you'll find more popular beaches.

(this page above) Lummus Park Beach volleyball; (opposite page upper right) Condos on Lummus Park Beach; (opposite page lower left) Bill Baggs Cape Florida State Park

Beaches tend to have golden, light brown, or gray-tinted sand with coarser grains than the fine white stuff on Florida's Gulf Coast beaches. Although pure white-sand beaches are many peoples' idea of picture-perfect, darker beach sand is much easier on the eyes on a sunny day and—bonus!—your holiday photos (and the people in them) will have a subtle warm glow rather than harsh highlights.

Expect gentle waves, which can occasionally turn rough, complete with riptides, depending on what weather systems are lurking out in the ocean—always check and abide by the warnings posted on the lifeguard's station. One thing that isn't perfect here is shelling, but for casual shell collectors Bal Harbour Beach is the best bet; enter at 96th Street and Collins Avenue.

SOUTH BEACH PARKING TIPS

On-street parking is scarce, tickets are given freely when meters expire, and towing charges are high. Check your meter to see when you must pay to park; times vary. It's $1/$1.25 for meters north/south of 23rd Street respectively. No quarters? You can buy a Parking Meter Card at Miami Beach Visitors Center and Publix supermarkets for $25. Or take the South Beach Local shuttle for a quarter.

LUMMUS PARK BEACH

Want glitz and glamour? On South Beach's Ocean Drive from 6th to 14th streets, this beach is crowded with beautiful people working hard on their tans, muscle tone, and social lives. It's also the place for golden sands, blue water, and gentle waves. However, as this place is all about seeing and being seen, the less-perfect among us may feel intimidated or bored.

MATHESON HAMMOCK PARK BEACH

Kids will thrill to the tender waves and warm water of the beach at 4000 Crandon Boulevard in Key Biscayne. The golden sands of this 3-mi beach are only part of the attraction: the park includes children's rides and a playground, picnic areas—even a golf course. The man-made lagoon is perfect for inexperienced swimmers, and it's the best place in Miami for a picnic. But the water can be a bit murky, and with the emphasis on families, it's not the best place for singles.

BILL BAGGS CAPE FLORIDA STATE PARK

All the way at the end of Key Biscayne, at 1200 South Crandon Boulevard, is a wide peachy-brown beach with usually gentle waves. The picnic area is popular with local families on weekends, but the beach itself never feels crowed. The park also includes miles of nature trails; bike, boat, beach chair/umbrella rentals; and

casual dining at the Lighthouse Café. You can fish off the piers by the marina, too. Come here for an escape from city madness.

HOLLYWOOD BEACH

Halfway between Miami and Fort Lauderdale, Hollywood Beach is a perfect retreat. Sun yourself on the pristine golden-white sands, join a volleyball game, take a tai chi or yoga lesson, then walk along the 2-mi boardwalk and visit its small shops, cafés, and restaurants. Head north on the boardwalk and you'll find North Beach Park's sea turtle hatchery (part of the Endangered Sea Turtle Protection Program—the kids will love it), meander south and you'll end up at the Ocean Walk Mall.

HAULOVER BEACH

Want to bare it all? Just north of Bal Harbour, at 10800 Collins Avenue in Sunny Isles, sits the only legal clothing-optional beach in the area. **Haulover** has more claims to fame than its casual attitude toward swimwear—it's also the best beach in the area for body-boarding and surfing as it gets what passes for impressive swells in these parts. Plus the sand here is fine-grain white, unusual for the Atlantic Coast.

THE FLORIDA KEYS

Because the Bahama Islands steal the Keys' offshore sand, the region has fewer natural beaches than one might expect. But the ones it does have are award-winning, specifically those at Bahia Honda State Park.

(this page above) Bahia Honda State Park; (opposite page upper right) Canoes for rent at Higgs Beach, Key West; (opposite page lower left) Zachary Taylor Historic State Park beach

Also, just because a beach is not natural doesn't mean it should be overlooked. Some of the Keys' public man-made beaches provide solid recreation and sunning options for visitors looking to work on their tan. Many resorts additionally provide their own private beachfronts.

The Keys may not have a surplus of beaches, but one nice perk is the availability of camping on some of them. It's one of many ways to enjoy nature while on the beach. Another is keeping an eye out for sea turtles. April through October female sea turtles lay their eggs into the sand for a nearly two-month period of nesting.

■ TIP➔ Don't let pests ruin your day at the beach. To avoid the stings of sea lice, remove your swimsuit and shower thoroughly upon exiting the water. Sand fleas (aka no-see-ums) are tiny insects with big teeth that are most likely to attack in the morning and around sunset.

BIRD-WATCHING ON THE BEACH

Residents include shorebirds—plovers, ruddy turnstones, willets, and short-billed dowitchers; wading birds—great blue herons, great white herons, snowy egrets, tricolored herons, and white ibis; brown pelicans; osprey; and turkey vultures. In autumn, hawks appear, while in winter ducks make their debut. In summer, white-crowned pigeons are common.

LONG KEY STATE PARK

The beach at **Long Key State Park** at MM 67.5 is typical of Middle Key's beaches, which are more like sand flats where low tide reveals the coral bedrock of the ecosystem. Here you can snorkel or fish (bonefishing is quite popular) during the day and then be lulled to sleep by the sound of gentle sea waves if you spend the night camping. (The beach is accessible only to campers.)

SOMBRERO BEACH

Something of a local hangout—especially on weekends, when it can get crowded—**Sombrero Beach** in Marathon is worth getting off the beaten Overseas Highway path (exit at MM 50 onto Sombrero Beach Road). Families will find much to do on the man-made coved beach and its grassy green, manicured lawn; playground area; and clear, calm waters. Separate sections also accommodate boaters and windsurfers.

BAHIA HONDA STATE PARK

This state park at MM 37 holds three beaches, all of different character. **Sandspur Beach** is the most removed from crowds with long stretches of powdery sands and a campground. **Loggerhead Beach** is closer to the park's concession area, where you can rent snorkel equipment and kayaks. Like Sandspur, it faces the Atlantic Ocean, but waves are typically wimpy. Near Loggerhead, Calusa Beach on the gulf side near the marina

is popular with families, offering a small and safe swimming venue and picnic facilities, as well as camping.

HIGGS BEACH, KEY WEST

Situated on Atlantic Boulevard, this is as urban as beaches in the Keys get, with lots of amenities, activities, and distractions. Visitors can check out a historic site; eat at a popular beachfront Italian restaurant; rent a kayak; play volleyball, tennis, or enjoy the playground—and all within walking distance of the long sweep of man-made beach and sparkling clear, shallow, calm water.

ZACHARY TAYLOR HISTORIC STATE PARK

This man-made beach is part of a Civil War–era fort complex at the end of Southard Street and is arguably the best beach in Key West with its typically small waves, swaying Australian pines, water-sports rentals, and shaded picnic grounds. It also hosts, from mid-January through mid-April, an alfresco collection of oversize art called Sculpture Key West, which changes annually and showcases artists from across the country.

UNDER THE SEA
SNORKELING AND DIVING
IN THE FLORIDA KEYS by Lynne Helm

Up on the shore they work all day...

> While we devotin',
>
> Full time to floatin',
>
> Under the sea...

–"Under the Sea,"
from Disney's *Little Mermaid*

All Floridians—even those long-accustomed to balmy breezes and swaying palms—turn ecstatic at the mere thought of tripping off to the Florida Keys. Add the prospect of underwater adventure, and hot diggity, it's unparalleled bliss.

Perennially laid back, the Keys annually attract nearly 800,000 snorkeling and scuba diving aficionados, and why not? There's arguably no better destination to learn these sports that put you up close to the wonders of life under the sea.

THE BARRIER REEF
The continental United States' only living coral barrier reef stretches 5 mi offshore of the Keys and is a teeming backbone of marine life, ranging from brilliant corals to neon-colored fish from blue-striped grunts to green moray eels. This is the prime reason why the Keys are where you descend upon intricate natural coral formations and encrusted shipwrecks, some historic, others sunk by design to create artificial reefs that attract divers

and provide protection for marine life. Most diving sites have mooring buoys (nautical floats away from shore, sometimes marking specific sites); these let you tie up your boat so you don't need to drop anchor, which could damage the reef. Most of these sites also are near individual keys, where dozens of dive operators can cater to your needs.

Reef areas thrive in waters as shallow as 5 feet and as deep as 50 feet. Shallow reefs attract snorkelers, while deeper reefs suit divers of varying experience levels. The Keys' shallow diving offers two benefits: longer time safely spent on the bottom exploring, and more vibrant colors because of sunlight penetration. Most divers log maximum depths of 20 to 30 feet.

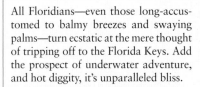

(left) Shallow-water coral reef, (top) Nine Foot Stake is a popular site for underwater photography.

WHERE TO SNORKEL AND DIVE

KEY WEST
Mile Marker 0–4

You can soak up a mesmerizing overview of submerged watery wonders at the Florida Keys Eco-Discovery Center, opened in 2007 on Key West's Truman

Nine Foot Stake

Annex waterfront. Both admission and parking are free at the 6,000 square–foot center (☉ 9–4 Tues.–Sat. ☎ 305/809–4670); interactive exhibits here focus on Keys marine life and habitats. Key West's offshore reefs are best accessed via professional charters, but it's easy to snorkel from shore at Key West Marine Park. Marked by a lighthouse, Sand Key Reef attracts snorkelers and scuba divers. Joe's Tug, at 65-foot depths, sets up encounters with Goliath grouper. Ten-Fathom Ledge, with coral caves and

dramatic overhangs, shelters lobster. The Cayman Salvor, a buoy tender sunk as an artificial reef in 1985, shelters baitfish. Patch reef Nine Foot Stake, submerged 10 to 25 feet, has soft corals and juvenile marine life. Kedge Ledge features a pair of coral-encrusted anchors from 18th-century sailing vessels. 🛈 Florida Keys main visitor line at ☎ 800/FLA-KEYS (352-5397).

BIG PINE KEY/LOWER KEYS
Mile Marker 4–47

Many devotees feel a Florida dive adventure would not be complete without heading 5 mi from Big Pine Key to Looe Key National Marine Sanctuary, an underwater preserve named for the HMS Looe running aground in 1744. If you time your visit for July, you might hit the one-day free underwater music festival for snorkelers

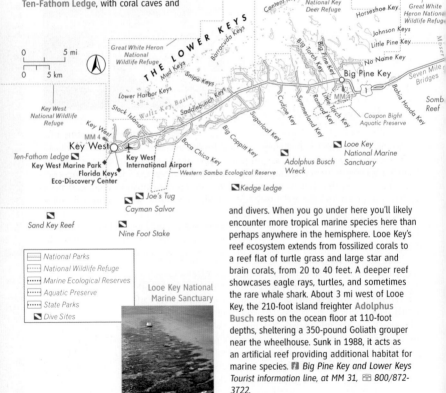

Looe Key National Marine Sanctuary

and divers. When you go under here you'll likely encounter more tropical marine species here than perhaps anywhere in the hemisphere. Looe Key's reef ecosystem extends from fossilized corals to a reef flat of turtle grass and large star and brain corals, from 20 to 40 feet. A deeper reef showcases eagle rays, turtles, and sometimes the rare whale shark. About 3 mi west of Looe Key, the 210-foot island freighter Adolphus Busch rests on the ocean floor at 110-foot depths, sheltering a 350-pound Goliath grouper near the wheelhouse. Sunk in 1988, it acts as an artificial reef providing additional habitat for marine species. 🛈 Big Pine Key and Lower Keys Tourist information line, at MM 31, ☎ 800/872-3722.

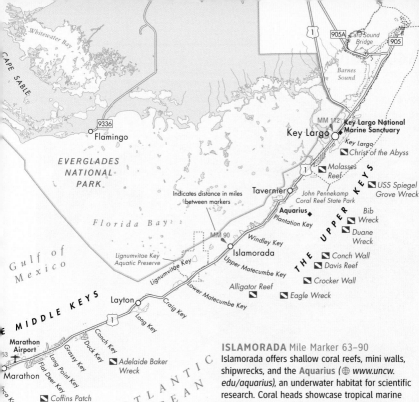

Whitewater Bay

CAPE SABLE

Flamingo 9336

EVERGLADES NATIONAL PARK

Florida Bay

Indicates distance in miles between markers

MM 90

Gulf of Mexico

Lignumvitae Key Aquatic Preserve

Lignumvitae Key

Layton

Craig Key

Long Key

MIDDLE KEYS

Conch Key

Duck Key

Long Point Key

Grassy Key

Marathon Airport

Flat Deer Key

Marathon

Coffins Patch

Delta Shoal

Thunderbolt Wreck

ATLANTIC OCEAN

Adelaide Baker Wreck

Barnes Sound

905A Card Sound Bridge 905

U.S. 1

MM 112 Key Largo National Marine Sanctuary

Key Largo

Key Largo

Christ of the Abyss

Molasses Reef

Tavernier

John Pennekamp Coral Reef State Park

USS Spiegel Grove Wreck

Aquarius

Plantation Key

THE UPPER KEYS

Bib Wreck

Duane Wreck

Windley Key

Islamorada

Upper Matecumbe Key

Conch Wall

Davis Reef

Crocker Wall

Alligator Reef

Lower Matecumbe Key

Eagle Wreck

MARATHON/MIDDLE KEYS
Mile Marker 47–63

The Middle Keys yield a marine wilderness of a spur-and-groove coral and patch reefs. The **Adelaide Baker** historic shipwreck has a pair of stacks in 25 feet of water.

Sombrero Reef

Popular **Sombrero Reef**, with coral canyons and archways, is marked by a 140-foot lighted tower. Six distinct patch reefs known as **Coffin's Patch** have shallow elkhorn forests. **Delta Shoals**, a network of coral canyons fanning seaward from a sandy shoal, attracts divers to its elkhorn, brain, and star coral heads. Marathon's **Thunderbolt**, a 188-foot ship sunk in 1986, sits upright at 115-foot depths, coated with sponge, coral, and hydroid, and attracting angelfish, jacks, and deep-water pelagic creatures. ⬛ *Greater Marathon Chamber and visitors center at MM 53.5,* ☎ *800/262-7284.*

ISLAMORADA Mile Marker 63–90

Islamorada offers shallow coral reefs, mini walls, shipwrecks, and the **Aquarius** (⊕ *www.uncw. edu/aquarius*), an underwater habitat for scientific research. Coral heads showcase tropical marine life, from grunt to regal queen angelfish. Green moray eels populate spur-and-groove channels, and nurse sharks linger around overhangs. Submerged attractions include the **Eagle**, a 287-foot ship in 110 feet of water; **Davis Reef**, with gorgonian coral; **Alligator Reef**, where the *USS Alligator* sank while fighting pirates; the sloping **Conch Wall**, with barrel sponges and gorgonian; and **Crocker Wall**, featuring spur-and-groove and block corals. ⬛ *Islamorada Chamber and visitor center at MM 83.2,* ☎ *800/322–5397.*

KEY LARGO Mile Marker 90–112

Key Largo marine conservation got a big leg up with creation of **John Pennekamp Coral Reef State Park** in 1960, the nation's first undersea preserve, followed by 1975's designation of the **Key Largo National Marine Sanctuary**. A popular underwater item to view is the bronze statue of **Christ of the Abyss** between coral formations. Explorers with a "lust for rust" can dive down to 60 to 90 feet and farther to see the murky cemetery for two twin 327-foot U.S. Coast Guard cutters, *Duane* and *Bibb*, used during World War II; *USS Spiegel Grove*, a 510-foot Navy transport ship sunk in 2002 to create an artificial reef; and **Molasses Reef**, showcasing coral heads. ⬛ *Key Largo Chamber at MM 106,* ☎ *800/822–1088.*

SCUBA DIVING

A diver explores the coral reef in the Florida Keys National Marine Sanctuary off Key Largo.

Florida offers wonderful opportunities to spend your vacation in the sun and become a certified diver at the same time. In the Keys, count on setting aside three to five days for entry-level or so-called "Open Water" certification offered by many dive shops. Basic certification (covering depths to about 60 feet) involves classroom work and pool training, followed by one or more open-water dives at the reef. After passing a knowledge test and completing the required water training (often starting in a pool), you become a certified recreational scuba diver, eligible to rent dive gear and book dive trips with most operations worldwide. Learning through video or online computer programs can enable you to complete classroom work at home, so you can more efficiently schedule time in the Keys for completing water skills and getting out to the reef for exploration.

Many would-be divers opt to take the classroom instruction and pool training at home at a local dive shop and then spend only two days in the Keys completing four dives. It's not necessarily cheaper, but it can be far more relaxing to commit to only two days of diving.

Questions you should ask: Not all dive shops are created equal, and it may be worthwhile to spend extra money for a better diving experience. Some of the larger dive shops take out large catamarans that can carry as many as 24 to 40 people. Many people prefer the intimacy of a smaller boat.

Good to know: Divers can become certified through PADI *(www.padi.com)*, NAUI *(www.naui.org)*, or SSI *(www.divessi.com)*. The requirements for all three are similar, and if you do the classroom instruction and pool training with a dive shop associated with one organization, the referral for the open water dives will be honored by most dive shops. Note that you are not allowed to fly for at least 24 hours after a dive, because residual nitrogen in the body can pose health risks upon decompression. While there are no rigid rules on diving after flying, make sure you're well-hydrated before hitting the water.

Cost: The four-day cost can range from $300 to $475, but be sure to ask if equipment, instruction manuals, and log books are extra. Some dive shops have relationships with hotels, so check for dive/stay packages. Referral dives (a collaborative effort among training agencies) run from $285 to $300 and discover scuba runs around $175 to $200.

SNUBA

Beyond snorkeling or the requirements of scuba, you also have the option of "Snuba." The word is a trademarked portmanteau or combo of snorkel and scuba. Marketed as easy-to-learn family fun, Snuba lets you breathe underwater via tubes from an air-supplied vessel above, with no prior diving or snorkel experience required.

NOT CERTIFIED?

Not sure if you want to commit the time and money to become certified? Not a problem. Most dive shops and many resorts will offer a discover scuba day-long course. In the morning, the instructor will teach you the basics of scuba diving: how to clear your mask, how to come to the surface in the unlikely event you lose your air supply, etc. In the afternoon, instructors will take you out for a dive in relatively shallow water—less than 30 feet. Be sure to ask where the dive will take place. Jumping into the water off a shallow beach may not be as fun as actually going out to the coral. If you decide that diving is something you want to pursue, the open dive may count toward your certification.

■**TIP→** You can often book the discover dives at the last minute. It may not be worth it to go out on a windy day when the currents are stronger. Also the underwater world looks a whole lot brighter on sunny days.

5

IN FOCUS UNDER THE SEA

(top) Scuba divers on Anna Maria Island; (bottom) Diver ascending line.

SNORKELING

Snorking lets you see the wonders of the sea from a new perspective.

The basics: Sure, you can take a deep breath, hold your nose, squint your eyes, and stick your face in the water in an attempt to view submerged habitats . . . but why not protect your eyes, retain your ability to breathe, and keep your hands free to paddle about when exploring underwater? That's what snorkeling is all about.

Equipment needed: A mask, snorkel (the tube attached to the mask), and fins. In deeper waters (any depth over your head), life jackets are advised.

Steps to success: If you've never snorkeled before, it's natural to feel a bit awkward at first, so don't sweat it. Breathing through a mask and tube, and wearing a pair of fins take getting used to. Like any activity, you build confidence and comfort through practice.

If you're new to snorkeling, begin by submerging your face in shallow water or a swimming pool and breathing calmly through the snorkel while gazing through the mask.

Next you need to learn how to clear water out your mask and snorkel, an essential skill since splashes can send water into tube openings and masks can leak. Some snorkels have built-in drainage valves, but if a tube clogs, you can force water up and out by exhaling through your mouth. Clearing a mask is similar: lift your head from water while pulling forward on mask to drain. Some masks have built-in purge valves, but those without can be cleared underwater by pressing the top to the forehead and blowing out your nose (charming, isn't it?), allowing air to bubble into the mask, pushing water out the bottom. If it sounds hard, it really isn't. Just try it a few times and you'll soon feel like a pro.

Now your goal is to get friendly with fins—you want them to be snug but not too tight—and learn how to propel yourself with them. Fins won't help you float, but they will give you a leg up, so to speak, on smoothly moving through the water or treading water (even when upright) with less effort.

Flutter stroking is the most efficient underwater kick, and the farther your foot bends forward the more leg power you'll be able to transfer to the water and the farther you'll travel with each stroke. Flutter kicking movements involve alternately separating the legs and then drawing them back together. When your legs separate, the leg surface encounters drag from the water, slowing you down. When your legs are drawn back together, they produce a force pushing you forward. If your kick creates more forward force than it causes drag, you'll move ahead.

Submerge your fins to avoid fatigue rather than having them flailing above the water when you kick, and keep your arms at your side to reduce drag. You are in the water—stretched out, face down, and snorkeling happily away—but that doesn't mean you can't hold your breath and go deeper in the water for a closer look at some fish or whatever catches your attention. Just remember that when you do this, your snorkel will be submerged, too, so you won't be breathing (you'll be holding your breath). You can dive head-first, but going feet-first is easier and less scary for most folks, taking less momentum. Before full immersion, take several long, deep breaths to clear carbon dioxide from your lungs.

If your legs tire, flip onto your back and tread water with inverted fin motions while resting. If your mask fogs, wash condensation from lens and clear water from mask.

TIPS FOR SAFE SNORKELING

■ Snorkel with a buddy and stay together.

■ Plan your entry and exit points prior to getting in the water.

■ Swim into the current on entering and then ride the current back to your exit point.

■ Carry your flippers into the water and then put them on, as it's difficult to walk in them.

■ Make sure your mask fits properly and is not too loose.

■ Pop your head above the water periodically to ensure you aren't drifting too far out, or too close to rocks.

■ Think of the water as someone else's home—don't take anything that doesn't belong to you, or leave any trash behind.

■ Don't touch any sea creatures; they may sting.

■ Wear a rash guard (e.g., a T-shirt); it will keep you from being fried by the sun.

■ When in doubt, don't go without a snorkeling professional; try a guided tour.

5

IN FOCUS UNDER THE SEA

Cayman Salvor

ALABAMA

Many people don't even realize that Alabama has beaches, and that's their loss. The soft, white sandy beaches rival those in Florida. But with fewer crowds, they can provide an ideal spot for family vacations.

(this page above) High-rise condominiums on Orange Beach; (opposite page upper right) A bastion at Ft. Gaines, Dauphin Island; (opposite page lower left) A dolphin off Gulf Shores

Alabama has two coastal counties—Mobile and Baldwin—that are separated by the brackish waters of Mobile Bay. Those seeking high-rise hotels and condominiums and water sports typically head east to Gulf Shores and Orange Beach in Baldwin County. People who want a quieter atmosphere (perhaps those who would rather rent a house on stilts and walk a few steps to the ocean) choose Dauphin Island in Mobile County. Fort Morgan, a 20-mi peninsula on the Baldwin side, offers a bit of both. A 45-minute ferry ride or a scenic drive around the bay connects the two counties. Tropical storms and hurricanes have taken their toll on the beaches, but millions of dollars worth of sand has been added and protective dunes rebuilt, so the beaches are beginning to recover. The area is known for bird-watching. Brown pelicans, sea skimmers, seagulls, sandpipers, and the occasional osprey are seen.

DEEP-SEA FISHING

Alabama's ocean waters can be a deep-sea fisherman's paradise. Just ask the thousands who participate in the Alabama Deep Sea Fishing Rodeo on Dauphin Island. Charter boats in both coastal counties offer anglers a chance to catch redfish, snapper, king mackerel, tarpon, and bluefish. Overnight trips take fishermen out farther for tuna, grouper, amberjack, and wahoo.

GULF SHORES

Gulf Shores offers beautiful beaches overlooking emerald waters, a water park, activities such as deep-sea fishing, and even a small zoo. A popular public beach—and the site of the National Shrimp Festival in October—is located where Alabama Highway 59 dead-ends into the gulf. There you'll find volleyball nets, beachside bars, and restaurants featuring such local favorites as shrimp po'boys and fried crab claws. **Gulf State Park,** on the eastern edge of Gulf Shores, offers a 2-mi stretch of public beaches, a freshwater lake, a resort, cabins, and campsites. The park boasts the longest fishing pier on the Gulf of Mexico, at 1,540 feet (saltwater fishing license required).

ORANGE BEACH

Just east of **Gulf Shores** is **Orange Beach.** Some popular beaches here include **Cotton Bayou** (at the intersection of Alabama Highways 182 and 161), **Romar Beach** (7 mi east of Alabama Highway 59), and **Florida Point** (3 mi east of the Perdido Pass Bridge). The city of Orange Beach offers upscale shopping and some big-name concerts at the Wharf. To the east of the city, right on the Alabama–Florida line, there's a regionally famous bar called the Florabama that features an annual mullet toss.

FORT MORGAN

Named for the early 19th-century fort at the end of the peninsula, **Fort Morgan** still offers some isolated, quiet beaches. Halfway down the peninsula (9 mi west of Gulf Shores) is the **Bon Secour National Wildlife Refuge,** which has public beaches and nature trails; the beaches here serve as nesting sites for endangered and threatened sea turtles, including the loggerhead and Kemp's ridley. The fort itself is open to the public. A ferry takes passengers to Fort Gaines on **Dauphin Island.** It was along these waters that Navy Admiral David Farragut said during the Civil War: "Damn the torpedoes. Full speed ahead."

DAUPHIN ISLAND

The water is usually a little murkier on this side of Mobile Bay, but the beautiful, natural scenery can more than make up for that. This barrier island offers about 8 mi of accessible beaches. On the east end, visitors can explore Fort Gaines, learn about the area's fish and wildlife at the Dauphin Island Estuarium, and hike trails in the bird sanctuary. There's a public beach near the center of the island with a fishing pier. Beach houses dot the road toward the west end, which has a new public park. Here, beachgoers can feel like they are at the edge of the world, with no other land in sight, just the occasional oil rig.

MISSISSIPPI

The beaches of the Mississippi Gulf Coast are well suited to fun in the sun—just don't expect great swimming. The waters of Mississippi Sound can be stagnant and very warm.

(this page above) Biloxi Beach; (opposite page upper right) West Ship island in Gulf Islands; National Seashore (opposite page lower left) Ocean Springs

Nevertheless, the picturesque beaches that front this string of coastal communities, long a honky-tonk vacation paradise, have their own charms. Kayaks and Jet Skis zip across the water, and charter boats head out for deep-sea fishing. Beachcombers enjoy the Gulf breezes and expansive views. If you're looking for more action, it can be found in Biloxi's casinos, just steps away from the beachfront. The entire area has been slowly rebuilding since Hurricane Katrina in 2005. Attractions, restaurants, and hotels have been steadily rising again from the flat, sandy soil facing the wide open waters. The area's barrier islands, coastal swamps, and bayous are home to a wide variety of wildlife—especially birds, including osprey, pelican, and great blue heron. Armadillo, opossum, and diamondback terrapin are just a few of the land creatures found here, while shrimp, crab, oyster, and numerous species of fish swim through the channels of Mississippi Sound.

BARRIER ISLANDS

Barrier Islands are essentially sandbars that are created offshore and help to protect the coastal regions from fierce storms. Over time, they can develop their own ecosystems. Shaped by wind and shifting seawater, the barrier islands on the Mississippi Gulf Coast are under constant assault by hurricanes and strong Gulf currents that erode beaches, toss about sand dunes, and sometimes move the islands themselves.

GULFPORT

Gulfport is the jumping-off point for the 11-mi trip to **West Ship Island**, with ferries departing regularly from the small craft harbor on U.S. 90. Keep an eye out for bottlenose dolphins in Mississippi Sound, which is also crisscrossed with shrimp boats, barges, and freighters. Away from the shoreline, **Gulfport** is home to a popular water park and children's museum. To the east, **Beauvoir** was home to Jefferson Davis, who settled there after the Civil War.

BILOXI

The bustling heart of the Mississippi Gulf Coast, **Biloxi** hums with some dozen casinos, as well as a historic downtown known as the Vieux Marché. A monument on the town green memorializes the destruction wrought by Hurricane Katrina in 2005. A short distance away is a monument to Hurricane Camille, which struck the coast in 1969. Beachfront strolls lead past Biloxi's historic lighthouse and boats bobbing on the waters of Mississippi Sound.

OCEAN SPRINGS

On the east side of the soaring Biloxi Bay Bridge, a popular spot for strollers and joggers, **Ocean Springs** is a genteel artists' colony with a charming downtown, where streets lined with quaint shops are shaded with drooping live oaks. **Davis Bayou**, part of **Gulf Islands National Seashore**, has campsites and a visitor center, as well as a nature trail, boat launch, and fishing pier.

PASCAGOULA

An industrial city with Mississippi's largest shipyard as well as oil and chemical companies and a naval base, **Pascagoula** offers some opportunities for getting in touch with nature. Swamp tours leave from the nearby towns of Gautier and Moss Point, site of the Pascagoula River Audubon Center. Pascagoula also has its Spanish fort, actually a colonial-era home and one of the oldest structures still standing in the United States.

GULF ISLANDS NATIONAL SEASHORE

Stretching like an old clothesline across Mississippi Sound are five barrier islands which make up this park's Mississippi district. **West Ship** has a popular beach, reachable by ferry from Gulfport (not to mention a Civil War–era fort), while **East Ship** is undeveloped and has been eroded by hurricanes. Part of **Cat** remains under private ownership, while **Horn** and **Petit Bois** ("Petty Boy") were designated wilderness areas in 1978, making them among the last untouched barrier islands on the Gulf or Atlantic coasts. Wildlife abounds on the islands. Trips to the wilderness areas can be arranged at the visitor center at **Davis Bayou** in **Ocean Springs**.

5

TEXAS

Fun is part of everyday life in south Texas. Mile after mile of beaches beckon families to play in the gentle surf. Locals make time to hunt, fish, golf, windsurf, and bird-watch.

(this page above) Port Aransas Beach; (opposite page upper right) Bob Hall Pier, Corpus Christi; (opposite page lower left) A surfer on the beach on Galveston Island

Historic Galveston, 50 mi south of Houston, is itself experiencing somewhat of a beachside boom, from its historic Strand District to new communities all along the waterfront. Padre Island, a long, skinny barrier island with sandy weather and persistent winds, stretches the more than 100 mi of south Texas coastline from Corpus Christi all the way to the mouth of the Rio Grande. It protects the region from the ravaging waves of the Gulf of Mexico. The northern end of the island is part of the city of Corpus Christi, and there are public, drive-on beaches that are convenient if you like hauling a ton of beach accoutrements and staying all day. The southern end makes up South Padre Island, one of the nation's most popular beach towns. Some of the beaches on this end are more protected and do not allow cars to drive on them. In between are miles and miles of protected shoreline and pristine beaches that belong to the National Park Service. Many south Texas beaches charge a few dollars per vehicle.

MARDI GRAS IN GALVESTON

Sure it's not as rowdy as the party in New Orleans (which may be a good thing if you have kids in tow), but Galveston throws a pretty nice little Mardi Gras bash. More than 250,000 people participate in the 12-day event, which features 11 parades. For more information, go to ⊕ *www. mardigrasgalveston.com.*

GALVESTON

A 17-foot-high seawall, built after a devastating hurricane in 1900, abuts a long ribbon of sand and provides a place for rollerblading, bicycling, and going on the occasional surrey ride. The island has several good beaches. The **seawall** itself on the Gulf-side waterfront attracts runners, cyclists, and rollerbladers. Just below it is a long, free beach near many big hotels and resorts. **Stewart Beach Park**, at 6th Street, has a bathhouse, amusement park, bumper boats, miniature-golf course, and a water coaster in addition to saltwater and sand. **Galveston Island State Park**, about 10 mi southwest of town, is a 2,000-acre natural beach habitat ideal for birding, walking, and renewing your spirit.

CORPUS CHRISTI

As beach communities around the United States become more and more expensive, Corpus Christi remains an affordable destination for sun and fun. Because of the constant winds, it's a major windsurfing destination. **Magee Beach** is right downtown next to the marina. **North Beach**, north of the Harbor Bridge, is on the calm bay. For locals, the drive-on beaches between JP Luby Park and Bob Hall Pier, on the northern end of **Padre Island**, are popular with both rowdy spring breakers and (for the rest of the year) families.

PORT ARANSAS

Port Aransas (or "Port A" as everyone here calls it) is about 45 minutes northeast of downtown Corpus Christi. You can drive on the beaches in Port A, but wooden posts keep the cars 50 pleasant feet from the Gulf water. The town has cute restaurants, swimsuit-'n'-souvenir shops, and places to rent little buggy carts to cruise the beaches and streets.

SOUTH PADRE ISLAND

For much of the year the island is quiet. Texan tourists visit their rental homes or the resort hotels and enjoy the serene beaches and the many outdoor activities, which include surfing, parasailing, snorkeling, diving, horseback riding, and windsurfing. Then for a few weeks each year spring break descends upon the area, injecting a monetary boon but also a youthful, reckless energy bent on partying, partying, and more partying. The prices for most things skyrocket in March, when debauchery reigns supreme. And then, just as suddenly, the storm lifts and the town quickly returns to its windswept calm, nothing but bright sunshine and crashing waves. The **beaches on the Gulf side** offer what most visitors are looking for: breezy winds, breaking surf, and pristine sand. The "bay side" on the **Laguna Madre** is mostly muddy, shallow, and calm. **Isla Blanca Park** sits on the southernmost tip of the island and offers clean beaches and a number of nearby activities.

Best Beaches in
the Bahamas

WHAT'S WHERE

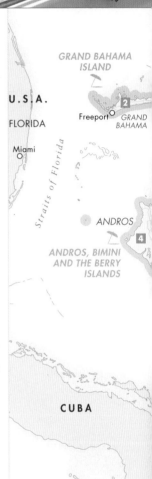

1 New Providence Islands. Nassau and nearby Paradise Island are the most action-packed places in the Bahamas. From flashy megaresort Atlantis to fine dining and high-end shopping, development here is unrivaled on any of the other islands.

2 Grand Bahama Island. Urban and deserted vibes mix to create a quieter alternative to fast-paced Nassau. Lucaya has great shopping, gambling, golfing, and beach parties, but old-island fishing settlements and vast expanses of untouched nature appeal to adventurous travelers.

3 The Abacos. Shallow, translucent waters, top-notch marinas, and idyllic, historic settlements spread over 120 mi of cays (some uninhabited) give the Abacos the apt title of sailing capital of the Bahamas.

4 Andros, Bimini, and the Berry Islands. In the northwest corner of the Bahamas, these islands share many characteristics, most notably their reputation for excellent fishing and diving. Each exudes a casual, old-island atmosphere and abundant natural beauty.

5 Eleuthera and Harbour Island. The Nantucket of the Bahamas, Harbour Island—rimmed by its legendary pink sand beach—is the most chic Out Island. Eleuthera is the opposite with historic churches and pretty fishing villages, unpretentious inns, and a few upscale, intimate beach resorts.

6 The Exumas. Hundreds of islands skip like stones across the Tropic of Cancer, all with gorgeous white beaches and the most beautiful water in the Bahamas. Mainland Great Exuma has friendly locals and great beach parties.

7 The Southern Out Islands. The Bahamas' southernmost islands have so few visitors and so many natural wonders. These islands are also known as the Family Islands, since many Bahamians have roots on these smaller and less populated cays.

GRAND BAHAMA ISLAND

U.S.A.

FLORIDA

Freeport ○ *GRAND BAHAMA*

Miami ○

Straits of Florida

● *ANDROS*

ANDROS, BIMINI AND THE BERRY ISLANDS

CUBA

ATLANTIC OCEAN

THE ABACOS

ABACO

3

**ELEUTHERA AND
HARBOUR ISLAND**

NEW
PROVIDENCE **5**

ELEUTHERA

1 ✪ **NASSAU**

**NEW PROVIDENCE
AND PARADISE
ISLAND**

CAT
ISLAND

SAN
SALVADOR

George
Town
○

THE EXUMAS **6**

GREAT and
LITTLE EXUMA

LONG
ISLAND

MAYAGUANA

CROOKED
and ACKLINS
ISLANDS

**THE SOUTHERN
OUT ISLANDS**

7

TURKS
and CAICOS
ISLANDS

*Bahamas National
Trust Park*

LITTLE
and
GREAT
INAGUA

Great Bahama Bank

Santiago
de Cuba
○

6

| 0 | | 100 mi |

| 0 | | 100 km |

NEW PROVIDENCE ISLAND

New Providence is the Bahamas' most urban island, but that doesn't mean you won't find beautiful beaches. Powdery white sand, aquamarine waves, and shade-baring palm trees are easy to come by, regardless how populated you like your beach to be. Whether you crave solitude or want to be in the middle of the action, there's a sand spot that's just right for you.

Cable Beach and the beaches near Atlantis are where you'll typically find loud music, bars serving tropical drinks, and vendors peddling everything from parasailing and Jet Ski rides to T-shirts and hair braiding. Nassau only has man-made beaches, the best being Junkanoo Beach just west of the British Colonial Hilton. But the capital city's beaches can't compare to the real thing. For a more relaxed environment, drive out of the main tourist areas. You'll likely find stretches of sand populated by locals only, or, chances are, no one at all.

(this page above) Cable Beach; (opposite page upper right) Blue Lagoon Island; (opposite page lower left) Love Beach

OFFSHORE ADVENTURES

For a true beach getaway, head to one of the tiny islands just off the coast of Paradise Island. A 20-minute boat ride from Nassau, Blue Lagoon Island has a number of beaches, including one in a tranquil cove lined with hammocks suspended by palm trees. Enjoy a grilled lunch and then rent a kayak or water bike if you're feeling ambitious.

ADELAIDE BEACH

Time your visit to this far-flung beach on the island's southwestern shore to catch low tide, when the ocean recedes, leaving behind sandbanks and seashells. It's a perfect place to take the kids for a shallow-water dip in the sea, or for a truly private rendezvous. Popular with locals, you'll likely have the miles-long stretch all to yourself unless it's a public holiday.

CABBAGE BEACH

Cabbage Beach is 3 mi of white sand lined with shady casuarina trees, sand dunes, and sun worshipers. This is the place to go to rent Jet Skis or get a bird's-eye view of Paradise Island while parasailing. Hair braiders and T-shirt vendors stroll the beach, and hotel guests crowd the areas surrounding the resorts, including Atlantis. For peace and quiet, stroll east.

CABLE BEACH

Hotels dot the length of this 3-mi beach, so don't expect isolation. Music from the hotel pool decks wafts out onto the sand, Jet Skis race up and down the waves, and vendors sell everything from shell jewelry to coconut drinks right from the shell. If you get tired of lounging around, join a game of beach volleyball.

JUNKANOO BEACH

Right in downtown Nassau, this beach is spring-break central from late February through April. The man-made beach isn't the prettiest on the island, but it's conveniently located if you only have a few quick hours to catch a tan. Music is provided by bands and DJs to guys with boom boxes; a few bars keep the drinks flowing.

LOVE BEACH

If you're looking for great snorkeling and some privacy, drive about 20 minutes west of town. White sand shimmers in the sun and the azure waves gently roll ashore. About a mile offshore is 40 acres of coral reef known as the Sea Gardens. Access is not marked, just look for a vacant lot.

6

GRAND BAHAMA ISLAND

Fluffy white sand carpets in-your-dream beaches, where water sparkles like sapphires, lapis, tanzanite, emeralds, aquamarines . . . you get the picture. Grand Bahama Island has more than its share of beautiful beaches fringing the south coast of its 96-mi length. Some are bustling with water sports activity, while others lie so far off the beaten path it takes a four-wheel-drive vehicle and local knowledge to find them.

(this page above and opposite page top) Lucaya Beach

BEACH-SHACKING

A dozen open-air, no-need-for-shoes shacks dot the island's sandy shores, with the largest concentration in the Freeport–Lucaya Taino Beach area. Here locals cook up beach eats and dispense cold beer and Bahama Mama rum cocktails. Grand Bahama has more beach shacks than any other island; Billy Joe's on Lucaya Beach and Tony Macaroni's on Taino Beach are our favorites.

Lucaya and Taino beaches are the most accessible to the general public. Further off the beaten path, some 60 mi of magnificent stretches of sand extend between Freeport–Lucaya and McLean's Town, the island's isolated eastern end. Most are used only by people who live in adjacent settlements along the way. The outlying beaches have no public facilities, so beachgoers often headquarter at one of the local beach bars. Some, such as Paradise Cove on the island's west end, have vans that will pick you up at your hotel.

DEADMAN'S REEF BEACH

The spectacular swim-to reef is the best asset of this beach, a 15-minute drive from Freeport. It's part of Paradise Cove, a small native-owned resort that will bus you out if you call ahead. The beach is short but wide with scrubby vegetation and swaying palm trees. Snorkel equipment and kayaks are available to rent, and refreshments flow at the Red Bar. This beach will give you a taste of what the Out Islands are like; come here when the crowds in Lucaya become too much.

LUCAYA BEACH

Although somewhat monopolized by the broad spread of Our Lucaya Resort, this beach is accessible to the public and a good place to visit if you like lots of options for drinking, dining, and water sports. Cruise-ship excursions add to the resort's crowds. The white-sand beach is interrupted by rocky protrusions, so it's not great for strolling. Instead, spend the day people-watching at one of the beach bars, swimming pools, or the famous Billy Joe's beach shack.

TAINO BEACH

Arguably the most marvelous beach on the island, **Taino** is just far enough removed from **Lucaya** to thin the crowds some, although cruise-ship passengers often make their way here en groupe. Junkanoo Beach Club has a small food menu (compared to its long menu of

34 different drinks) and water-sports operators are on hand. With lapping water that puts gemstones to shame, this fluffy-sand beach begs for explorations. A short walk down the long, gently coved beach takes you to Tony Macaroni's Conch Experience.

WILLIAM'S TOWN BEACH

When the tide is high, this slice of relatively hidden beach (off East Sunrise Highway and down Beachway Drive) can get a little narrow, but there's a wide area at its east end, where a pig roast-jerk pit stand does business. Across the road, a number of beach shacks have names such as Bikini Bottom and Toad's on the Bay. Island Seas Resort, next to the pig roast stand, has its own modern interpretation of the local beach shack, called CoCoNuts Grog & Grub.

XANADU BEACH

The old Xanadu Resort of Howard Hughes fame has now morphed into a time-share vacation club, but the beach club on wide powdery sands remains vibrant with guests from other Freeport resorts that bus them here. The scent of grilling burgers in the open-air kitchen and restaurant is as luring as the mile-long, fluffy stretch of beach itself.

6

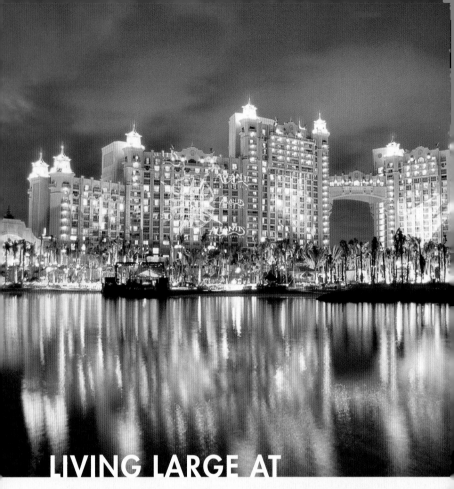

LIVING LARGE AT
ATLANTIS

by Jessica Robertson

The unmistakable sight of this peach fantasia comes into view long before you cross the Paradise Island Bridge. With a glitzy shopping mall, the biggest casino and water park in the country, and seemingly unlimited choices for dining and drinking (40 restaurants and bars), the Bahamas' largest resort is as much a tourist attraction as a hotel.

Royal Towers entrance

Atlantis at night

Water Paradise

Aura Nightclub

Poseidon's Kids Pool

✉ Casino Dr., Paradise Island ☎ 888/528–7155 or 242/363–3000 💲 Discover Atlantis tour $35; Aquaventure day pass $110; beach day pass $60; casino admission free ⏱ Tours daily 9–4:45, casino daily 24 hrs.

CUTTING-EDGE EXPERIENCES

As kid friendly as Atlantis is, the resort has recently upped its sophistication levels. Trendy clubs and private pool areas ensure adults have their own space. Below are our top picks for family and adult activities.

Pirates Cove

Pirates Cove Beach

1 Aquaventure

4 The Cove Atlantis

Paradise Beach

Paradise Island

Leap of Faith

Club Med Village

✕ **Mesa Grill**
8

Blue Project

Royal Towers

Pirates Cove Drive

Sivananda Ashram Yoga Retreat

7
Dolphin Cay

Casuarina Dr.

The Pink House

Paradise Island Dr.

Werner Gren Canal

Casuarina Beach

Tennis Centre

Nassau Harbour

1 Aquaventure. At the 63-acre water park, adults and kids over 48" tall can take the **Leap of Faith**, meander along a lazy river, or paddle in fun-filled themed pools like Poseidon and Splasher's Island. ⟲

2 Atlantis Kids Adventures. Check the kids into this 8,000-sq-foot wonderland, and they might not come out until it's time to head back to the airport. Interactive activities include a **gaming center, Lego room, performance stage, and cooking classes.** ⟲

⟲ Great for families

🍸 Perfect for adults

3 Aura. Hot tunes, sexy people, and topshelf drinks are all at the country's trendiest (and most expensive) nightclub. If you're really a big spender, invest in a VIP table with bottle service. 🍸

4 Cain at the Cove. A DJ orchestrates the mood from morning 'til night at this adults-only pool lounge, while concierges keep the food and drinks coming. For a totally decadent experience, book a private cabana, and have it stocked with whatever your heart desires. 🍸

Miss USA and Miss Universe DJing at Cain

5 Casino. The largest casino in the Bahamas and the Caribbean never closes. Test your luck on one of the 850 slot machines, play a hand of blackjack or Caribbean stud poker, or place a bet on major sporting events at Pegasus Race and Sports Book. 🍸

6 The Dig. You don't have to get wet to get up close and personal with some of the ocean's most incredible creatures. The Dig houses everything from spiny lobster to lionfish, seahorses, and even piranha in a 2½ million gallon habitat, the world's largest aquarium. ⟲

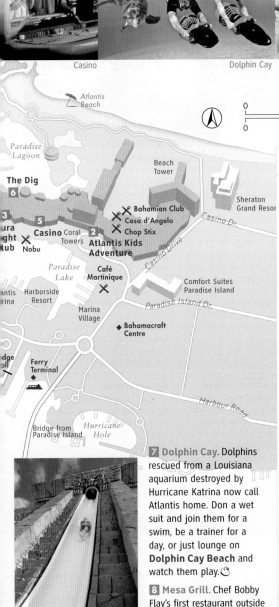

Casino　　　　　　　Dolphin Cay　　　　　Aquaventure

Atlantis Beach

0   220 yards
0   200 meters

Paradise Lagoon

The Dig
6

Beach Tower

Sheraton Grand Resort

Casino Dr.

3
5
ura
ght ✕
lub

✕ **Bahamian Club**
✕ Casa d'Angelo
✕ **Chop Stix**

Casino Coral
Towers **2**
Nobu **Atlantis Kids Adventure**

Casino Drive

Paradise Lake

Café **Martinique**

Comfort Suites Paradise Island

ntis Harborside
rina Resort

Marina Village

Paradise Island Dr.

♦ **Bahamacraft Centre**

dge
oll Ferry
Terminal

Harbour Road

Bridge from Paradise Island

Hurricane Hole

7 Dolphin Cay. Dolphins rescued from a Louisiana aquarium destroyed by Hurricane Katrina now call Atlantis home. Don a wet suit and join them for a swim, be a trainer for a day, or just lounge on **Dolphin Cay Beach** and watch them play. ☾

8 Mesa Grill. Chef Bobby Flay's first restaurant outside the United States serves up his signature southwestern dishes, many with a Bahamian twist. ☾

Leap of Faith

SAVE VS. SPLURGE

Save at Paradise Lagoon

Splurge at the casino

ACTIVITY	SAVE	SPLURGE
Dining	So long as everyone in your group can settle on a dish or two, Carmine's (242/363–3000 Ext. 29) is a great deal. Italian food is served up family style, which means portions large enough to share. Desserts like the chocolate cannoli and the tiramisu are wonderful, so save room and order your own.	For the ultimate in fine dining, try Café Martinique. Select your courses from the exquisite menu, which includes a market-price mixed-seafood appetizer and Chateaubriand for two. Or order the chef's tasting menu for $145 per person.
Underwater Adventures	Pack your mask, snorkel, and swimsuit, and hit the 7-acre Paradise Lagoon or the reefs just off Cove Beach.	Sign up to be an Aquarist for a Day and get hands-on experience helping care for the thousands of marine animals that call Atlantis home. Prices start at $179, and it's limited to 12 people.
A Night Out	Take a leisurely stroll through Marina Village for some great people watching, "ooh" and "ahh" at the luxurious yachts docked there, and grab a seat across from Bimini Road to listen to live music.	Aura Nightclub, upstairs from the casino, is one of the hottest nightspots in the country. Admission can range from nothing to $100, drinks cost a pretty penny, and tables are only available to groups buying a bottle of top-shelf liquor.
Entertain the Kids	The Atlantis Theater shows recent Hollywood blockbusters and is free for resort guests. Make it a family affair, or the kids can catch a flick while you dine at a nearby restaurant.	The newly overhauled Atlantis Kids Adventures offers kids ages 3–12 more activities than they could ever take advantage of. It costs $40–$65 per session.
Souvenirs	Head over to the Bahama Craft Centre and pick up a locally made straw bag or a T-shirt to remind you of your time in Paradise. Bartering is the norm in the markets.	Marina Village and the main shopping court at Atlantis are lined with stores selling many of the world's most exclusive brands. A duty-free regime ensures that even when splurging, you'll often land a deal.

(opposite) Atlantis

THE ABACOS

From island-long stretches to strips as short as your boat, with powder-white to warm-cream sand, the roar of the surf or the silence of a slow rising tide, the Abacos have a beach suited to everyone's liking. And most likely, you'll find a secluded spot to call your own.

(this page above and opposite page bottom) Treasure Cay Beach

Ocean-side beaches are long expanses of white powder that change their form throughout the year depending on the surge brought in by weather. Beaches sheltered from strong winds, on the lee sides of islands, are small, narrow, and stable. Trees are taller on the lee sides of the islands and provide shaded areas for picnics. On the outer cays, beaches make popular surf spots and snorkel sites, with the barrier reef running along the shore. Most Abaco beaches are secluded, but if you're looking for a beach party, head to Great Guana Cay for the Sunday pig roast.

RED BAYS

Just north of Marsh Harbour, eroded rocks offshore give the beaches a distinct red-brown color. Some people think this is the result of ancient deposits of wind-blown soil from the Sahara. These beaches are smaller than the more popular beaches, and run along the shore in a series of small scalloped curves. They are only accessible through old logging trails, but are secluded and unique to the area.

GUANA CAY BEACH

The **beaches on Guana Cay** stretch along much of the island's ocean side and are often only separated by rocky outcroppings. The sand here is slightly courser and is more cream colored, with speckles of pink from wave-ground corals. Surfing is popular here too, especially on the northern beaches. The **North Side Beach,** as it is known by locals, offers both long quiet walks and Sunday pig roasts at Nippers restaurant, one of the best beach parties in the Bahamas.

PELICAN CAY BEACH

In a protected park, this is a great spot for snorkeling and diving on nearby Sandy Cay Reef. The cay is small and between two ocean cuts, so the water drops off quickly but its location is also what nurtures the beach's pure white sand. If you get restless, ruins of an old house are hidden in overgrowth at the top of the cay, and offers fantastic views of the park.

TAHITI BEACH

This small beach at the southern tip of Elbow Cay is a popular boater's stop. The soft white sand is well protected from the close ocean cut by thick vegetation, a few barrier cays, and shallow water. This shallow area is popular for shelling, and of course simply relaxing and watching the tide rise. At low tide, the true beauty of this beach is revealed when a long sand spit emerges, perfect

for picnics. It's great for young children, as the water on one side of the spit is ankle deep, stays calm, and remains warm. During peak season the beach can become a bit crowded.

TREASURE CAY BEACH

This beach is world famous for its expanse of truly powder-like sand and turquoise water. On the beach's southern end is a bar and grill with a couple shade-baring huts. The rest of the beach is clear from development, since the land is privately owned, and almost clear of footprints. With a top-notch marina across the road and lunch a short stroll away, you have luxury; a walk farther down the beach gives you a quiet escape.

6

ANDROS, BIMINI, AND THE BERRY ISLANDS

Because they're famous for their off-the-chart fishing and diving, the islands of Andros, Berry, and Bimini often get shorted when talk turns to beaches. This is a great injustice, especially in the case of the abandoned way-white sand beaches of South Andros, Great Harbour Cay (in the Berry Islands), and South Bimini.

(this page above) North Bimini beach; (opposite page top) Coco Cay Beach, Berry Islands; (opposite page bottom) Berry Island

BLUE HOLES

Mystical and mesmerizing, blue holes pock Andros' marine landscape in greater concentration than anywhere else on earth—an estimated 160-plus. They provide explorers entry into the islands' extensive network of coral-rock caves. Offshore, some holes drop off to 200 feet or more. Inland blue holes reach depths of 120 feet, layered with fresh, brackish, and salt water.

Seclusion is these islands' forte, with the exception of North Bimini, which spring breakers and weekend warriors swarm with their coolers of Kalik beer. South Bimini, because of its convenient boat docks right at the beach, also grabs a party crowd, but there's more room to spread out here. Andros beaches as a whole are, like Berry's, ungroomed and wild. Some take a bit of searching to find, others front resorts and lodges.

BERRY ISLAND BEACHES

Two crescent beaches scoop the coastline of Great Harbour Cay. Within walking distance of the airport and town, a 5-mi sweep appeals to beachgoers who like the conveniences of food, drink, and hotel with their sand. Beach Villa, the Beach Club restaurant, and houses line its length. For more seclusion, move 5 mi north to **Sugar Beach,** where rock bluffs divide the gorgeous, fine white sand into "private" beaches roughly 1 mi in length. Exploring the caves is an added attraction. The calm waters along these coved beaches make them a natural for snorkeling.

MORGAN'S BLUFF BEACH, ANDROS

At the north end of North Andros near Nicholl's Town, this wide lovely beach is normally quiet except around regatta time. Otherwise, it's an entirely natural stretch with no facilities and sparkling gem-colored waters. It's adjacent to the harbor, so boaters sometimes make use of the beach. Australian pines and palms provide a bit of shade inland at its edges.

NORTH BIMINI BEACHES

North Bimini's three downtown beaches—**Radio Beach, Blister Beach,** and **Spook Hill Beach** (named for the cemetery across the street)—stretch several miles on the island's windward side at the top of a dune ridge. Australian pine trees line the sand—what Hemingway

described as "floury white" in *Islands in the Stream*—on one side, glorious gem-hued waters on the other. The iron wreck of an old salvage ship rusts at the beach's south end. At the north end, a string of beach bars provide the only facilities.

SMALL HOPE BAY BEACH, ANDROS

Small Hope Bay Lodge is planted squarely on this coved beach where from-shore snorkeling is excellent, the sand is white, and tidal limestone pools make for fun tiny sea creature exploration at low tide. It's a good, long walking beach, and you can also sign up for a resort course or diving excursion at the resort, or simply enjoy a beachside lunch buffet.

SOUTH BIMINI BEACHES

South Bimini claims the island's prettiest beaches, with some of the best from-shore snorkeling around. Beachgoers can set up headquarters at the Bimini Sands Beach Club, where public boat docks, volleyball, tiki umbrellas, restaurants, and bars await. For more seclusion, head to **Shell Beach,** around the point on the island's west side. The beach stretches long and natural, and calm waters typically prevail. The snorkeling is also good here.

ELEUTHERA AND HARBOUR ISLAND

Eleuthera and Harbour Island beaches are some of the best in the world, thanks to their pristine beauty and dazzling variety. Deep-blue ocean fading to aqua shallows make gorgeous backdrops for gourmet restaurants and the wooden decks of fishing shacks. The sand is for bonfires, celebrity watching, Friday night fish fries, dancing, and music, as much as it is for afternoon naps and stargazing.

(this page above and opposite page top) Pink Sands Beach, Harbour Island

BLUSHING BEACHES

Contrary to popular opinion, pink sand comes primarily from the crushed pink and red shells of microscopic insects called foraminifera, not coral. Foraminifera live on the underside of reefs and the sea floor. After the insects die, the waves smash the shells, which wash ashore along with sand and bits of pink coral. The intensity of the rosy hues depends on the slant of the sun.

Tranquil coves' sparkling white sand are as calm as a pool on the west side of Eleuthera, while the Atlantic's winter waves challenge skilled surfers on the east side, which has long stretches of pink sand. On Harbour Island, pink sand is on the ocean side and the white-sand coves face the calm channel. Home to shells that tumble in with every wave and starfish resting just offshore, the island's occasional glitz can't compete with the beaches' natural beauty.

CLUB MED BEACH

This stretch of pink sand was Club Med's famed beach before the resort was destroyed by a hurricane in 1999. But the gorgeous Atlantic-side beach remains, anchored by fantastic bistros like the Beach House and Tippy's. The wide expanse, ringed by casuarina trees, is often deserted and makes a great outpost for romantics.

COCODIMAMA BEACH

Many necklaces and shell decorations come from **Cocodimama**, which, along with **Ten Bay Beach** at South Palmetto Point, is well-known for perfect small shells. The water at Cocodimama, a secluded beach 6 mi north of Governor's Harbour, has the aqua and sky blue shades you see on Bahamas posters, and is shallow and calm, perfect for children and sand castles. The Cocodimama Resort is next to the beach, and makes a perfect lunchtime respite for shrimp spinach salad or pasta and wine.

GAULDING'S CAY BEACH

Snorkelers and divers will want to spend time at this beach, 3 mi north of Gregory Town. You'll most likely have the long stretch of white sand and shallow aqua water all to yourself, and it's great for shelling. At low tide, you can walk or swim to **Gaulding's Cay,** a tiny rock island with a few casuarina trees. There's great snorkeling around the island; you'll see a concentration of sea

anemones so spectacular it dazzled even Jacques Cousteau's biologists.

PINK SANDS BEACH, HARBOUR ISLAND

This is the fairest pink beach of them all: 3 mi of pale pink sand behind some of the most expensive and posh inns in the Bahamas. Its sand is of such a fine consistency that it's almost as soft as talcum powder, and the gentle slope of the shore makes small waves break hundreds of yards offshore; you have to walk out quite a distance to get past your waist. This is the place to see the rich and famous in designer resort wear or ride a horse bareback across the sand and into the sea.

SURFER'S BEACH

This is Gregory Town's claim to fame and one of the few beaches in the Bahamas known for surfing. Serious surfers have gathered here since the 1960s for decent waves from December to April. If you don't have a jeep, you can walk the ¾ mi to this Atlantic-side beach—follow rough-and-bumpy Ocean Boulevard at Eleuthera Island Shores just south of town. Look for a young crowd sitting around bonfires at night.

6

THE EXUMAS

You can't go wrong with the beaches in the Exumas. They're some of the prettiest in the Bahamas—powdery bleach-white sand sharply contrasts the glittery emerald and sapphire waves. You can even stake your umbrella directly on the Tropic of Cancer. And the best part of all? You'll probably be the only one there.

(this page above) Staniel Cay; (opposite page top) Chat 'N' Chill, Stocking Island

The Exumas are made up of 365 cays, each and every one with pristine white beaches. Some cays are no bigger than a footprintless sandbar. But you won't stay on the sand long; Perrier-clear waters beckon, and each gentle wave brings new treasures—shells, bits of blue-and-green sea glass, and starfish. Beaches won't be hard to find on the tiny cays; on Great Exuma, look for BEACH ACCESS signs on the Queen's Highway.

PICTURE PERFECT

"My pictures will never show the incredible shades of blue in this water." You're likely to hear this on your vacation, maybe straight from your own mouth. Here are a few tips: shoot early—before 9—on a sunny day, or late in the afternoon. Make sure the sun is behind you. Use a tripod, or hold the camera still. Find a contrasting color—a bright red umbrella or a yellow fishing boat.

CHAT 'N' CHILL, STOCKING ISLAND

The restaurant and 9-acre playground—an amazing white-sand beach—is the Exumas' party central, particularly for the famous all-day Sunday pig roasts. Play volleyball in the powdery sand, order what's cooking on the outdoor grill—fresh fish, ribs—or chat and chill. There are dances on the beach from January to the end of April when 200-plus sailboats populate the harbor. The new Conch Bar on the beach serves conch fritters, conch salad, and lobster fritters. The beach is quieter on weekdays, and usually not crowded in summer and fall.

JOLLY HALL BEACH, GREAT EXUMA

Snorkeling, swimming, running; you can do it all on this long beach, a curve of sparkling white sand shaded by casuarina trees, just north of Palm Bay Beach Club. It's quiet and the shallow azure water makes it a great spot for families or romantics. When it's time for lunch, walk over to Palm Bay, Coconut Cove, or Augusta Bay, three small nearby inns. Watch your bags when high tide comes in; much of the beach is swallowed by the sea. That's the signal for a cold Kalik and grouper sandwich.

PELICAN'S BAY BEACH, LITTLE EXUMA

This is the beach most visitors come to the Exumas for, although don't be surprised if you're the only one on it at noon on a Saturday. It's right on the Tropic of Cancer; a helpful line marking the spot on the steps leading down to the sand makes a great photo op. The beach is a white-sand crescent in a protected cove, where the water is usually as calm as a pond. A shady wooden cabana makes a comfortable place to admire the beach and water. *Pirates of the Caribbean* 2 and 3 were filmed on nearby **Sandy Cay.** Have lunch at the cast's favorite place, the open-air Santana's in Williams Town, a 10-minute drive from the beach.

WARDERICK WELLS CAY, EXUMA CAYS

Next to the Park Headquarters in Exuma Cays Land and Sea Park is a lovely white beach, but you won't be looking at the sand when you first arrive. The beach is dominated by the stunningly huge skeleton of a sperm whale that died in 1995 because of consumed plastic. The skeleton was fortified in its natural form and makes an emotion-packed statue that no artist could duplicate. Equally striking is the gorgeous blue shades of water and the glistening white sand. Check out the snorkel trail in the park when you've soaked in enough sun.

6

THE SOUTHERN OUT ISLANDS

Beach connoisseurs come to the southern Out Islands to walk luscious pink and sparkling white-sand beaches that have no footprints but their own, and maybe a heron's odd step—three toes facing forward, one backward. These are the things you notice when there's no one on the beach but you.

(this page above) Cape Santa Maria Beach, Long Island; (opposite page top) Fernandez Bay Beach, Cat Island; (opposite page bottom) Greenwood Beach, Cat Island

Shells tumble in on gentle waves in a rhythmic splash that becomes the soundtrack for your vacation. Beach lovers sit cross-legged around bonfires at night, entertained by Rake 'n' Scrape musicians; mesmerized by the starry sky (hello, no light pollution!); and curled up on lounge chairs to watch the pale pink rays of the morning sun peek over the horizon, then later set in the west in fiery reds and oranges. You can swim in water as clear and soothing as a pool, or relax in the shade of a coconut tree with a cold Kalik in sybaritic bliss.

HISTORIC LIGHTHOUSES

Powerful lighthouse beacons have rotated over the southern islands since the 1800s to help ships navigate the treacherous reefs that surround them. Visit the 115-foot Bird Rock Lighthouse (1872) on Crooked Island; the Castle Island Lighthouse (1867) on Acklins Island; the Inagua Lighthouse (1870); and San Salvador's 160-foot Dixon Hill Lighthouse (1856), which is still hand-operated.

BONEFISH BAY, SAN SALVADOR

The 3-mi beach in front of Club Med has bright white sand as fine as talcum powder, and calm water such a neon shade of turquoise it seems to glow. It might possibly be the most gorgeous water you ever lay eyes on. There are activities, such as waterskiing and snorkeling, in front of Club Med, but the beach is long enough that you'll be able to find an isolated spot.

CAPE SANTA MARIA BEACH, LONG ISLAND

Located on the leeward side of the island in the north at Cape Santa Maria Resort, the water colors here range from pale blue to aqua to shades of turquoise. The 4-mi stretch of soft white sand beckons you to stroll, build sand castles, or sun worship. The resort has a beachside restaurant and lounge chairs for guests, but there's also plenty of sand to find a secluded stretch all your own.

FERNANDEZ BAY BEACH, CAT ISLAND

Imagine the perfect calm cove in the tropics—a 1-mi stretch of glistening, pristine white sand, inviting shade under coconut palms and sea grape trees, and a couple of boutique resorts with cottages and verandas facing the spectacular sand and azure water. You'll never want to leave; restaurants and bars built on decks overlooking the water are a blessing. The beach is often deserted, so dinner for two might really mean just that.

GALLOWAY LANDING, LONG ISLAND

This remarkable beach south of Clarence Town is known only by the locals, but no one will mind if you come. Swim and sun at the first beach, or walk a short distance south to an even more wonderful and secluded stretch of sand. Here, canals carved into the limestone hills by the now defunct Diamond Salt Mine are filled with the palest blue ocean water and are home to small marine life. It's a wonderful area to kayak, snorkel, and swim. A bit further south, a narrow bridge leads to beyond-stunning lagoons and ocean flats.

GREENWOOD BEACH, CAT ISLAND

An 8-mi stretch of pink sand makes this one of the most spectacular beaches in the Bahamas. It is by far the best pink-sand beach on the island. Hypnotized by the beauty, most visitors walk the entire beach, some even farther to an adjoining sandy cove accessible only by foot. After such a long walk, a dip in the shallows of the turquoise ocean is pure bliss. The beach is on the remote southeastern end of the island and has just one resort; stay here for a heavenly escape, but nonguests are welcome on the sand, too.

Best Beaches in the Northern Caribbean

THE GREATER ANTILLES

WHAT'S WHERE

THE
BAHAMAS

CUBA

CAYMAN ISLANDS
(U.K.)

Cayman
Brac

George
Town

1 Little
Cayman

Grand Cayman

Santiago
de Cuba

JAMAICA

Montego
Bay

JAMAICA

2 Kingston

0   100 mi
0   100 km

Caribbean Sea

Northern Caribbean. The islands closest to the United States mainland—composed of Cuba, Jamaica, Haiti, the Dominican Republic, and Puerto Rico—are also the largest in the chain that stretches in an arc from the southern coast of Florida down to Venezuela. Haiti and Cuba aren't covered in this book. The Cayman Islands, just south of Cuba, are usually included in this group.

1 Cayman Islands. Vacationers appreciate the mellow civility of the islands, and Grand Cayman's exceptional Seven Mile Beach has its share of fans. Divers come to explore the pristine reefs or perhaps to swim with friendly stingrays. Go if you want a safe, family-friendly vacation spot. Don't go if you're trying to save money, because there are few real bargains here.

2 Jamaica. Easy to reach and with resorts in every price range, Jamaica is also an easy choice for many travelers. Go to enjoy the music, food, beaches, and sense of hospitality that's made it one of the Caribbean's most popular destinations. Don't go if you can't deal with the idea that a Caribbean paradise still has problems of its own to solve.

3 Dominican Republic.
Dominicans have beautiful smiles and warm hearts and are proud of their island, which is blessed with pearl-white beaches and a vibrant, Latin culture. Go for the best-priced resorts in the Caribbean and a wide range of activities that will keep you moving day and night. Don't go if you can't go with the flow. Things don't always work here, and not everyone speaks English.

4 Puerto Rico. San Juan is hopping day and night; beyond the city, you'll find a sunny escape and slower pace. Party in San Juan, relax on the beach, hike the rain forest, or play some of the Caribbean's best golf courses. You have the best of both worlds here, with natural and urban thrills alike. So go for both. Just don't expect to do it in utter seclusion.

5 Turks and Caicos Islands.
Miles of white-sand beaches surround this tiny island chain, only eight of which are inhabited. The smaller islands seem to come from some long-forgotten era of Caribbean life. Go for deserted beaches and excellent diving on one of the world's largest coral reefs. Don't go for nightlife and a fast pace. And don't forget your wallet. This isn't a budget destination.

CAYMAN ISLANDS

Limestone, coral, shells, water, and wind collaborated to fashion the Cayman Islands beaches. It's a classic example of the interaction between geology and marine biology.

(this page above) A beach lounger at the Ritz-Carlton, Grand Cayman; (opposite page bottom) Horseback riding at Barkers; (opposite page top) Snorkelers at Stingray Sandbar

Most of the beaches in Cayman, especially on Grand and Little Cayman, resemble powdered ivory. A few, including those on Cayman Brac, are more dramatic, a mix of fine beige sand and rugged rocky "ironshore," which often signals the healthiest reefs and best snorkeling. The islands are limestone outcroppings, the thrusting summits of a submarine mountain range called the Cayman Ridge. Grand Cayman's beaches range from cramped, untrammeled coves to long stretches basking like a cat in the sun, lined with bustling bars and water-sports concessions. There are some sandy beaches on Cayman Brac, especially along the southwest coast, but these beaches are also lined with turtle grass. Little Cayman has some spectacular white-sand beaches. All beaches are public, though access can be restricted by resorts. Remember that the Cayman Islands is a conservative place: nudity is strictly forbidden and punishable by a hefty fine and/ or prison time.

CORAL SAND

On most limestone-coral-based islands around the world, the hue and texture of the sand are derived from various micro-skeletons, like the coral-like foraminifera and the calcareous algae halimeda (a genus embracing a dozen species), which flourish in offshore reefs and sea-grass beds. These form the powdery, pearly sand on Seven Mile Beach and Rum Point, as well as Point of Sand on Little Cayman.

GRAND CAYMAN

East End Beaches. Just drive along and look for any sandy beach, park your car, and enjoy a stroll. The vanilla-hue stretch at **Colliers Bay,** by the Reef and Morritts resorts, is a good clean one with superior snorkeling. ⊠ *Queen's Hwy., East End.*

Rum Point. This North Sound beach has hammocks slung in towering casuarina trees, picnic tables, the Wreck Bar and Grill for dining, well-stocked shop for seaworthy sundries, and Red Sail Sports, which offers various water sports and boats to explore Stingray City. The barrier reef ensures safe snorkeling and soft sand. The bottom remains shallow for a long way from shore, but it's littered with small coral heads, so kids shouldn't wrestle in the water here. The Wreck is ablaze with color—yellow with navy blue trim and lime and mango picnic tables—as if trying to upstage the snorkeling just offshore; an ultracasual hangout turns out outstanding pub grub from fish-and-chips to wings, as well as lethal mudslide cocktails. Showers are available. Just around the bend, another quintessential beach hangout, Kaibo, rocks during the day. ⊠ *Rum Point, North Side.*

Fodor's Choice ★ **Seven Mile Beach.** Grand Cayman's west coast is dominated by the famous **Seven Mile Beach**—actually a 6½-mi-long (10-km-long) expanse of powdery white sand overseeing lapis

water stippled with a rainbow of parasails and kayaks. The width of the beach varies with the season; toward the south end it narrows and disappears altogether south of the Marriott, leaving only rock and ironshore. It starts to broaden into its normal silky softness anywhere between Tarquyn Manor and the Reef Grill at Royal Palms. Free of litter and pesky peddlers, it's an unspoiled (though often crowded) environment. At the public beach toward the north end you can find chairs for rent ($10 for the day, including a beverage), a playground, water toys aplenty, two beach bars, restrooms, and showers. The best snorkeling is at either end, by the Marriott and Treasure Island or off the northern section called **Cemetery Reef Beach.** ⊠ *West Bay Rd., Seven Mile Beach.*

Smith's Cove. South of the Grand Old House, this tiny but popular protected swimming and snorkeling spot makes a wonderful beach wedding location. The bottom drops off quickly enough to allow you to swim and play close to shore. Although slightly rocky, there's little debris and few coral heads, plenty of shade, picnic tables, restrooms, and parking. Surfers will find some decent swells just to the south. Local scuttlebutt calls it a place for dalliances during work hours; it's also a romantic sunset spot. ⊠ *Off S. Church St., George Town.*

7

(this page above) A view of Own Island from Little Cayman; (opposite page) Kayaks on a beach at Rum Point, Grand Cayman

South Sound Cemetery Beach. A narrow, sandy driveway takes you past the small cemetery to a perfect beach. The dock here is primarily used by dive boats during winter storms. You can walk in either direction; the sand is talcum-soft and clean, the water calm and clear (though local surfers take advantage of occasional small reef breaks; if wading, wear reef shoes since the bottom is somewhat rocky and dotted with sea urchins). You'll definitely find fewer crowds than at the more popular beaches. ⊠ *S. Sound Rd., Prospect.*

Water Cay. For an unspoiled beach, bear left at Rum Point on the North Side and follow the road to the end. When you pass a porte cochere for an abandoned condo development and see a soft, sandy beach, stop your car. Wade out knee deep and look for the large flame-hued starfish. (Don't touch—just look.) ⊠ *North Side.*

CAYMAN BRAC

The island has several sandy beaches, mostly along the southwest coast. In addition to the hotel beaches, where everyone is welcome, there is a public beach with good access to the reef; it's well marked on tourist maps. The north-coast beaches, predominantly rocky ironshore, offer excellent snorkeling.

LITTLE CAYMAN

Fodor's Choice ★ Owen Island. This private, forested island can be reached by rowboat, kayak, or an ambitious 200-yard swim. Anyone is welcome to come across and enjoy the deserted beaches and excellent snorkeling. Nudity is forbidden as "idle and disorderly" in the Cayman Islands, though that doesn't always stop skinny-dippers (who may not realize they can be seen quite easily from shore on the strands facing Little Cayman).

DOMINICAN REPUBLIC

Its beaches are what put the D.R. on the touristic sonar. The east coast beaches (near Punta Cana, Juanillo, Bavaro), which are washed by the Caribbean, rival any in the Antilles . . . possibly the world. The government partnered with the hospitality industry and beautified many beaches not as naturally endowed. Think cosmetic surgery. Think hundreds of millions of dollars.

The Dominican Republic has more than 1,000 mi (1,600 km) of beaches, including the Caribbean's longest stretch of white sand: Punta Cana–Bavaro. Many beaches are accessible to the public (in theory, all beaches in this country, from the high-water mark down, are open to everyone) and may tempt you to stop for a swim. That's part of the uninhibited joy of this country. Do be careful, though: some have dangerously strong currents, which may be the reason why they are undeveloped.

(this page above) Kitesurfing the waters of Punta Cana; (opposite page bottom) Kiteboarding the waves of Cabrete; (opposite page top) Looking down on Cabrete Beach

WHAT'S YOUR PREFERENCE?

Is white sand a must? Then you are talking the Punta Cana region. If you can go nearly white, say, a light taupe, then it's the southeast coast. Bayahibe, with its half-crescent beaches, is a charmer. Juan Dolio's Villas de Mar beach has been reborn with tons of white sand trucked in. The amber sands of Playa Dorada and Cabarete have also been enhanced with truckloads of white sand.

Playa Bahoruco. This isolated, gorgeous stretch of virgin beach goes on for miles in either direction, with rugged cliffs dropping to golden sand and warm, blue water. It's a wild, undeveloped Caribbean beach, but many sections are pebbly, so you need surf shoes for swimming. In nearby San Rafael are beach shacks where you can buy meals of fresh fish, even whole sea bass in coconut sauce. ⊠ *Carretera La Costa, Km 17, 8 mi (13 km) south of Barahona.*

Playa Boca Chica. You can walk far out into the gin-clear waters protected by coral reefs. Unfortunately, some areas are cluttered with plastic furniture, pizza stands, and cottages. If you're staying in the capital, this is the closest good beach. Grab lunch at one of the larger beach-front restaurants like El Pelicano or nearby, the trendy waterfront restaurants Boca Marina or Neptuno's Club. ⊠ *Autopista Las Americas, 21 mi (34 km) east of Santo Domingo, Boca Chica.*

Playa Cabarete. Follow the coastal road east from **Playa Dorada** to find this beach, which has strong waves and ideal, steady winds (from 15 to 20 knots), making it an integral part of the international windsurfing circuit. Segments are strips of golden sand punctuated only by palm trees. In the most commercial area, restaurants and bars are back-to-back, spilling onto the sand. The informal scene is young and fun, with expats and

tourists from every imaginable country. ⊠ *Sosúa–Cabarete road, Cabarete.*

Playa Dominicus. This southeast coast beach near Bayahibe has gin-clear water and just a very few waves at the entrance but absolutely no undertow. The Iberostar, Viva Wyndham, and Oasis Canoa resorts all share this beach, and there's a small public section where the locals venture on weekends. The beach has some huts to purchase souvenirs and two restaurants on the sand as well. *Dominicus Americanus.*

Playa Dorada. On the north's Amber Coast, this is one of the D.R.'s most established resort areas. Each hotel has its own slice of the beach, which is soft beige sand, with lots of reefs for snorkeling. **Gran Ventana Beach Resort,** which is on a point, marks the end of the major hotel development. The Atlantic waters are great for windsurfing, waterskiing, and fishing. ⊠ *Off Autopista Luperon, 10 mins east of Puerto Plata, Playa Dorada.*

Playa Grande. On the North Coast, between the towns of Río San Juan and Cabrera, is this long stretch of powdery sand. The public entrance is about a mile after Playa Grande Golf Course, at Km 9. Here, the beach is on a lovely cove, with towering cliffs on both sides. A few beach shacks fry up fresh fish and keep the beer on ice. An outcropping separates this beach from **Playa Precioso.** During the week you'll have little

7

(this page above) Isla Saona; (opposite page) Windsurfing off Cabarete Beach

company, but on Sunday afternoons the locals are here in full force. ⊠ *Carretera Río San Juan–Cabrera, Km 11.*

Playa Las Terrenas. On the north coast of the Samaná Peninsula, tall palms list toward the sea, and the beach is extensive and postcard perfect, with crystalline waters and soft, golden sand. There's plenty of color—vivid blues, greens, and yellows—as well as colorful characters. To the west is Playa El Cosón, opposite Cayo Ballena, a great whale-watching spot (from January to April). Samaná has some of the country's best beaches and drop-dead scenery, the rough roads notwithstanding. ⊠ *Carretera Las Terrenas, Las Terrenas.*

Playa Sosúa. Sosúa Bay is a gorgeous, natural harbor with coral reefs and dive sites, about a 20-minute drive from Puerto Plata. Swimming is delightful, except after a heavy rain when litter floats in. From the beach you can see mountains in the background, the cliffs that surround the bay, and seemingly miles of coastline. Snorkeling from the beach is good, but the best spots are farther offshore, closer to the reefs. (Don't bother going to Three Rocks)

Unfortunately, the backdrop is a string of tents where hawkers push souvenirs, snacks, drinks, and water-sports equipment rentals. Lounge chairs can usually be had for RD$75. ⊠ *Carretera Puerto Plata–Sosúa, Sosúa.*

Punta Cana. The area encompasses Cabeza de Torres, Playa Bavaro, and continues all the way around the peninsula to Playa de Uvero Alto. Each hotel has its own strip of sand with rows of chaise longues, and you can call in advance for a day pass. The stretch between Club Med and the Puntacana Resort & Club is one of the most beautiful. Playa El Cortecito, where Capitan Cook restaurant sits, is more how life used to be, with fishermen bringing in their catch. The public beach at Macao is no longer a good option, having been taken over by four-wheeler excursions and a new Westin resort rising from its sands. A rough road leads to more-deserted stretches in the Uvero Alto area, but outside of the resorts there are few services. ⊠ *Off Autopista Las Americas, east of Higüey, Punta Cana.*

JAMAICA

As the Caribbean's third-largest island, Jamaica has no shortage of beaches, ranging from the North Coast's tourist-filled stretches of sand lined by exclusive resorts to the nearly deserted beaches of the South Coast, where beach action often means a fisherman cleaning his catch.

(this page above) The beach at Sandals Whitehouse, on the South Shore; (opposite page bottom) Doctor's Cave Beach, Montego Bay; (opposite page top) Dunn's River Falls, Ocho Rios

North and west coast beaches tend to be busy, well supplied with amenities, and blessed with large expanses of sand. Both Negril (and its lovely Seven Mile Beach) and Montego Bay (which has both Doctor's Cave and Half Moon Bay) are renowned for their beaches, and both have many resorts directly on the beach to choose from. Beaches on the South Coast are generally less crowded but are smaller, with fewer services. The best South Coast beaches are in the Treasure Beach area near Calabash Bay. Kingston-area beaches are generally congested; ask your hotel concierge before heading out to any of them. Some of the best beaches are private, owned by the resorts and accessible only to resort guests or travelers who have purchased a day pass to gain access to the facilities.

BEST BEACHES?

Most of Jamaica's beaches are coral based, creating a medium-coarse, light-colored sand. In general, the best Jamaican beach sand is on the north and west sides of the island. The softest and most beautiful beaches are in Negril, on the island's west coast, and in the Montego Bay area. Those on the South Coast are narrower and wilder, with coarser, darker sand.

While hotel beaches are generally private and restricted to guests of the property, other beaches are public and are open to all kinds of vendors, which have a reputation of being rather aggressive. At resort areas, even if the beach area is considered private, the area below the high-water mark is always public, so vendors will roam longer beaches looking for business. In most cases, a simple "no thanks" will do.

MONTEGO BAY

★ **Doctor's Cave Beach.** Montego Bay's tourist scene has its roots right on the Hip Strip, the bustling entertainment district along Gloucester Avenue. Here a sea cave's waters were said to be curative and drew many travelers to bathe in them. Though the cave was destroyed by a hurricane generations ago, the beach is always busy and has a perpetual spring-break feel. It's the best beach in Jamaica outside one of the more-developed resorts, thanks to its plantation-style clubhouse with changing rooms, showers, gift shops, a bar, a grill, and even a cybercafé. There's a $5 fee for admission; beach chairs and umbrellas are also for rent. Its location within the Montego Bay Marine Park—where there are protected corals and marine life—makes it a good spot for snorkeling. More-active travelers can opt for parasailing, glass-bottom boat rides, or jet skiing. ✉ *Gloucester Ave., Montego Bay.*

Walter Fletcher Beach. Though not as pretty as **Doctor's Cave Beach**, or as tidy, Walter Fletcher Beach is home to Aquasol Theme Park, which offers a large beach (with lifeguards and security), water trampolines, Jet Skis, Wave Runners, glass-bottom boats, snorkeling, tennis, go-kart racing, a disco at night, a bar, and a grill. The park is open daily from 9 to 6; admission is $5, with à la carte pricing for most activities. Near the center of town, the beach has protection from the surf on a windy day. This means you can find unusually fine swimming here; the calm waters make it a good bet for children. ✉ *Gloucester Ave., Montego Bay.*

RUNAWAY BAY

Puerto Seco Beach. This public beach looks out on Discovery Bay, the location where, according to tradition, Christopher Columbus first came ashore on this island. The explorer sailed in search of freshwater but found none, naming the stretch of sand Puerto Seco, or "dry port." Today the beach is anything but dry; concession stands sell Red Stripe beer and local food, including jerk and patties, to a primarily local beach crowd. ✉ *Discovery Bay, 5 mi (8 km) west of Runaway Bay.*

OCHO RIOS

Dunn's River Falls Beach. You'll find a crowd (especially if there's a cruise ship in town) at the small beach at the foot of

(opposite page above) The Blue Lagoon, near Port Antonio; (this page) Negril Beach

the falls. Although tiny—especially considering the crowds that pack the falls—it's got a great view, as well as a beach bar and grill. Look up from the sands for a spectacular view of the cascading water, whose roar drowns out the sea as you approach. ⊠ *Rte. A1 between St. Ann's Bay and Ocho Rios.*

Turtle Beach. One of the busiest beaches in Ocho Rios is usually lively, and has a mix of both residents and visitors. It's next to the Sunset Jamaica Grande and looks out over the cruise port. ⊠ *Main St.*

PORT ANTONIO

Blue Lagoon. Though the beach is small, the large lagoon has to be seen to be believed. The cool, spring-fed waters cry out to swimmers and are a real contrast to the warmer sea waters. Floating docks encourage you to sun a little, or you can lie out on the small beach. Just how deep is the Blue Lagoon? You might hear it's bottomless (Jacques Cousteau verified that it is not), but the lagoon has been measured at a depth of 180 feet. At present, freelance operators at the gates sometimes offer entry but, for current (and official) conditions, call the Jamaica Tourist Board. ⊠ *9 mi (13 km) east of Port Antonio, 1 mi (2 km) east of San San Beach.*

Boston Beach. Considered the birthplace of Jamaica's famous jerk-style cooking, it's the beach where some locals visit just to buy dinner. You can get peppery jerk pork at any of the shacks spewing scented smoke along the beach. While you're there, you'll also find a small beach perfect for an after-lunch dip, although these waters are occasionally rough and much more popular for surfing. ⊠ *11 mi (18 km) east of Port Antonio.*

★ **Frenchman's Cove.** This beautiful, somewhat secluded beach is petite perfection. Protected by two outcroppings that form the cove, the inlet's calm waters are a favorite with families. A small stream trickles into the cove. You'll find a bar and restaurant serving fried chicken right on the beach. If this stretch of sand looks a little familiar, it just might be because you've seen it in the movies; it has starred in *Club Paradise*, *Treasure Island* (the Charlton Heston version), and *The Mighty Quinn*. If you are not a guest of Frenchman's Cove, admission is $4.50 ($2.50

for children). ⊠ *Rte. A4, 5 mi (8 km) east of Port Antonio.*

San San Beach. This small beach ($5 admission fee) has beautiful blue water. Just offshore, **Monkey Island** is a good place to snorkel (and, sometimes, surf). ⊠ *5 mi (8 km) east of Port Antonio.*

THE SOUTH COAST

If you're looking for something off the main tourist routes, head for Jamaica's largely undeveloped southwest coast. Because the population in this region is sparse, these isolated beaches are some of the island's safest, with hasslers practically nonexistent. You should, however, use common sense; never leave valuables unattended on the beach.

Treasure Beach. The most atmospheric beach in the southwest is in the community of Treasure Beach, which comprises four long stretches of sand as well as many small coves. Though it isn't as pretty as those to the west or north—it has more rocks and darker sand—the idea that you might be discovering a bit of the "real" Jamaica more than makes up for the small negatives. Both locals and visitors use the beaches here, though you're just as likely to find it completely deserted save for a friendly beach dog. ⊠ *Treasure Beach township.*

Word of Mouth. "We just returned from Treasure Beach and had the best, most relaxing time. Having traveled all over Jamaica, we fell in love with the area and cannot wait to return. It is the perfect spot to immerse yourself in the culture and enjoy everything wonderful about Jamaica."—RobynBou

NEGRIL

Fodor's Choice ★ **Negril Beach.** Stretching for 7 mi (11 km), the long, white-sand beach in Negril is arguably Jamaica's finest. It starts with the white sands of **Bloody Bay** north of town and continues along **Long Bay** all the way to the cliffs on the southern edge of town.

Some stretches remain undeveloped, but these are increasingly few. Along the main stretch of beach, the sand is public to the high-water mark, so a non-stop line of visitors and vendors parade from end to end. The walk is sprinkled with many good beach bars and open-air restaurants, some of which charge a small fee to use their beach facilities. Bloody Bay is lined with large all-inclusive resorts, and these sections are mostly private. Jamaica's best-known nude beach, at Hedonism II, is always among the busiest; only resort guests or day-pass holders may sun here. ⊠ *Norman Manley Blvd.*

Word of Mouth. "[In] Negril, you immediately get a different vibe. Felt like we were somewhere special in the Carribean, a feeling we didn't really get [in Ocho Rios] and MoBay. Seven Mile [Beach] was beautiful."—jpniner.

7

REGGAE

Julie Schwietert Collazo
& Eric Wechter

There's an undeniable, universal appeal to reggae music. Its feel-good beat and impassioned lyrics resonate with listeners across the globe, but experiencing reggae in the country of its birth is the best way to enjoy the music.

Widely considered to be Jamaica's seminal music form, reggae was born out of other genres, including ska and rocksteady, and is relatively young compared to other Jamaican musical styles. In fact, the history of Jamaican music is as long as the history of the island itself. Reggae's origins are firmly rooted in traditions of African music, and its lyrics are inspired by Jamaicans' fervid resistance to colonialism and imperialism. Reggae can be distinguished from earlier music forms by its comparatively faster beat, its experimental tendencies, and a more prominent role for the guitar. Reggae is also more "ragged"—both in sound and in concept. That is it's both more earthy and down to earth, or folkloric. Lyrically, reggae is rife with social themes, primarily those that explore the plight of the working classes.

(opposite) Bob Marley, (top) Akon performs at Sumfest

BUILDING A BEAT

Sly Dunbar, touring with Peter Tosh, 1979

Robbie Shakespeare, on tour with Peter Tosh, 1978

Pioneering reggae musicians, such as drummer **Sly Dunbar** and bassist **Robbie Shakespeare**, shaped the genre by distilling what they viewed as the best elements of ska and rocksteady. Reggae is not complex in terms of chord structure or rhythmic variation. There may be only one to three chords in a typical reggae song, and the danceable feel is propelled most commonly by a rhythm—or "riddim"—called the "drop beat" or "one drop." The bass drum emphasizes the third beat in a four-beat cycle, creating an anchor, or a pull, that the guitar and bass play on top of. For a more propulsive feel, the drummer may equally emphasize all four beats in each measure. Layered on top of this repetitive, solid foundation are socially conscious lyrics, which often preach resistance to the establishment or beseech listeners to love one another.

REGGAE AND RASTA

Reggae is a musical genre of, by, and for the people, and the influence of Rastafarianism has expanded its folk appeal. Rasta became pervasive in Jamaica in the 1950s, when resistance to colonialism peaked. Rasta, combining spiritual, political, and social concerns, had its origins in the crowning of **Hailie Selassie I** as the emperor of Ethiopia in 1930. Selassie, the only black man to head an independent African nation at the time, became a vital figure and symbol of freedom for Africans in the diaspora. Greatly inspired by Selassie, Jamaicans integrated his empowering messages into many aspects of their culture. Musically, the Rasta influence is felt in reggae in two ways. The lyrics often advocate the idea of returning to Africa, and minor chords and a simple "riddim" structure characterize the songs. In the words of music historian Lloyd Bradley, Rastas were the "underclass of the underclass," and by 1959 more than one in every 25 Jamaicans identified with Rastafarianism. One of them was Bob Marley.

Haile Selassie I of Ethiopia

BOB MARLEY

Bob Marley is reggae's oracle, a visionary who introduced the world to the music of Jamaica and the struggles of its people. A stirring performer with a preternatural talent for connecting with audiences, Marley revealed the oppression of his countrymen and their indomitable spirit through his songs of hope, freedom, and redemption. His legacy extends far beyond reggae, influencing generations of artists across multiple genres.

Born in February 1945, Robert Nesta Marley left his home in rural St. Ann's Parish, Jamaica at 14 to pursue a music career in Kingston. In 1963 Marley joined with singers Peter Tosh and Bunny Livingston to form the group the Wailers, and they began recording singles with a renowned local producer. After a series of stops and starts and a strengthened devotion to the teachings of the Rastafari faith, Bob Marley and the Wailers released *Catch a Fire* in 1973. It was their first release outside of Jamaica, and nearly instantly it became an international success. Marley's global popularity and acclaim grew with albums like *Burnin'* and *Natty Dread*. As Marley's stardom increased abroad, his influence at home became transcendent. Regarded by many of his countrymen as a prophet, Marley, whose songs of freedom and revolution reverberated throughout Jamaica, was perceived as threat in some corridors. In December 1976, he was wounded in an assassination attempt. Marley left Jamaica for more than a year and in 1977 released his biggest record thus far, *Exodus*, which included the hits "Jammin" and "One Love/People Get Ready." By 1980, Marley was poised to reach even greater heights with an extensive U.S. tour, but while jogging in New York he suddenly collapsed. Cancer had silently invaded his brain and lungs. He died in May, 1981, at age 36. Marley's spirit and music endure in the hearts and minds of fans worldwide. His greatest hits collection, *Legend*, is the top-selling reggae album of all time.

Bob Marley at Reggae Sunsplash

7

IN FOCUS REGGAE

COMMUNING WITH THE SPIRIT

Bob Marley Museum, Kingston

Whether you're a serious enthusiast or have just a passing curiosity, Jamaica offers visitors plenty of opportunities to experience the music and culture of reggae.

Zion Bus Line Tour to Nine Mile. Marley fans won't want to miss this bus pilgrimage to the reggae icon's birthplace and final resting place. With the sounds of familiar reggae tunes thumping through the bus speakers, the guided tour takes you through the mountains to the small town of Nine Mile. The half-day tour includes a visit to Marley's house, a stop at Mount Zion (a rock where Marley meditated) and the opportunity to view Marley's mausoleum. The tour leaves from Ocho Rios. On the return trip from Nine Mile, the group stops at the Jerk Center for an authentic Jamaican lunch.

Reggae Sumfest in Montego Bay. This week-long reggae festival is held each July. In addition to featuring musical line-ups of the most popular reggae, dance hall, R&B, and hip hop acts, the Sumfest offers traditional Jamaican food and local crafts. Recent festivals have featured local favorite Tarrus Riley, as well as international performers, like LL Cool J and Mary J. Blige.

DID YOU KNOW?

The first appearance of the word *reggae* is widely attributed to the 1968 single by the Maytals called "Do the Reggay."

Burning Spear

Jimmy Cliff

The Congos

At **Reggae Yard & Island Life** (☎ *876/675–8795*) in Ocho Rios you'll find an extensive selection of reggae CDs as well as other types of Caribbean music.

Bob Marley Museum in Kingston. If the Zion Bus Tour only whets your appetite for Marley, visit the Bob Marley Museum for a glimpse at another chapter of his life. Housed inside the former headquarters of Marley's label, Tuff Gong Records, it is also the site of the failed attempt on Marley's life that inspired his song, "Ambush."

And, of course, your Jamaican reggae experience would not be complete without catching some live bands. Local acts play at **Bourbon Beach** (☎ *876/957–4405*) in Negril on Monday, Thursday, and Saturday nights. Also in Negril is **Rick's Cafe** (☎ *876/957–0380*), which features an in-house reggae band nightly.

7

IN FOCUS REGGAE

REGGAE LINGO

Dancehall. A modern style that introduces elements of electronic dance music and improvised singing or rapping by DJs to raw reggae tracks.

Dub. A form of reggae characterized by the use of remixes of previously recorded material.

One-drop rhythm. The definitive beat of reggae characterized by a steady "drop" of the bass drum on the strong beat in each measure.

Ragamuffin (ragga). Similar to dancehall, ragga combines electronic dance music, hip-hop, and R&B with reggae for a more contemporary, club feel.

Riddim. The rhythmic foundation for nearly all reggae styles, characterized by a repetitive, driving drum and bass feel.

Rocksteady. A style of reggae that followed ska, rocksteady is marked by a slower tempo.

Ska. Precursor to reggae that combines traditional Caribbean rhythms, jazz, and calypso.

RECOMMENDED LISTENING

Bob Marley
Uprising, Legend, Exodus, Burnin', Catch a Fire

Peter Tosh
Legalize It

Toots and the Maytals
Funky Kingston

Jimmy Cliff
The Harder They Come

Burning Spear
Marcus Garvey

Alton Ellis
Alton Ellis Sings Rock and Soul

The Congos
The Heart of the Congos

PUERTO RICO

With 365 different beaches in Puerto Rico, choosing where to spread out your towel might seem like a daunting task. The decision is easier now that four have been designated with a Blue Flag.

(this page above) Playa Luquillo; (opposite page bottom) Playa Luquillo; (opposite page top) Playa Flamenco

Playa Flamenco, on the island of Culebra, made the cut. After all, it's rated one of the world's best beaches. More surprisingly, two of the beaches are in San Juan: Balneario Escambrón, in Puerta de Tierra, and Balneario Carolina, in Isla Verde. The fourth is Luquillo's Balneario Monserrate (Playa Luquillo). This means that three of Puerto Rico's finest beaches are within an hour's drive of the capital. The government maintains 13 *balnearios* (public beaches), including two in the San Juan metro area. They're gated and equipped with dressing rooms, lifeguards, parking, and, in some cases, picnic tables, playgrounds, and camping facilities.

BLUE FLAG

Chosen by the Foundation for Environmental Education, a nonprofit agency, Blue Flag beaches have to meet 27 criteria, focusing on water quality, the presence of a trained staff, and the availability of facilities such as water fountains and restrooms.

SAN JUAN

The city's beaches can get crowded, especially on weekends. There's free access to all of them, but parking can be an issue in the peak sun hours—arriving early or in the late afternoon is a safer bet.

Balneario de Carolina. When people talk of a "beautiful Isla Verde beach," this is the one they're talking about. A government-maintained beach, this *balneario* east of Isla Verde is so close to the airport that the leaves rustle when planes take off. The long stretch of sand, which runs parallel to Avenida Los Gobernadores, is shaded by palms and almond trees. There's plenty of room to spread out and lots of amenities: lifeguards, restrooms, changing facilities, picnic tables, and barbecue grills. ⊠ *Carolina* ⌸ *Parking $3* ⊙ *Daily 8–5.*

Balneario de Escambrón. In Puerta de Tierra, this government-run beach is just off Avenida Muñoz Rivera. The patch of honey-colored sand is shaded by coconut palms and has surf that's generally gentle. Favored by families, it has lifeguards, bathhouses, bathrooms, and restaurants. ⊠ *Puerta de Tierra* ⌸ *Parking $4.28* ⊙ *Daily 6–7.*

EASTERN PUERTO RICO

A long stretch of powdery sand near the Reserva Natural Las Cabezas de San Juan, **Balneario Seven Seas** may turn out to be the best surprise of your trip.

Facilities include picnic tables, changing areas, restrooms, and showers. Many restaurants are just outside the gates. Its calm, clear waters are perfect for swimming. ⊠ *Rte. 987, Las Croabas.*

Fodor's Choice ★ Just off Route 3, gentle **Playa Luquillo** (or Balneario La Monserrate) is a magnet for families. It's well equipped with restrooms, showers, lifeguards, guarded parking, food stands, picnic areas, and even cocktail kiosks. Lounge chairs and umbrellas are available to rent. Its most distinctive facility is the Mar Sin Barreras (Sea Without Barriers), a low-sloped ramp leading into the water that allows wheelchair users to take a dip. The beach is open daily. Admission is $2 per car, $3 for minivans. ⊠ *Off Rte. 3.*

VIEQUES AND CULEBRA

Playa Caracas. Located on former U.S. Navy land on the eastern end of Vieques, this tiny yet beautiful beach is reached via a well-maintained dirt road. The water is crystal clear, and its location in Bahía Corcho means that it is sheltered from waves. ⊠ *Off Rte. 997, east of Playa Media Luna.*

Fodor's Choice ★ **Playa Flamenco.** Consistently ranked one of the most beautiful in the world. Snow-white sands, turquoise waters, and lush hills that rise on all sides, make it feel miles away from civilization. During the week it's pleasantly uncrowded; on weekends it

7

(this page above) Surfing near Rincón; (opposite page) Isla Verde Beach, San Juan

fills up fast with day-trippers from the mainland. It's the only beach on Culebra with amenities such as camping, restrooms, showers, and kiosks selling simple fare. ⊠ *Rte. 251, west of the airport.* ☏ *787/742–0700* ☺ *Daily dawn–dusk.*

Playa Sun Bay. The 1-mi-long (1½-km-long) white sands skirt a crescent-shaped bay. You'll find food kiosks, picnic tables, and changing facilities. It gets packed on holidays and weekends. On weekdays, when the crowds are thin, you might see wild horses grazing among the palm trees. Parking is $3, but often no one is at the gate to take your money. ⊠ *Rte. 997, east of Esperanza.* ☏ *787/741–8198.*

SOUTHERN PUERTO RICO
Caja de Muertos *(Coffin Island).* This island a few miles off the coast has the best beaches in the Ponce area and is, perhaps, the second-best spot in southern Puerto Rico for snorkeling, after **La Parguera**. Ask one of the many boatmen at La Guancha to take you out for about $30 round-trip. ⊠ *Boats leave from La Guancha, at the end of Rte. 14, Ponce.*

WESTERN PUERTO RICO
Balneario de Rincón. Swimmers can enjoy the tranquil waters at this beach. The beautiful facility has a playground, changing areas, restrooms, and a clubhouse. It's within walking distance of the center of town. Parking is $2. ⊠ *Rte. 115.*

Playa Crashboat. Here you'll find the colorful fishing boats that are portrayed on postcards all over the island. The sand is soft and sugary, and the water's smooth as glass. Named after rescue boats used when Ramey Air Force Base was in operation, there are picnic huts, showers, parking, and restrooms. There's a food stand run by locals where the catch of the day is served with cold beer. ⊠ *End of Rte. 458, off Rte. 107.*

TURKS AND CAICOS ISLANDS

If you're on a quest for the world's best beaches, then Turks and Caicos is your destination. They are blessed with stunning strands and shallow waters protected by outer reefs, a combination that makes for the most amazing turquoise water.

(this page above) Beach palapas on Grace Bay, Providenciales; (opposite page bottom) Half Moon Bay at Donna Cay, off Providenciales; (opposite page top) Sapodilla Bay, Providenciales

Grace Bay Beach in Providenciales has the best of the best, and most of the island's resorts clustered here. On the rare occasions that storms bring seaweed, it is quickly raked and buried. The water is protected by an outer reef, so it's often as still as glass. There is never an undertow or litter, and there are no beach vendors, so the opportunities for relaxation are optimal. Grand Turk is spoiled for choices when it comes to beach options: sunset strolls along miles of deserted beaches, picnics in secluded coves, beachcombing on the coralline sands, snorkeling around shallow coral heads close to shore, and admiring the impossibly turquoise-blue waters. There are also great beaches on several other less-visited islands.

BEACH LOGISTICS

Although there is no charge for parking at any beach, come prepared. Umbrellas are provided by resorts for guests only, and resorts generally don't share with nonguests, even for a price. Grace Bay has the busiest sections of beachfront, especially at Beaches Resort and Club Med, but there are still plenty of secluded areas if you wish to explore beyond your own resort.

All the beaches of Turks and Caicos have bright white sand that's soft like baby powder. An added bonus is that no matter how hot the sun gets, your feet never burn. The sand is soft and clean, even in the water, so there is no fear of stepping on rocks or corals. Even the beach areas with corals for snorkeling have clear, clean sand for entry until you reach them.

THE CAICOS

PROVIDENCIALES

Grace Bay. The 12-mi (18-km) sweeping stretch of ivory-white, powder-soft sand on Provo's north coast is simply breathtaking, and home to migrating starfish as well as shallow snorkeling trails. The majority of Provo's beachfront resorts are along this shore. ✉ *Grace Bay Rd., on the north shore, Grace Bay.*

Half Moon Bay. A natural ribbon of sand linking two uninhabited cays is only inches above the sparkling turquoise waters and one of the most gorgeous beaches on the island. There are limestone cliffs to explore as well as small, private sand coves; there's even a small wreck offshore for snorkeling. It's only a short boat ride away from Provo, and most of the island's tour companies run excursions here or simply offer a beach drop-off. These companies include Silverdeep and Caicos Dream Tours. ✉ *15 mins from Leeward Marina, between*

Pine Cay and Water Cay, accessible only by boat,

Fodor'sChoice ★ Malcolm's Beach. It's one of the most stunning beaches you'll ever see, but you'll need a high-clearance vehicle to reach it. Bring your own food and drinks, because it doesn't have any facilities or food service unless you have made a reservation with Amanyara to eat at the resort. ✉ *Malcolm's Beach Rd.; keep straight after passing the Amanyara turnoff.*

Sapodilla Bay. The best of the many secluded beaches and pristine sands around Provo can be found at peaceful quarter-mile cove protected by Sapodilla Hill, with its soft strand lapped by calm waves, where yachts and small boats move with the gentle tide. ✉ *North of South Dock, at end of South Dock Rd., Sapodilla Bay.*

NORTH CAICOS

The beaches of North Caicos are superb for shallow snorkeling and sunset strolls, and the waters offshore have excellent scuba diving. **Horse Stable Beach** is the main beach for annual events and beach parties. **Whitby Beach** usually has a gentle tide, and its thin strip of sand is bordered by palmetto plants and taller trees.

SOUTH CAICOS

The beaches at **Belle Sound** on South Caicos will take your breath away, with lagoonlike waters. Expect the beach to

7

(this page above) Pillory Beach, Grand Turk (opposite page) Grace Bay, Providenciales

be natural and rustic—after storms you will see some seaweed. Due south of South Caicos is **Little Ambergris Cay**, an uninhabited cay about 14 mi (23 km) beyond the Fish Cays, with excellent bonefishing on the second-largest sandbar in the world. On the opposite side of the ridge from Belle Sound, **Long Bay** is an endless stretch of beach, but it can be susceptible to rough surf; however, on calmer days, you'll feel like you're on a deserted island.

THE TURKS

GRAND TURK

Governor's Beach. A beautiful crescent of powder-soft sand and shallow, calm turquoise waters front the official British governor's residence, called Waterloo, framed by tall casuarina trees that provide plenty of natural shade. To have it all to yourself, go on a day when cruise ships are not in port. On days when ships are in port, the beach is lined with lounge chairs.

Little Bluff Point Beach. Just west of the Grand Turk Lighthouse is a low, limestone-cliff-edged, shell-covered beach that offers more of a beachcombing experience and looks out onto shallow waters, mangroves, and often flamingos, especially in spring and summer.

Pillory Beach. With sparkling neon turquoise water, this is the prettiest beach on Grand Turk; it also has great off-the-beach snorkeling.

SALT CAY

North Beach. The north coast of Salt Cay has superb beaches, with tiny, pretty shells and weathered sea glass, but North Beach is the reason to visit Salt Cay; it might be the finest beach in Turks and Caicos, if not the world. Part of the beauty lies not just in the soft, powdery sand and bright blue water but in its isolation; it's very likely that you will have this lovely beach all to yourself.

Big Sand Cay. Accessible by boat with the on-island tour operators, Big Sand Cay, 7 mi (11 km) south of Salt Cay, is tiny and totally uninhabited; it's also known for its long, unspoiled stretches of open sand.

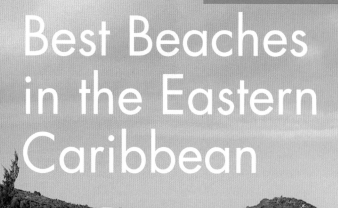

Best Beaches in the Eastern Caribbean

WHAT'S WHERE

Eastern Caribbean. Larger in number but smaller in size than the Greater Antilles, they make up the bulk of the Caribbean arc. Beginning with the Virgin Islands but going all the way to Grenada, the islands of the Eastern Caribbean form a barrier between the Atlantic Ocean and the Caribbean Sea. The best beaches are usually on the Caribbean side.

1 US Virgin Islands. A perfect combination of the familiar and the exotic, the U.S. Virgin Islands are a little bit of America set in an azure sea. Go to St. Croix if you like history and interesting restaurants. Go to St. John if you crave a back-to-nature experience. Go to St. Thomas if you want a shop-till-you-drop experience and a big selection of resorts, activities, and nightlife.

2 British Virgin Islands. The lure of the British Virgins is exclusivity and personal attention, not lavish luxury. Even the most expensive resorts are selling a state of mind

rather than state-of-the-art. So go with an open mind, and your stress may very well melt away. Don't go if you expect glitz or stateside efficiency. These islands are about getting away, not getting it all.

3 Anguilla. With miles of brilliant beaches and a range of luxurious resorts (even a few that mere mortals can afford), Anguilla is where the rich, powerful, and famous go to chill out. Go for the fine cuisine in elegant surroundings, great snorkeling, and funky late-night music scene. Don't go for shopping and sightseeing. This island is all about relaxing and reviving.

4 St Maarten/St Martin. Two nations (Dutch and French), many nationalities, one small island, a lot of development. But there are also more white, sandy beaches than days in a month. Go for the awesome restaurants, excellent shopping, and wide range of

activities. Don't go if you're not willing to get out and search for the really good stuff.

5 St Barthélemy. If you come to St. Barth for a taste of European village life, not for a conventional full-service resort experience, you will be richly rewarded. Go for excellent dining and wine, great boutiques with the latest hip fashions, and an active, on-the-go vacation. Don't go for big resorts, and make sure your credit card is platinum-plated.

6 St Kitts and Nevis. Things are unhurried on lush, hilly St. Kitts and Nevis. And the locals seem more cordial and courteous—eager to share their paradise with you—than on more touristy Caribbean islands. Go to discover Caribbean history, to stay in a small plantation inn, or just to relax. Don't go for

ANGUILLA
(U.K.)

ST. MAARTE/ ST. MARTIN

3

St. Martin (Fr.)

4

Sint Maarten
(Neth.)

ST. BARTHÉLEMY
(Fr.)

5

Saba (Neth.)

Barbuda

Sint Eustatius
(Neth.)

St. Kitts

ANTIGUA
& BARBUDA

Basseterre

St. John's

9

6

Nevis

ST. KITTS & NEVIS

Antigua

ATLANTIC OCEAN

nightlife or shopping. These islands are about laid-back "liming" and maybe buying some local crafts.

Plymouth
Montserrat
(U.K.)

GUADELOUPE
(Fr.)

Désirada(Fr.)

8

7 Guadeloupe. An exotic, tropical paradise, Guadeloupe is covered by a lush rain forest and blessed with a rich, creole culture that influences everything from its dances to its food. Go if you want to experience another culture—and still have your creature comforts and access to fine beaches. Don't go if you want five-star luxury, because it's rare here.

7

Basse-Terre

Marie Galante

style. Don't go if you are looking for a bargain and don't have patience. Getting here is a chore, but there are definitely rewards for the persistent.

Dominica

Roseau

8 Martinique. Excellent cuisine, fine service, highly touted rum, and lilting Franco-Caribbean music are the main draws in Martinique. Go if you're a Francophile drawn to fine food, wine, and sophisticated

9 Antigua and Barbuda. Beaches, bone-white and beckoning—one for every day of the year—can be secluded or hopping with activity. History buffs and nautical nuts will appreciate English Harbour, which sheltered Britain's Caribbean fleet in the 18th and 19th centuries. Go for

Martinique
(Fr.)

8

those beaches but also for sailing. Don't go for local culture, because all-inclusives predominate. Lovely as it is, Antigua is more for tourists than travelers.

ANGUILLA

You can always tell a true beach fanatic: say "Anguilla" and watch for signs of ecstasy. They say there are 33 beaches on the island's 34 square miles; we say, "Who's counting? Pack the sunscreen!"

(this page above) Shoal Bay; (opposite page bottom) Cove Bay; (opposite page top) Shoal Bay

Renowned for their beauty, Anguilla's 30-plus beaches are among the best in the Caribbean. You can find long, deserted stretches suitable for sunset walks, or beaches lined with lively bars and restaurants—all surrounded by crystal clear warm waters in several shades of turquoise. The sea is calmest at 2½-mile-long Rendevous Bay, where gentle breezes tempt sailors. But Shoal Bay (East) is the quintessential Caribbean beach. The white sand is so soft and abundant that it pools around your ankles. Cove Bay and Maundays Bay, both on the southeast coast, must also rank among the island's best beaches. Maundays is the location of the island's top resort, Cap Juluca, while smaller Cove Bay is just a walk away. Unlike on the French islands, topless sunbathing is not permitted.

DAZZLING WHITE

The dazzling white sand of Anguilla's famous beaches, as fine and soft as confectioners' sugar, is a result of calcareous marine algae called Halimeda, which thrive in the rich offshore sea-grass beds and reefs. Its coral-like skeleton is broken down by wave action and swept ashore by swift currents where it mixes with the eroded tertiary limestone of Anguilla's surface.

NORTHEAST COAST

Captain's Bay. On the north coast just before the eastern tip of the island, this quarter-mile stretch of perfect white sand is bounded on the left by a rocky shoreline where Atlantic waves crash. If you make the tough, four-wheel-drive-only trip along the dirt road that leads to the northeastern end of the island toward Junk's Hole, you'll be rewarded with peaceful isolation. The surf here slaps the sands with a vengeance, and the undertow is strong—so wading is the safest water sport.

Island Harbour. These mostly calm waters are surrounded by a slender beach. For centuries Anguillians have ventured from these sands in colorful handmade fishing boats. It's not much of a beach for swimming or lounging, but there a several restaurants (Hibernia, Arawak Café, Côtée Mer, and Smitty's), and this is the departure point for the three-minute boat ride to Scilly Cay, where a thatched beach bar serves seafood. Just hail the restaurant's free boat and plan to spend most of the day (the all-inclusive lunch starts at $40 and is worth the price—Wednesday, Friday, and Sunday only).

NORTHWEST COAST

Sandy Island. A popular day trip for Anguilla visitors, tiny Sandy Island shelters a pretty lagoon, nestled in coral reefs about 2 mi (3 km) from Road Bay.

Most of the operators in Sandy Ground can bring you here.

Fodor's Choice ★ **Shoal Bay.** Anchored by sea grape and coconut trees, the 2-mi powdered-sugar strand at Shoal Bay (not to be confused with Shoal Bay West at the other end of the island) is universally considered one of the world's prettiest beaches. You can park free at any of the restaurants, including Elodia's, Uncle Ernie's, or Gwen's Reggage Grill, most of which either rent or provide chairs and umbrellas for patrons for about $20 a day per person. There is plenty of room to stretch out in relative privacy, or you can bar-hop, take a ride on Junior's Glass Bottom Boat, or arrange a wreck dive at PADI-certified Shoal Bay Scuba near Kú, where ZaZaa, the island's chic-est boutique will satisfy fans of St. Barth shopping. The relatively broad beach has shallow water that is usually gentle, making this a great family beach; a coral reef not far from the shore is a wonderful snorkeling spot. Sunsets over the water are spectacular. You can even enjoy a beachside massage at Malakh, a little spa near Madeariman's.

SOUTHWEST COAST

Fodor's Choice ★ **Cove Bay.** Follow the signs to Smokey's at the end of Cove Road, and you will find water that is brilliantly blue and sand that is as soft as sifted flour. It's just as spectacular as its

(this page above) Maundays Bay (opposite page) Meads Bay

neighbors **Rendezvous Bay** and **Maundays Bay**. You can walk here from Cap Juluca for a change of pace, or you can arrange a horseback ride along the beach. Weekend barbecues with terrific local bands at Smokey's are an Anguillian must.

Fodor'sChoice ★ Maundays Bay. The dazzling, mile-long platinum-white beach is especially great for swimming and long beach walks. It's no wonder that Cap Juluca, one of Anguilla's premier resorts, chose this as its location. Public parking is straight ahead at the end of the road near Cap Juluca's Pimms restaurant. You can have lunch or dinner at Cap Juluca (just be prepared for the cost), and if you dine, you can also rent chaises and umbrellas from the resort for the day. Depending on the season you can book a massage in one of the beachside tents.

Rendezvous Bay. Follow the signs to Anguilla Great House for public parking at this broad swath of pearl-white sand that is some 1½ mi (2½ km) long. The beach is lapped by calm, bluer-than-blue water and a postcard-worthy view of St. Martin. The expansive crescent is home to three resorts; stop in for a drink or a meal at one of the hotels, or rent a chair and umbrella at one of the kiosks. Don't miss the daylong party at the tree-house Dune Preserve, where Bankie Banx, Anguilla's most famous musician, presides and where Dale Carty (of Tasty's fame) cooks delicious barbecue and fixes great salads.

Shoal Bay West. This glittering bay bordered by mangroves and sea grapes is a lovely place to spend the day. The mile-long beach is home to the dazzling Covecastles and Altamer villas. The tranquillity is sublime, with coral reefs for snorkeling not too far from shore. Punctuate your day with a meal at beachside Trattoria Tramonto. Reach the beach by taking the main road to the West End and bearing left at the fork, then continuing to the end. Note that similarly named **Shoal Bay** is a separate beach on a different part of the island.

ANTIGUA AND BARBUDA

Antigua and Barbuda proudly offer 365 beaches, one for every day of the year. And you could probably spend a year beach-hopping its beautiful shores—some lined with bars and sports concessions and some virtually deserted.

(this page above) Half Moon Bay; (opposite page bottom) Darkwood Beach; (opposite page top) Jet skiing in Dickenson Bay

Antigua's beaches are public, and many are lined with resorts that have water-sports outfitters and beach bars. The government does a fairly good job of cleaning up seaweed and garbage. Most restaurant and bars on beaches won't charge for beach-chair rentals if you buy lunch or drinks; otherwise the going rate is $3 to $5. Access to some of the finest stretches, such as those at the Five Islands Peninsula resorts, is somewhat restricted by security gates. Sunbathing topless is strictly illegal except on one small beach at Hawksbill by Rex Resorts. When cruise ships dock in St. John's, buses drop off loads of passengers on most of the west-coast beaches. Choose such a time to visit one of the more-remote east-end beaches, or take a day trip to Barbuda.

EASY, BREEZY

Most Antiguan beaches feature talcum-powdery sand right out of a brochure. Those on the windward side, such as Dutchman's Bay in the north, and Nonsuch, Long, and Half Moon Bays to the east, receive brisk breezes, making them favorites of windsurfers and boarders. Blissfully undeveloped Barbuda seems like one big beach; indeed sand exceeds lobster as its primary export.

ANTIGUA

Darkwood Beach. This ½-mi (1-km) beige ribbon on the southwest coast has stunning views of Montserrat. Although popular with locals on weekends, it's virtually deserted during the week. Waters are generally calm, but there's scant shade, no development other than a basic beach bar, and little to do other than bask in solitude. ⊠ *2 mi (3 km) south of Jolly Harbour and roughly ½ mi (1 km) southwest of Valley Church off main coast road.*

Dickenson Bay. Along a lengthy stretch of powder-soft white sand and exceptionally calm water you can find small and large hotels, water sports, concessions, and beachfront restaurants. There's decent snorkeling at either point. ⊠ *2 mi (3 km) northeast of St. John's, along main coast road.*

Half Moon Bay. This ½-mi (1-km) ivory crescent is a prime snorkeling and windsurfing area. On the Atlantic side, the water can be rough at times, attracting intrepid hard-core surfers and wakeboarders. The northeastern end, where a protective reef offers spectacular snorkeling, is much calmer. A tiny bar has restrooms, snacks, and beach chairs. Half Moon is a real trek, but one of Antigua's showcase beaches. ⊠ *On southeast coast, 1½ mi (2½ km) from Freetown.*

Johnson's Point/Crabbe Hill. This series of connected, deserted beaches on the southwest coast looks out toward Montserrat, Guadeloupe, and St. Kitts. Notable beach bar–restaurants include OJ's, Gibson's, and Turner's. The water is generally placid, though not good for snorkeling. ⊠ *3 mi (5 km) south of Jolly Harbour complex on main west-coast road.*

Pigeon Point. Near Falmouth Harbour lie two fine white-sand beaches. The leeward side is calmer, the windward side is rockier, and there are sensational views and snorkeling around the point. Several restaurants and bars are nearby, though Bumpkin's satisfies most on-site needs. ⊠ *Off main south-coast road, southwest of Falmouth.*

BARBUDA

Fodor's Choice ★ **Pink Beach.** You can sometimes walk miles of this classic strand without encountering another footprint. It has a champagne hue, with sand soft as silk; crushed coral often imparts a rosy glint in the sun, hence its (unofficial) name. The water can be rough with a strong-ish undertow in spots, though it's mainly protected by the reefs that make the island a diving mecca. Hire a taxi to take you here, since none of the roads are well marked. ⊠ *1 mi (2 km) from ferry and airstrip along unmarked roads.*

BRITISH VIRGIN ISLANDS

With a couple of exceptions, restful and relaxing best describe most beaches across the British Virgin Islands. If peace and quiet are your goals, avoid popular beaches such as Cane Garden Bay on Tortola and the Baths on Virgin Gorda on days when cruise ships are in port.

(this page above) White Bay, Jost Van Dyke; (opposite page bottom) Beef Island, Tortola; (opposite page top) Spring Bay Beach, Virgin Gorda

The best BVI beaches are on deserted islands reachable only by boats, so take a snorkeling or sailing trip at least once. Tortola's north side has several perfect palm-fringed, white-sand beaches that curl around turquoise bays and coves, but none really achieves greatness. Nearly all are accessible by car (preferably a four-wheel-drive vehicle), albeit down bumpy roads that corkscrew precipitously. Some of these beaches are lined with bars and restaurants as well as water-sports equipment stalls; others have absolutely nothing.

Anybody going to Virgin Gorda must experience swimming or snorkeling among its unique boulder formations, which can be visited at several sites along Lee Road. The most popular is the Baths, but there are several other similar places nearby that are easily reached.

THE SAND

Soft, white talcum-powder strands of sand predominate across the British Virgin Islands, but beachgoers will find an occasional patch of yellowish sand here and there. If you have to draw a line in the sand, Virgin Gorda has the best selection of beaches, but you'll find similar beaches out near the airport on Tortola.

TORTOLA

Apple Bay, including nearby Little Apple Bay and Capoon's Bay, is your spot if you want to surf—although the white, sandy beach itself is narrow. If you're swimming and the waves are up, take care not to get dashed on the rocks. **Cane Garden Bay** is a silky stretch of sand with exceptionally calm, crystalline waters—except when storms at sea turn the water murky. Snorkeling is good along the edges. **Long Bay, Beef Island** has superlative scenery: the beach stretches seemingly forever, and you can catch a glimpse of Little Camanoe and Great Camanoe islands. If you walk around the bend to the right, you can see little Marina Cay and Scrub Island. Long Bay is also a good place to search for seashells. Swim out to wherever you see a dark patch for some nice snorkeling. **Long Bay West** is a stunning, mile-long stretch of white sand; have your camera ready to snap the breathtaking approach. The entire beach is open to the public. **Smuggler's Cove**, a beautiful, palm-fringed beach, is down a pothole-filled dirt road. You probably won't be alone on weekends, though, when the beach fills with snorkelers and sunbathers. There's a fine view of Jost Van Dyke from the shore.

VIRGIN GORDA

The Baths is a national park that features a stunning maze of huge granite boulders that extend into the sea. It's usually

crowded midday with day-trippers. The snorkeling is good, and you're likely to see a wide variety of fish, but watch out for dinghies coming ashore from the numerous sailboats anchored offshore. **Nail Bay**, at the island's north tip, will reward you with a trio of beaches within the Nail Bay Resort complex that are ideal for snorkeling. Mountain Trunk Bay is perfect for beginners, and Nail Bay and Long Bay beaches have coral caverns just offshore. **Savannah Bay** is a wonderfully private beach close to Spanish Town. It may not always be completely deserted, but you can find a spot to yourself on this long stretch of soft, white sand. **Spring Bay Beach** is a national-park beach that gets much less traffic than the nearby Baths, and has the similarly large, imposing boulders that create interesting grottoes for swimming. The snorkeling is excellent, and the grounds include swings and picnic tables.

JOST VAN DYKE

Sandy Cay is a gleaming scimitar of white sand, with marvelous snorkeling. **White Bay** has a long stretch of white sand that is especially popular with boaters who come ashore for a libation at one of the beach bars.

TRY A YACHT CHARTER
IT'S SURPRISINGLY AFFORDABLE

By Carol M. Bareuther

Savoring a freshly brewed mug of coffee, I sat on the front deck of our chartered 43-foot catamaran and watched the morning show. Laserlike rays of sunlight streamed through a cottony cloud bank, bringing life to the emerald islands and turquoise seas. What would it have been like to sail with Columbus and chart these waters for the first time? How would it feel to cast about the deserted beaches for the perfect place to bury plundered treasure? The aroma of freshly made banana pancakes roused me from my reverie.

Once considered an outward-bound adventure or exclusive domain of the rich and famous, chartering a boat can be a surprisingly affordable and attractive vacation alternative. Perhaps you're already a sailor and want to explore beyond your own lake, river, or bay. Or maybe your idea of sailing has always been on a cruise ship, and now you're ready for a more intimate voyage. Or perhaps you've never sailed before, but you are now curious to cast off and explore a whole new world.

(opposite and top) Sailboating in the British Virgin Islands.

CREWED CHARTER

On a crewed charter, you sit back and relax while the crew provides for your every want and need. Captains are licensed by the U.S. Coast Guard or the equivalent in the British maritime system. Cooks—preferring to be called chefs—have skills that go far beyond peanut butter and jelly sandwiches. There are four meals a day, and many chefs boast certificates from culinary schools ranging from the Culinary Institute of America in New York to the Cordon Bleu in Paris.

The advantage of a crewed yacht charter, with captain and cook, is that it takes every bit of stress out of the vacation. With a captain who knows the local waters, you get to see some of the coves and anchorages that are not necessarily in the guidebooks. Your meals are prepared, cabins cleaned, beds made up every day—and turned down at night, too. Plus, you can sail and take the helm as often as you like. But at the end of the day, the captain is the one who will take responsibility for anchoring safely for the night while the chef goes below and whips up a gourmet meal.

COSTS	PROS	CONS
$3,850–$6,200 for 2 people for 5 days	■ Passengers just have to lay back and relax with no work (unless they want to help sail)	■ More expensive than a bareboat, especially if you get a catamaran
$4,900–$7,900 for 2 people for 7 days		■ Less privacy for your group than on a bareboat
$7,000–$12,500 for 6 people for 5 days	■ Most crewed charter yachts are catamarans, offering more space than monohulls	■ Captain makes ultimate decisions about the course
$9,000–$16,000 for 6 people for 7 days		■ Chance for personality conflicts: you have to get along with the captain and chef
Prices are all-inclusive for a 50- to 55-foot yacht in high season except for 10%–15% gratuity.	■ You have an experienced, local hand on board if something goes wrong	
	■ Water toys and other extras are often included	

(top) Family sailing in the British Virgin Islands

BAREBOAT

If you'd like to bareboat, don't be intimidated. It's a myth that you must be a graduate of a sailing school in order to pilot your own charter boat. A bareboat company will ask you to fill out a resume. The company checks for prior boat-handling experience, the type of craft you've sailed (whether powerboat or sailboat), and in what type of waters. Real-life experience, meaning all those day and weekend trips close to home, count as valuable know-how. If you've done a bit of boating, you may be more qualified than you think to take out a bareboat.

Costs can be very similar for a bareboat and crewed charter, depending on the time of year and size of the boat. You'll pay the highest rates between Christmas and New Year's, when you may not be allowed to do a charter of less than a week. But there are more than 800 bareboats between the USVI and BVI, so regardless of your budget, you should be able to find something in your price range. Plus, you might save a bit by chartering an older boat from a smaller company instead of the most state-of-the-art yacht from a larger company.

COSTS	PROS	CONS
$2,600–$4,400 for a small monohull (2–3 cabins)	■ The ultimate freedom to set the yacht's course	■ Must be able to pass a sailing test
$4,400–$8,000 for a large monohull (4–5 cabins)	■ A chance to test your sailing skills	■ Those unfamiliar with the region may not find the best anchorages
$4,000–$5,000 for a small catamaran (2 cabins)	■ Usually a broader range of boats and prices to choose from	■ You have to cook for and clean up after yourself
$6,000–$12,000 for a large catamaran (4 cabins)	■ More flexibility for meals (you can always go ashore if you don't feel like cooking)	■ You have to do your own provisioning and planning for meals
Prices exclude food, beverages, fuel, and other supplies. Most bareboat rates do not include water toys, taxes, insurance, and permits.	■ You can always hire a captain for a few days	■ If something goes wrong, there isn't an experienced hand onboard

Three women rigging the sails.

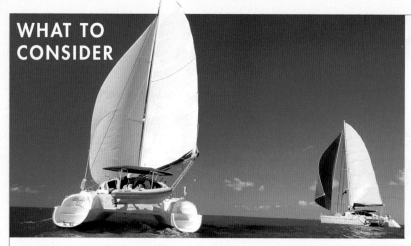

WHAT TO CONSIDER

Whether bareboat or a crewed yacht, there are a few points to ponder when selecting your boat.

HOW BIG IS YOUR GROUP?

As a general rule, count on one cabin for every two people. Most people also prefer to have one head (bathroom) per cabin. A multihull, also called a catamaran, offers more space and more equal-size cabins than a monohull sailboat.

WHAT TYPE OF BOAT?

If you want to do some good old traditional sailing, where you're heeling over with the seas at your rails, monohulls are a good option. On the other hand, multihulls are more stable, easier to board, and have a big salon for families. They're also ideal if some people get seasick or aren't as gung-ho for the more traditional sailing experience. If you'd like to cover more ground, choose a motor yacht.

DO YOU HAVE A SPECIAL INTEREST?

Some crewed charter boats specialize in certain types of charters. Among these are learn-to-sail excursions, honeymoon cruises, scuba-diving adventures, and family-friendly trips. Your broker can steer you to the boats that fit your specific needs.

WHAT KIND OF EQUIPMENT DO YOU WANT ONBOARD?

Most charter boats have satellite navigation systems and autopilots, as well as regulation safety gear, dinghies with motors, and even stereos and entertainment systems. But do you want a generator or battery-drive refrigeration system? How about a/c? Do you want a satellite phone? Do you want water toys like kayaks, boogie boards, and Windsurfers?

Now that you've decided on bareboat versus crewed charter and selected your craft, all you need to do is confirm the availability of the date with the company or broker and pay a nonrefundable deposit equal to 50% of the charter price.

TO SAIL OR NOT TO SAIL?

If you're not sure whether a charter yacht vacation is right for you, consider this: would you enjoy a floating hotel room where the scenery outside your window changed according to your desires? A "yes" may entice wary companions to try chartering. A single one-week trip will have them hooked.

Two catamaran sailboats seen from behind.

CATAMARANS
Multihulls are more stable, easier to board and have a big salon for families. Seasickness is less of an issue.

MOTOR YACHT
Best if you want to cover more ground, but costs a lot more than a sailboat.

MONOHULLS
Good for more traditional and active sailing, but the movement may not appeal to non-sailors.

CHOOSING A CHARTER

Information on charters is much easier to find now than even a decade ago. Websites for bareboat companies show photos of different types of boats—both interiors and exteriors—as well as layout schematics, lists of equipment and amenities, and sample itineraries. Many sites will allow you to book a charter directly, while others give you the option of calling a toll-free number to speak with an agent first.

There are two types of Websites for crewed charters. If you just want some information, the **Virgin Islands Charteryacht League** (⊕*www.vicl.org*) and the **Charter Yacht Society of the British Virgin Islands** (⊕*www.bvicrewedyachts.com*) both help you understand what to look for in a crewed charter, from the size of the boat to the amenities. You can't reserve on these sites, but they link to the sites of brokers, who are the sales force for the charter yacht industry. Most brokers, whether they're based in the Caribbean, the United States, or Europe, attend annual charter yacht shows in St. Thomas, Tortola, and Antigua. At these shows, brokers visit the boats and meet the crews. This is what gives brokers their depth of knowledge for "matchmaking," or linking you with a boat that will meet your personality and preferences.

The charter companies also maintain Websites. About 30% of the crewed charter yachts based out of the U.S. and British Virgin Islands can be booked directly. This saves the commission an owner has to pay to the broker. But while "going direct" might seem advantageous, there is usually little difference in pricing, and if you use a broker, he or she can help troubleshoot if something goes wrong or find a replacement boat if the boat owner has to cancel.

Timing also matters. Companies may offer last-minute specials that are available only online. These special rates—usually for specific dates, destinations, and boats—are updated weekly or even daily.

PREPARING FOR YOUR CHARTER

British Virgin Islands - anchorage in a tropical sea with breakfast on board.

PROVISIONING

Bareboaters must do their own provisioning. It's a good idea to arrange provisioning at least a week in advance.

Bobby's Market Place (✉ *Wickham's Cay I, Road Town, Tortola* ☎*284/494–2189* ⊕*www.bobbysmarketplace.com*) offers packages from $18 to $28 per person per day. **Ample Hamper** (✉*Inner Harbour Marina, Road Town, Tortola* ☎*284/494–2494* ✉*Frenchmans Cay Marina, West End, Tortola* ☎*284/495–4684* ⊕*www.amplehamper.com*) offers more than 1,200 items but no pre-arranged packages.

Provisioning packages from the charter company are usually a bit more expensive, at $25 to $35 per person per day, but they save you the hassle of planning the details. You can also shop on arrival. Both St. Thomas and Tortola have markets, though larger grocery stores may require a taxi ride. If you shop carefully, this route can still save you money. Just be sure to allow yourself a few hours after arrival to get everything done.

PLANNING

For a crewed charter, your broker will send a preference sheet for both food and your wishes for the trip. Perhaps you'd like lazy days of sleeping late, sunning, and swimming. Or you might prefer active days of sailing with stops for snorkeling and exploring ashore. If there's a special spot you'd like to visit, list it so your captain can plan the itinerary accordingly.

PACKING TIPS

Pack light for any type of charter. Bring soft-sided luggage (preferably a duffle bag) since space is limited and storage spots are usually odd shapes. Shorts, T-shirts, and swimsuits are sufficient. Bring something a bit nicer if you plan to dine ashore. Shoes are seldom required except ashore, but you might want beach shoes to protect your feet in the water. Most boats provide snorkel equipment, but always ask. Bring sunscreen, but a type that will not stain cockpit cushions and decks.

WHAT YOU'LL SEE IN THE USBVI

Cruz Bay in St. John

MAIN CHARTER BASES

The U.S. and British Virgin Islands boast more than 100 stepping-stone islands and cays within a 50-nautical-mi radius. This means easy line-of-sight navigation and island-hopping in protected waters, and it's rare that you'll spend more than a few hours moving between islands.

Tortola, in the British Virgin Islands, is the crewed charter and bareboat mecca of the Caribbean. This fact is plainly apparent from the forest of masts rising out from any marina.

The U.S. Virgin Islands fleet is based in **St. Thomas.** Direct flights from the mainland, luxurious accommodations, and duty-free shopping are drawing cards for departures from the U.S. Virgin Islands, whereas the British Virgins are closer to the prime cruising grounds.

POPULAR ANCHORAGES

On a typical weeklong charter you could set sail from Red Hook, St. Thomas, then cross Pillsbury Sound to St. John, which offers popular north-shore anchorages in Honeymoon, Trunk, or Francis bays.

But the best sailing and snorkeling always includes the British Virgin Islands (which require a valid passport or passport card). After clearing customs in West End, Tortola, many yachts hop along a series of smaller islands that run along the south side of the Sir Francis Drake Channel. But some yachts will also visit Guana Island, Great Camanoe, or Marina Cay off Tortola's more isolated east end.

The islands south of Tortola include **Norman Island,** the rumored site of Robert Lewis Stevenson's *Treasure Island.* The next island over is **Peter Island,** famous for it's posh resort and a popular anchorage for yachters. Farther east, off Salt Island, is the wreck of the **RMS *Rhone***—the most magnificent dive site in the eastern Caribbean. Giant boulders form caves and grottos called The Baths at the southern end of **Virgin Gorda.**

A downwind run along Tortola's north shore ends at **Jost Van Dyke,** where that famous guitar-strumming calypsonian Foxy Callwood sings personalized ditties that make for a memorable finale.

GUADELOUPE

Guadeloupe is an archipelago of five paradises surrounded by both the Caribbean and the Atlantic. It's beaches run the spectrum from white to black and everything in between.

(this page above) La Grande Anse, overlooking Les Saintes Islands; (opposite page bottom) Club Med Beach at Plage Caravalle; (opposite page top) La Grande Anse

There are idyllic beaches, long stretches of unspoiled beach shaded by coconut palms, with soft warm sand. Admittedly, hotels beaches are generally narrow, although well maintained. Some hotels allow nonguests who patronize their restaurants to use their beach facilities. The popular public beaches tend to be cluttered with campers-turned-cafés and cars parked in impromptu lots on the sand. Sunday is the big day, but these same (free) beaches are often quiet during the week.

On the southern coast of Grande-Terre, from Ste-Anne to Pointe des Châteaux, you can find stretches of soft white sand and some sparsely visited stretches. The Atlantic waters on the northeast coast are too rough for swimming. Along the western shore of Basse-Terre signposts indicate small beaches. The sand starts turning gray in Malendure; it becomes volcanic black farther south. There's only one official nude beach, Pointe Tarare, but topless bathing is common.

SAND IN A BOTTLE

Guadeloupe's sand profile is literally encapsulated in one of its popular souvenirs—an airtight glass cylinder displaying variegated stratum of sand. *St-François* is the lightest, followed by the blonde of St. Anne. Next down is the golden sands of Gosier and Moule. Malendure presents dark-gray, volcanic sand that farther along the coast is black. North of Basse-Terre, Deshaies has both black and nearly white sand.

GRANDE-TERRE

L'Autre Bord. The waves on this Atlantic beach give the long expanse of sand a wild look. The beach, which is protected by an extensive coral reef, is a magnet for surfers and windsurfers. You can stroll on the seaside promenade fringed by flamboyant trees. ⊠ *Le Moule.*

Plage Caravelle. Just southwest of Ste-Anne is one of Grande-Terre's longest and prettiest stretches of sand, the occasional dilapidated shack notwithstanding. Protected by reefs, it's also a fine snorkeling spot. Club Med occupies one end of this beach, and nonguests can enjoy its beach and water sports, as well as lunch and drinks, by buying a day pass. You can also have lunch at La Toubana, then descend the stairs to the beach and their beach restaurant. ⊠ *Rte. N4, southwest of Ste-Anne.*

Plage de la Chapelle à Anse-Bertrand. If you want a delightful day trip to the northern tip of Grande-Terre, aim for this spot, one of the loveliest white-sand beaches, whose gentle midafternoon waves are popular with families. When the tide rolls in, it's equally popular with surfers. Several little terrace restaurants at the far end of the beach sate your appetite, but you might want to bring your own shade, because none rent chaise longues. ⊠ *4 mi (6.5 km) south of La Pointe de la Grand Vigie.*

Pointe Tarare. This secluded strip just before the tip of Pointe des Châteaux is the island's only nude beach. Small bar–cafés are in the parking area, but it's still best to bring some water, snacks, and beach chairs, as there's no place to rent them. What you do have is one of the coast's most dramatic landscapes; looming above are rugged cliffs topped by a huge crucifix. When approaching St-François Marina, go in the direction of Pointe des Châteaux at the roundabout and drive for about 10 minutes. ⊠ *Rte. N4, southeast of St-François.*

BASSE-TERRE

La Grande-Anse. One of Guadeloupe's widest beaches has soft beige sand sheltered by palms. To the west it's a round verdant mountain. It has a large parking area and some food stands, but no other facilities. The beach can be overrun on Sunday, not to mention littered. Right after the parking lot, you can see signage for the creole restaurant Le Karacoli; if you have lunch there (it's not inexpensive), you can *sieste* on the chaise longues. ⊠ *Rte. N6, north of Deshaies.*

Malendure. Across from Pigeon Island and the Jacques Cousteau Underwater Park, this long, gray volcanic beach on the Caribbean's calm waters has restrooms, a few beach shacks offering cold drinks and snacks, and a huge parking lot. There might be some litter, but the beach is cleaned regularly. Don't

8

(this page above) Les Pompierres, Iles des Saintes (opposite page) La Soufrière volcano, Basse-Terre

come here for solitude, as the beach is a launch point for many boats. The snorkeling here is good. Le Rocher de Malendure, a fine seafood restaurant, is perched on a cliff over the bay. ✉ *Rte. N6, Bouillante.*

ILES DES SAINTES

Les Pompierres. This beach is particularly popular with families with small children, as there's a gradual slope, no drop-off, and a long stretch of shallow water. To get here, go to the seamen's church near the main plaza, and then head in the direction of Marigot. Continue until you see Le Salako Snack Bar and some scurrying chickens, and—voilà!—you'll spot a palm-fringed stretch of tawny sand. The morning sun is the best. ✉ *Terre-de-Haut.*

LA DÉSIRADE

Le Soufleur Plage. To reach one of La Désirade's longest and best beaches from the ferry dock, face town and follow the main road to the right. It's about 15 minutes by car or motor scooter (about €20 a day). White sand, calm waters, and snacks and cold drinks from the beach restaurant await, but there are no

chaises, so BYO beach towel. ✉ *Dpmt. Rd. 207, Le Soufleur.*

MARIE-GALANTE

Anse de Vieux Fort. This gorgeous Marie-Galante beach stretches alongside crystal clear waters that border a large body of freshwater that is ideal for canoeing. It's a surprising contrast from the nearby mangrove swamp you can discover on the hiking trails. The beaches in this area are wide because of the erosion of the sand dunes. It's known as a beach for lovers because of the solitude. Bring your own everything, because this is virgin territory. ✉ *Rte. D205, just past Pointe Fleur d'Épée, Vieux Fort.*

Petite-Anse. This long, golden beach on Marie-Galante is punctuated with sea grape trees. It's idyllic during the week, but on weekends the crowds of locals and urban refugees from the main island arrive. Le Touloulou's great creole seafood restaurant provides the only facilities. The golden sands are ideal for shelling. ✉ *6.5 mi (10 km) north of Grand-Bourg via rte. D203, Petite-Anse.*

MARTINIQUE

Take to the beach in Martinique. A Caribbean vacation can be a rough ride on Atlantic surf or a swim in calm Caribbean waters as tranquil as a blue lagoon. Experience the white sandbars known as Josephine's Baths, where Napoleon's Josephine would bathe.

(this page above) Anse Corps de Garde; (opposite page bottom) Les Salines; (opposite page top) Diamant Beach

All of Martinique's beaches are open to the public, but hotels charge a fee for nonguests to use changing rooms and other facilities. There are no official nudist beaches, but topless bathing is prevalent, as is the case on most French islands. Unless you're an expert swimmer, steer clear of the Atlantic waters, except in the area of Cap Chevalier (Cape Knight) and the Presqu'île du Caravelle (Caravelle Peninsula). The white-sand beaches are south of Fort-de-France; to the north, the beaches are silvery black volcanic sand. Some of the most pleasant strips of sand are around Ste-Anne, Ste-Luce, and Havre du Robert. And one wonders how, some 15 minutes from Le François harbor, the white sandbars that form Josephine's Baths were created in the middle of the sea.

SHIFTY SANDS

Martinique's sand often belies its environment. The long tawny stretches of beach in Carbet and the neighboring town of St-Pierre, where the infamous volcano Mont Pelée is located, are not volcanic black sand. The famous black-sand beach of Diamant is nowhere near Mont Pelée. It is, however, across from Diamond Rock, a volcanic outcropping.

Anse Corps de Garde. On the southern Caribbean coast, this is one of the island's best long stretches of white sand. The public beach has picnic tables, restrooms, sea grape trees, and crowds, particularly on weekends, when you can find plenty of wandering food vendors. The water is calm, with just enough wave action to remind you it's the sea. From Fort-de-France, exit to the right before you get to the town of Ste-Luce. You first see signs for the Karibea Hotels and then one for Corps de Garde, which is on the right. At the stop sign take a left. ⊠ *Ste-Luce*.

Anse-Mitan. This is not the French Riviera, though there are often yachts moored offshore. This long stretch of beach can be particularly fun on Sunday. Small, family-owned seaside restaurants are half hidden among palm trees and are footsteps from the lapping waves. Nearly all offer grilled lobster and some form of music, perhaps a zouk band. Inexpensive waterfront hotels line the clean, golden beach, which has excellent snorkeling just offshore. Chaise longues are available for rent from hotels for about €6. When you get to Pointe du Bout, take a left at the yellow office of Budget Rent-A-Car, then the next left up a hill, and park near the little white church. ⊠ *Pointe du Bout, Les Trois-Ilets*.

Anse Tartane. This patch of sand is on the wild side of the Presqu'île du Caravelle. It's what the French call a *sauvage* (virgin) beach, and the only people you are likely to see are brave surfers who ride the high waves or some local families. The surf school here has taught many kids the ropes. Résidence Oceane looks down on all of this action but doesn't have a restaurant. Turn right before you get to La Trinité, and follow the route de Château past the Caravelle hotel. Instead of following the signs to Résidence Oceane, veer left and go downhill when you see the ocean. The road runs right beside the beach. There are several bays and *pointes* here, but if you keep heading to the right, you can reach the surf school. ⊠ *Tartane*.

Diamant Beach. The island's longest beach has a splendid view of Diamond Rock, but the waters are rough, with lots of wave action. Often the beach is deserted, especially midweek, which is more reason to swim with prudence. Happily, it's a great place for picnicking and beachcombing; there are shade trees aplenty, and parking is abundant and free. The hospitable, family-run Diamant les Bains hotel is a good lunch spot; if you eat lunch there, the management may let you wash off in the pool overlooking the beach. From Les Trois-Ilets, go in the direction of Rivière Salée, taking the secondary road to the east,

(this page above and opposite page) Les Salines

toward Le Diamant. A coastal route, it leads to the beach. ✉ *Le Diamant.*

Les Salines. A short drive south of Ste-Anne brings you to a mi-long (2-km-long) cove lined with soft white sand and coconut palms. The beach is awash with families and children during holidays and on weekends but quiet during the week. The far end—away from the makeshift souvenir shops—is most appealing. The calm waters are safe for swimming, even for the kids. You can't rent chaise longues, but there are showers. Food vendors roam the sand. From Le Marin, take the coastal road toward Ste-Anne. You will see signs for Les Salines. If you see the sign for Pointe du Marin, you have gone too far. ✉ *Ste-Anne.*

☾ **Pointe du Bout.** The beaches here are small, man-made, and lined with resorts, including the Hotel Bakoua. Each little strip is associated with its resident hotel, and security guards and closed gates make access difficult. However, if you take a left across from the main pedestrian entrance to the marina—after the taxi stand—then go left again, you will reach the beach for Hotel Bakoua,

which has especially nice facilities and several options for lunch and drinks. If things are quiet—particularly during the week—one of the beach boys may rent you a chaise; otherwise, just plop your beach towel down, face forward, and enjoy the delightful view of the Fort-de-France skyline. The water is dead calm and quite shallow, but it eventually drops off if you swim out a bit. ✉ *Pointe du Bout, Les Trois-Ilets.*

Pointe du Marin. Stretching north from Ste-Anne, this is a good windsurfing and waterskiing spot. It's also a popular family beach, with restaurants, campsites, and clean facilities available for a small fee. Club Med is on the northern edge, and you can purchase a day pass. From Le Marin, take the coastal road to Ste-Anne. Make a right before town, toward Domaine de Belfond. You can see signs for Pointe du Marin. ✉ *Marin.*

ST. BARTHÉLEMY

There is a beach in St. Barth to suit every taste. Whether you are looking for wild surf, a dreamy white-sand strand, or a spot at a chic beach club close to shopping and restaurants, you will find it within a 20-minute drive.

(this page above) Snorkeling at Anse à Colombier; (opposite page bottom) Anse à Colombier; (opposite page top) Anse des Flamands

There are many *anses* (coves) and nearly 20 *plages* (beaches) scattered around the island, each with a distinctive personality; all are open to the public, even if the beach fronts the toniest of resorts. Because of the variety and number of beaches, even in high season you can find a nearly empty beach, despite St. Barths tiny size. That's not to say that all the island's beaches are equally good or even equally suitable for swimming, but each beach has something unique to offer. Unless you are having lunch at a beachfront restaurant that has lounging areas set aside for its patrons, you should bring your own umbrella, beach mat, and water (all of which are easily obtainable all over the island if you haven't brought yours with you on vacation). Topless sunbathing is common, but nudism is supposedly forbidden—although both Grande Saline and Gouverneur are de facto nude beaches. Shade is scarce.

THE RIGHT BEACH

For long stretches of talcum-soft pale sand choose La Saline, Gouverneur, or Flamands. For seclusion in nature, pick the tawny grains of Corossol. But the most remarkable beach on the island, Shell Beach, is right in Gustavia and hardly has sand at all! Millions of tiny pink shells wash ashore in drifts, thanks to an unusual confluence of ocean currents, sea-life beds, and hurricane action.

Anse à Colombier. The beach here is the least accessible, thus the most private, on the island; to reach it you must take either a rocky footpath from Petite Anse or brave the 30-minute climb down (and back up) a steep, cactus-bordered trail. But this is a good place to snorkel. Boaters favor this beach and cove for its calm anchorage.

Anse de Grand Cul de Sac. The shallow, reef-protected beach is especially nice for small children, fly-fishermen, kayakers, and windsurfers—and lots of the amusing pelicanlike frigate birds that dive-bomb the water fishing for their lunch.

Fodor'sChoice ★ Anse de Grande Saline. Secluded, with its sandy ocean bottom, this is just about everyone's favorite beach and is great for swimmers, too. However, there can be a bit of wind here, so you can enjoy yourself more if you go on a calm day. In spite of the prohibition, young and old alike go nude. The beach is a 10-minute walk up a rocky dune trail, so be sure to wear sneakers or water shoes. Although there are several good restaurants for lunch near the parking area, once you get there, the beach is just sand, sea, and sky.

Anse de Lorient. This beach is popular with St. Barths families and surfers, who like its rolling waves and central location. Be aware of the level of the tide, which can come in very quickly. Hikers

and avid surfers like the walk over the hill to Point Milou in the late afternoon sun when the waves roll in.

Anse des Flamands. This is the most beautiful of the hotel beaches—a roomy strip of silken sand. Come here for lunch and then spend the afternoon sunning, taking a long beach walk, and swimming in the turquoise water. From the beach, you can take a brisk hike along a paved sidewalk to the top of the now-extinct volcano believed to have given birth to St. Barth.

★ Anse du Gouverneur. Because it's so secluded, this beach is a popular place for nude sunbathing. It is truly beautiful, with blissful swimming and views of St. Kitts, Saba, and St. Eustatius. Venture here at the end of the day and watch the sun set behind the hills. The road here from Gustavia also offers spectacular vistas. Legend has it that pirates' treasure is buried in the vicinity. There are no restaurants or other services here, so plan accordingly.

Baie de St-Jean. Like a mini–Côte d'Azur—beachside bistros, terrific shopping, bungalow hotels, bronzed bodies, windsurfing, and day-trippers who tend to arrive on BIG yachts—the reef-protected strip is divided by Eden Rock promontory. You can rent chaises and umbrellas at La Plage restaurant or at Eden Rock, where you can lounge for hours over lunch.

8

ST. KITTS AND NEVIS

St. Kitts and Nevis aren't noted for seemingly endless sensuous strands, yet beachcombers will find enough variety during their holiday. The finest beaches are fairly developed (Frigate Beach on the Caribbean side, with one bar after another, is a party-hearty destination on weekends), but both islands offer surf-lashed Atlantic stretches fine for R&R à deux if not swimming.

(this page above) Pinney's Beach, Nevis; (opposite page bottom) Friar's Bay, St. Kitts; (opposite page top) Frigate Bay, St. Kitts

Beaches on St. Kitts are free and open to the public (even those occupied by hotels). The best beaches, with powdery white sand, are in the Frigate Bay area or on the lower peninsula. The Atlantic waters are rougher, and many black-sand beaches northwest of Frigate Bay double as garbage dumps, though locals bodysurf at Conaree Bay.

All beaches on Nevis are free to the public (the plantation inns cordon off "private" areas on Pinney's Beach for guests), but there are no changing facilities, so wear a swimsuit under your clothes.

THE SAND

Both islands have appealing beige-hue beaches, such as Pinney's or those garlanding St. Kitts's Southeast Peninsula. Many abutting the Atlantic feature earthier colors, ranging from warm mocha to taupe-gray. Some Atlantic beaches are wind-whipped and wilder, such as Conaree, ideal for bodysurfing, though they're not regularly maintained so otherwise soft sand competes with seaweed, shells, and driftwood.

ST. KITTS

Banana/Cockleshell Bays. These twin connected eyebrows of glittering champagne-color sand—stretching nearly 2 mi (3 km) total at the southeastern tip of the island—feature majestic views of Nevis and are backed by lush vegetation and coconut palms. The Rasta-hue Lion Rock Beach Bar (order the knockout Lion Punch) and Reggae Beach Bar & Grill bracket either end of Cockleshell. The water is generally placid, ideal for swimming. The downside is irregular maintenance, with seaweed (particularly after rough weather) and occasional litter, especially on Banana Bay. Follow Simmonds Highway to the end and bear right, ignoring the turnoff for Turtle Beach. ⊠ *Banana Bay*.

Friar's Bay. Locals consider Friar's Bay, on the Caribbean (southern) side, the island's finest beach. It's a long, tawny scimitar where the water always seems warmer and clearer. Unfortunately, the new Marine World development has co-opted nearly half the strand. Still, several happening bars, including Shipwreck, Mongoose, and Sunset Grill, serve terrific, inexpensive local food and cheap, frosty drinks. Chair rentals cost around $3, though if you order lunch, you can negotiate a freebie. Friar's is the first major beach along Southeast Peninsula Drive (aka Simmonds Highway), approximately a mile (1½ km) southeast of **Frigate Bay**. ⊠ *Friar's Bay*.

Frigate Bay. The Caribbean side offers talcum-powder-fine beige sand framed by coconut palms and sea grapes, and the Atlantic side (a 15-minute stroll)—sometimes called North Frigate Bay—is a favorite with horseback riders. **South Frigate Bay** is bookended by Sunset Café and Oasis. In between are several other lively beach spots, including Cathy's (fabulous jerk ribs), the Monkey Bar, and Mr. X Shiggidy Shack. Most charge $3 to $5 to rent a chair, though they'll often waive the fee if you ask politely and buy lunch. Locals barhop late into Friday and Saturday nights. Waters are generally calm for swimming; the rockier eastern end offers fine snorkeling. The incomparably scenic Atlantic side is—regrettably—dominated by the Marriott (plentiful dining options), attracting occasional pesky vendors. The surf is choppier and the undertow stronger here. On cruise-ship days, groups stampede both sides. Frigate Bay is easy to find, just less than 3 mi (5 km) from downtown Basseterre. ⊠ *Frigate Bay*.

Sand Bank Bay. A dirt road, nearly impassable after heavy rains, leads to a long mocha crescent on the Atlantic. The shallow coves are protected here, making it ideal for families, and it's usually deserted. Brisk breezes lure the occasional windsurfer, but avoid the rocky far left area because of fierce sudden swells and currents. This exceptionally pretty beach lacks facilities and shade.

WELCOME

8

(this page above) Pinney's Beach, Nevis (opposite page) Shells on Frigate Bay Beach, St. Kitts

As you drive southeast along Simmonds Highway, approximately 10 mi (16 km) from Basseterre, look for an unmarked dirt turnoff to the left of the Great Salt Pond. ⊠ *Sand Bank Bay*.

White House Bay. The beach is rocky, but the snorkeling, taking in several reefs surrounding a sunken tugboat, as well as a recently discovered 18th-century British troop ship, is superb. It's usually deserted, though the calm water (and stunning scenery) makes it a favorite anchorage of yachties. There are no facilities and little shade, but there's also little seaweed. A dirt road skirts a hill to the right off Simmonds Highway approximately 2 mi (3 km) after Friar's. ⊠ *White House Bay*.

NEVIS

Newcastle Beach. This broad swath of soft ecru sand shaded by coconut palms is near Nisbet Plantation, on the channel between St. Kitts and Nevis. It's popular with snorkelers, but beware stony sections and occasional strong currents that kick up seaweed and roil the sandy bottom. ⊠ *Newcastle*.

Oualie Beach. South of Mosquito Bay and north of Cades and Jones bays, this beige-sand beach lined with palms and sea grapes is where the folks at Oualie Beach Hotel can mix you a drink and fix you up with water-sports equipment. There's excellent snorkeling amid calm water and fantastic sunset views with St. Kitts silhouetted in the background. Several beach chairs and hammocks (free with lunch, $3 rental without) line the sand and the grassy "lawn" behind it. Oualie is at the island's northwest tip, approximately 3 mi (5 km) west of the airport. ⊠ *Oualie Beach*.

Pinney's Beach. The island's showpiece has soft, golden sand on the calm Caribbean, lined with a magnificent grove of palm trees. The Four Seasons Resort is here, as are the plantation inns' beach clubs and casual beach bars such as Sunshine's, Chevy's and the Double Deuce. Regrettably, the waters can be murky and filled with kelp if the weather has been inclement anywhere within a hundred miles, depending on the currents. ⊠ *Pinney's Beach*.

ST. MAARTEN/ST. MARTIN

For such a small island, St. Maarten/St. Martin has a wide array of beaches, from the long expanse of Baie Orientale on the French side to powdery-soft Mullet Bay on the Dutch side.

(this page above) Beachgoers watching the Heineken Regatta; (opposite page bottom) The cliffs at Cupecoy Beach; (opposite page top) Mullet Bay Beach

Warm surf and a gentle breeze can be found at the island's 37 beaches, and every one of them is open to the public. What could be better? Each is unique: some bustling and some bare, some refined and some rocky, some good for snorkeling and some for sunning. Whatever you fancy in the beach landscape department, it's here, including a clothing-optional one at the south end of Baie Orientale, one of the Caribbean's most beautiful beaches. The key to enjoying beach life on St. Maarten and St. Martin is to try out several beaches; one quickly discovers that several of the island's gems don't have big hotels lining their shores. Petty theft from cars in beach parking lots is an unfortunate fact of life in St. Maarten and St. Martin. Leave nothing in your parked car, not even in the glove compartment or the trunk.

THE SAND

Although the best beaches, including Baie Orientale, Mullet Bay, Anse Marcel, and Ilêt Pinel, are lined with soft, white sand, some of the nicer beaches have small rocks, including Happy Bay and Baie des Péres. Atlantic-facing Le Galion has soft sand and gentle surf because it is protected by a reef, but soft sand (in the case of Guana Bay and Cupecoy) can also be accompanied by heavy surf.

DUTCH SIDE

Several of the best Dutch-side beaches are developed and have large-scale resorts. But others, including **Simpson Bay** and **Cupecoy**, have little development. You'll sometimes find vendors or beach bars to rent chairs and umbrellas (but not always).

Cupecoy Beach. This picturesque area of sandstone cliffs, white sand, and shoreline caves is a necklace of small beaches that come and go according to the whims of the sea. Even though the western part is more developed, the surf can be rough. It's popular with gay locals and visitors. Break-ins have been reported in cars, so don't leave anything at all in your vehicle. ⊠ *Cupecoy, between Baie Longue and Mullet Bay.*

★ **Dawn Beach**. True to its name, Dawn Beach is the place to be at sunrise. On the Atlantic side of Oyster Pond, just south of the French border, this is a first-class beach for sunning and snorkeling. It's not usually crowded, and there are several good restaurants nearby. To find it, follow the signs to Mr. Busby's restaurant. ⊠ *South of Oyster Pond, Dawn Beach.*

Great Bay. This is probably the easiest beach to find because it curves around Philipsburg. A bustling, white-sand beach, Great Bay is just behind Front Street. Here you'll find boutiques, eateries, and a pleasant boardwalk. Busy with

cruise-ship passengers, the beach is best west of Captain Hodge Pier or around Antoine Restaurant. ⊠ *Philipsburg.*

Little Bay. Despite its popularity with snorkelers and divers as well as kayakers and boating enthusiasts, Little Bay isn't usually crowded. Maybe the gravelly sand is the reason. But, it does boast panoramic views of St. Eustatius, Philipsburg, the cruise-ship terminal, Saba, and St. Kitts. The beach is west of Fort Amsterdam and accessible via the Divi Little Bay Beach Resort. ⊠ *Little Bay Rd., Little Bay.*

Mullet Bay Beach. Many believe that this mile-long, powdery white-sand beach near the medical school is the island's best. Swimmers like it because the water is usually calm. When the swell is up, the surfers hit the beach. ⊠ *South of Cupecoy, Mullet Bay.*

Simpson Bay Beach. This secluded, half-moon stretch of white-sand beach on the island's Caribbean side is a hidden gem. It's mostly surrounded by private residences. There are no big resorts, no Jet Skiers, no food concessions, and no crowds. Southeast of the airport, follow the signs to Mary's Boon and the Horny Toad guesthouses. ⊠ *Simpson Bay.*

FRENCH SIDE

Almost all the French-side beaches, whether busy Baie Orientale or less busy Baie des Pères (Friars Bay), have beach clubs and restaurants. For about $25 a

8

(opposite page) Baie Orientale, St. Martin; (this page) Baie Rouge, St. Martin

couple you get two chaises (*transats*) and an umbrella (*parasol*) for the day, not to mention chair-side service for drinks and food. Only some beaches have bathrooms and showers, so if that is your preference, inquire.

Anse Heureuse (*Happy Bay*). Not many people know about this romantic, hidden gem. Happy Bay has powdery sand, gorgeous luxury villas, and stunning views of Anguilla. The snorkeling is also good. To get here, turn left on the rather rutted dead-end road to Baie des Péres (Friars Bay). The beach itself is a 10- to 15-minute walk from the last beach bar. ✉ *Happy Bay.*

Baie de Grand Case. Along this skinny stripe of a beach bordering the culinary capital of Grand Case, the old-style gingerbread architecture sometimes peeps out between the bustling restaurants. The sea is calm, and there are tons of fun lunch options from bistros to beachside barbecue stands (called *lolos*). Several of the restaurants rent chairs and umbrellas; some include their use for lunch patrons. ✉ *Grand Case.*

Baie des Péres (*Friars Bay*). This quiet cove close to Marigot has beach grills and bars, with chaises and umbrellas, calm waters, and a lovely view of Anguilla. Kali's Beach Bar, open daily for lunch and (weather permitting) dinner, has a Rasta vibe and color scheme—it's the best place to be on the full moon, with music, dancing, and a huge bonfire, but you can get lunch, beach chairs, and umbrellas there in any moon phase. To get to the beach, take National Road 7 from Marigot, go toward Grand Case to the Morne Valois hill, and turn left on the dead-end road at the sign. ✉ *Friar's Bay.*

Baie Longue (*Long Bay*). Though it extends over the French Lowlands, from the cliff at La Samanna to La Pointe des Canniers, the island's longest beach has no facilities or vendors. It's the perfect place for a romantic walk. But car break-ins are a particular problem here. To get here, take National Road 7 south of Marigot. The entrance marked LA SAMANNA is the first entrance to the beach. For a splurge, lunch at the resort or sunset drinks are a must. ✉ *Baie Longue.*

Fodor's Choice ★ **Baie Orientale** (*Orient Bay*). Many consider this the island's most beautiful beach, but its 2 mi (3 km) of satiny white sand, underwater marine reserve, variety of water sports, beach clubs, and hotels also make it one of the most crowded. Lots of "naturists" take advantage of the clothing-optional policy, so don't be shocked. Early-morning nude beach walking is de rigueur for the guests at Club Orient, at the southeastern end of the beach. Plan to spend the day at one of the clubs; each bar has different color umbrellas, and all boast terrific restaurants and lively bars. You can have an open-air massage, try any sea toy you fancy, and stay until dark. To get to Baie Orientale from Marigot, take National Road 7 past Grand Case, past the Aéroport de L'Espérance, and watch for the left turn. ⊠ *Baie Orientale.*

Baie Rouge (*Red Bay*). At this home to a couple of beach bars, complete with chaises and umbrellas, you can bask with the millionaires renting the big-ticket villas in the "neighborhood" and take advantage of the gorgeous beach they came for. Baie Rouge and its salt ponds make up a nature preserve, the location of the oldest habitations in the Caribbean. This area is widely thought to have the best snorkeling beaches on the island. You can swim the crystal waters along the point and explore a swim-through cave. The beach is fairly popular with gay men in the mornings and early afternoons. There are two restaurants here; only Chez Raymond is open every day, and cocktail hour starts when the conch shell blows, so keep your ears open. There is a sign and a right turn after you leave Baie Nettlé. ⊠ *Baie Rouge.*

Le Galion. A coral reef borders this quiet beach, part of the island's nature preserve, which is paradise if you are traveling with children. The water is calm, clear, and quite shallow, so it's a perfect place for families with young kids. It's a full-service place, with chair rentals, restaurants, and water-sports operators. Kite-boarders and windsurfers like the trade winds at the far end of the beach. On Sunday there are always groups picnicking and partying. To get to Le Galion, follow the signs to the unmissable Butterfly Farm and continue toward the water. ⊠ *Quartier d'Orleans.*

Ilêt Pinel. A protected nature reserve, this kid-friendly island is a five-minute ferry ride from French Cul de Sac ($7 per person round-trip). The ferry runs every half hour from midmorning until dusk. The water is clear and shallow, and the shore is sheltered. If you like snorkeling, don your gear and paddle along both coasts of this pencil-shape speck in the ocean. You can rent equipment on the island or in the parking lot before you board the ferry for about $10. Plan for lunch any day of the week at the water's edge at a palm-shaded beach hut at Karibuni (except in September, when it's closed) for the freshest fish, great salads, tapas, and drinks—try the frozen mojito for a treat. ⊠ *Ilêt Pinel.*

U.S. VIRGIN ISLANDS

The beaches of the USVI are like pearly-white smiles that outline the curve of the bays on both the Atlantic Ocean to the north and Caribbean Sea to the south. The brilliant sand provides a beaming contrast to the deep turquoise seas and the lush green palms and sea grape trees that line the shores.

(this page above) Trunk Bay, St. John; (opposite page bottom) Coki Beach, St. Thomas; (opposite page top) Magens Bay, St. Thomas

The three islands of the USVI offer a wide range of beach experiences and activities. St. Thomas and St. John are widely known for having the best beaches in the U.S. Virgin Islands, but there is one more island that you shouldn't miss if you're visiting St. Thomas. Water Island, a half-mi ferry ride from Crown Bay Marina on St. Thomas, has Honeymoon Beach, one of the most perfect powdery beaches you'll find (though some say that Sprat Beach, which is much farther away from the ferry dock, is better); there are restrooms on the beach as well as a restaurant that serves lunch, but it's a half-mi hike from the ferry dock (some of it up a rather steep hill).

DON'T MISS

St. Thomas is the busiest and most developed of the U.S. Virgin Islands. Don't miss watching the planes land from Brewer's Beach, eating fish and fungi (a cornmeal polenta-like side dish) at Coki Beach, renting a paddleboat at Magens Bay, bodysurfing in the winter at Hull Bay, and enjoying a rum and Coke from beachside bar service at Morningstar Beach.

ST. THOMAS

All 44 St. Thomas beaches are open to the public, although you can reach some of them only by walking through a resort. Hotel guests frequently have access to lounge chairs and floats that are off-limits to nonguests; for this reason you may feel more comfortable at one of the beaches not associated with a resort, such as **Magens Bay** (which charges an entrance fee to cover beach maintenance) or **Coki Beach**, the latter abutting Coral World Ocean Park and offering the island's best off-the-beach shorkeling. **Morningstar Beach** sits between the twin Marriott Resorts on St. Thomas's south shore. **Sapphire Beach** is another of the island's better beaches, and it offers both soft, silky sand as well as access to a good reef for snorkeling.

ST. JOHN

St. John is blessed with many beaches, and all of them fall into the good, great, and don't-tell-anyone-else-about-this-place categories. Some are more developed than others—and many are crowded on weekends, holidays, and in high season—but by and large they're still pristine. Beaches along the south and eastern shores are quiet and isolated.

Two of the island's stand-out beaches can be found in the national park. **Trunk Bay** is the beach you often seen pictured

on postcards from the Virgin Islands; a long, white sandy beach is fronted by a coral reef that makes waves smooth and steady. **Cinnamon Bay**, which is next to the national park campground, has a water sports center and excellent snorkeling; there are also a couple of hiking trails that start at the beach. St. John's other excellent beach is **Hawksnest Bay**. Close to Cruz Bay, it's often busy with locals and tourists alike, but it's a great spot for off-shore snorkeling.

ST. CROIX

St. Croix's beaches are not quite as spectacular as those on St. John or St. Thomas. But that's not to say you won't find some good places to spread out for a day on the water. The best beach is on nearby **Buck Island**, a national monument where a marked snorkeling trail leads you through an extensive coral reef while a soft, sandy beach beckons a few yards away. Other great beaches are the unnamed **west end beaches** both south and north of Frederiksted. You can park yourself at Sunset Grill, about a mi north of Frederiksted, where you can rent a lounger and get food and drinks from the restaurant.

8

Best Beaches in the Southern Caribbean

WHAT'S WHERE

The Southern Caribbean.
The Souhern Caribbean including St. Lucia, St. Vincent, and Grenada—complete the main Caribbean arc. These dramatically scenic southern islands face the trade winds head-on. The Grenadines—a string of small islands between Grenada and St. Vincent—is heaven for sailors. The Southern Caribbean islands—Trinidad, Tobago, Aruba, Bonaire, and Curaçao—are rarely bothered by hurricanes.

1 Aruba. Some Caribbean travelers seek an undiscovered paradise, some seek the familiar and safe: Aruba is for the latter. On the smallest of the ABC islands, the waters are peacock blue, and the white beaches are beautiful and powdery soft. For Americans, Aruba offers all the comforts of home: English is spoken universally, and the U.S. dollar is accepted everywhere.

2 Bonaire. With only 15,000 year-round citizens and huge numbers of visiting divers, Bonaire still seems largely untouched by tourism. Divers come for the clear water, profusion of marine life, and great dive shops. With a surreal, arid landscape, immense flamingo population, and gorgeous turquoise vistas, you can also have a wonderful land-based holiday.

3 Curaçao. Rich in heritage and history, Curaçao offers a blend of island life and city savvy, wonderful weather, spectacular diving, and charming beaches. Dutch and Caribbean influences are everywhere, but there's also an infusion of touches from around the world, particularly noteworthy in the great food. Willemstad, the picturesque capital, is a treat for pedestrians, with shopping clustered in areas around the waterfront.

4 St Lucia. One of the most green and beautiful islands in the Caribbean is, arguably, the most romantic. The scenic south and central regions are mountainous and lush, with dense rain forest, endless banana plantations, and fascinating historic sites. Along the west coast, some of the region's most interesting resorts are interspersed with dozens of delightful inns, appealing to families as well as lovers and adventurers.

5 St Vincent and the Grenadines. Thirty-two perfectly endowed islands and cays have no mass tourism but a lot of old-style Caribbean charm; several have not a small sense of

ARUBA
(Neth.)

CURAÇAO
(Neth.)

BONAIRE
(Neth.)

○ **1**
Oranjestad

3
○
Willemstad

○ Rincón
2

Isla Las Roques
(Ven.)

Isla La Orchila
(Ven.)

Isla La Tortuga
(Ven.)

VENEZUELA

0		100 mi
0	100 km	

○
Caracas

luxury. Tourism isn't even the biggest business in lush, mountainous St. Vincent. Throughout the chain, wildlife trusts protect rare species of flora and fauna, and villa walls ensure privacy for the islands' rich and famous human visitors.

6 Grenada. The spice business is going strong, but tourism is just as important. On the laid-back island, the only sounds are the occasional abrupt call of a cuckoo in the lush rain forest, the crash of surf in the secluded coves, and the slow beat of a big-drum dance. Resorts are mostly small and charming. St. George's, the island's capital, is often called the most beautiful city in the Caribbean.

7 Trinidad and Tobago. Trinidad and Tobago, the most southerly Caribbean islands, are two different places. Trinidad is an effervescent mix of cultures—mostly descendants of African slaves and East Indian indentured workers—who like to party but also appreciate the island's incredibly diverse ecosystem. Little sister Tobago is laid-back and rustic, with beaches that can match any in the Caribbean.

8 Barbados. Broad vistas, sweeping seascapes, craggy cliffs, and acre upon acre of sugarcane make up the island's varied landscape. A long, successful history of tourism has been forged from the warm, Bajan hospitality, welcoming hotels and resorts, sophisticated dining, lively nightspots, and, of course, magnificent sunny beaches.

ATLANTIC OCEAN

Castries
4 ST. LUCIA

St. Vincent
Kingstown
Bequia
5 Mustique
Canouan
Union
Carriacou

ST. VINCENT & THE GRENADINES

THE GRENADINES

6
GRENADA St. George's

8
Bridgetown
BARBADOS

9

Isla La Blanquilla (Ven.)

Tobago

Isla de Margarita (Ven.)

TRINIDAD & TOBAGO **7**

Port of Spain

Trinidad

Puerto La Cruz

ARUBA

There are few destinations that can match the glorious beach vistas of Aruba. Virtually every popular beach has a resort attached but as all beaches are public there is never a problem with access. The constant breezes are a lovely cool counterpoint to the intense sunshine.

(this page above) Eagle Beach; (opposite page bottom) Baby Beach; (opposite page top) Fisherman's Huts

The beaches on Aruba are legendary: white sand, turquoise waters, and virtually no litter—everyone takes the NO TIRA SUSHI (no littering) signs very seriously, especially considering the island's $280 fine. The major public beaches, which back up to the hotels along the southwestern strip, are usually crowded. You can make the hour-long hike from the Holiday Inn to the Tamarijn without ever leaving sand. Make sure you're well protected from the sun—it scorches fast despite the cooling trade winds. Luckily, there's at least one covered bar (and often an ice-cream stand) at virtually every hotel. On the island's northeastern side, stronger winds make the waters too choppy for swimming, but the vistas are great and the terrain is wonderful for exploring.

BRING YOUR SHADES

Aruba's most popular beaches, from Druif Beach to the end of the High Rise Resort area, are wide, white and pristine. The powdery sand is highly reflective so you'll need your sunglasses. Beaches on the island's North Coast are much rockier and swimming is not advisable. Baby Beach on the south-western tip of the island is a bit of a drive but the wide stretch of sugar-icing sand make it worthwhile.

Arashi Beach. Just after **Malmok Beach**, this is a ½-mi (1-km) stretch of gleaming white sand. Although it was once rocky, nature—with a little help from humans—has turned it into an excellent place for sunbathing and swimming. Despite calm waters, the rocky reputation has kept most people away, making it relatively uncrowded. ✛ *West of Malmok Beach, on west end.*

Baby Beach. On the island's eastern tip (near the refinery), this semicircular beach borders a placid bay that's just about as shallow as a wading pool—perfect for tots, shore divers, and terrible swimmers. Thatched shaded areas are good places to cool off. Down the road is the island's rather unusual pet cemetery. Stop by the nearby snack truck for burgers, hot dogs, beer, and soda. The road to this beach (and several others) is through San Nicolas and along the road toward Seroe Colorado. Just before reaching the beach, keep an eye out for a strange 300-foot natural seawall made of coral and rock that was thrown up overnight when Hurricane Ivan swept by the island in 2004. ✉ *Near Seroe Colorado, on east end.*

Boca Prins. You'll need a four-wheel-drive vehicle to make the trek to this strip of coastline, which is famous for its backdrop of enormous vanilla sand dunes. Near the Fontein Cave and Blue Lagoon, the beach itself is about as large

as a Brazilian bikini—but with two rocky cliffs and tumultuously crashing waves, it's as romantic as Aruba gets. The water is rough and swimming is prohibited (with good reason), however. Bring a picnic, a beach blanket, and sturdy sneakers, and descend the rocks that form steps to the water's edge. ✉ *Off 7 A/B, near Fontein Cave.*

Fodor's Choice ★ Eagle Beach. On the southwestern coast, across the highway from what is quickly becoming known as Time-Share Lane, is one of the Caribbean's—if not the world's—best beaches. Not long ago it was a nearly deserted stretch of pristine sand with the occasional thatched picnic hut. Now that the resorts have been completed, this mile-plus-long beach is always hopping. The white sand is literally dazzling, and sunglasses are essential. Many of the hotels have facilities on or near the beach, and refreshments are never far away. ✉ *J.E. Irausquin Blvd., north of Manchebo Beach.*

Fisherman's Huts *(Hadicurari).* Next to the Holiday Inn is a windsurfer's haven with good swimming conditions and a decent, slightly rocky, white sand beach. Take a picnic lunch (tables are available) and watch the elegant purple, aqua, and orange sails struggle in the wind. ✉ *1 A/B, at Holiday Inn SunSpree Aruba.*

Grapefield Beach. To the southeast of San Nicolas, a sweep of blinding-white

9

(this page above) Palm Beach (opposite page) Windsurfing in Aruba

sand in the shadow of cliffs and boulders is marked by an anchor-shape memorial dedicated to all seamen. Pick sea grapes from January to June. Swim at your own risk; the waves here can be rough. This is not a popular tourist beach so finding a quiet spot is almost guaranteed, but the downside of this is a complete lack of facilities or nearby refreshments. ✉ *Southwest of San Nicolas, on east end.*

Malmok Beach *(Boca Catalina)*. On the northwestern shore, this small, nondescript beach borders shallow waters that stretch 300 yards from shore. There are no snack or refreshment stands here, but shade is available under the thatched umbrellas. It's the perfect place to learn to windsurf. Right off the coast here is a favorite haunt for divers and snorkelers—the wreck of the German ship *Antilla*, scuttled in 1940. ✉ *At end of J.E. Irausquin Blvd., Malmokweg.*

Manchebo Beach *(Punta Brabo)*. Impressively wide, the white sand shoreline in front of the Manchebo Beach Resort is where officials turn a blind eye to the occasional topless sunbather. This beach merges with **Druif Beach**, and most locals use the name Manchebo to refer to both. ✉ *J.E. Irausquin Blvd., at Manchebo Beach Resort.*

Palm Beach. This stretch runs from the Westin Aruba Resort, Spa & Casino to the Marriott Aruba Ocean Club. It's the center of Aruban tourism, offering good swimming, sailing, and other water sports. In some spots you might find a variety of shells that are great to collect, but not as much fun to step on barefoot—bring sandals. ✉ *J.E. Irausquin Blvd. between Westin Aruba Resort, Spa & Casino and Marriott Aruba Ocean Club.*

Rodger's Beach. Near Baby Beach on the island's eastern tip, this beautiful curving stretch of sand is only slightly marred by its proximity to the oil refinery at the bay's far side. Swimming conditions are excellent here. The snack bar at the water's edge has beach-equipment rentals and a shop. Drive around the refinery perimeter to get here. ✉ *Next to Baby Beach, on east end.*

BARBADOS

Geologically, Barbados is a coral-and-limestone island (not volcanic) with few rivers, and as a result has beautiful beaches, particularly along the island's southern and southeastern coastlines.

(this page above) Bathsheba, Barbados; (opposite page bottom) Surfers at Soup Bowl, Bathsheba; (opposite page top) couple on the beach in Barbados

The west coast has some lovely beaches as well, but they're more susceptible to erosion after major autumn storms, if any, have taken their toll. With long stretches of open beach, crashing ocean surf, rocky cliffs, and verdant hills, the Atlantic (windward) side of Barbados is where Barbadians spend their holidays, but these aren't beaches for swimming. The surf and currents are too strong, even for experienced swimmers. All Bajan beaches have fine white sand, and all are open to the public. Most have access from the road, so nonguest bathers don't have to pass through hotel properties. When the surf is too high and swimming may be dangerous, a red flag will be hoisted on the beach. A yellow flag—or a red flag at half-staff—means swim with caution. Topless sunbathing—on the beach or at the pool—is not allowed anywhere in Barbados by government regulation.

LOTS OF BEACHES

All along the south and west coasts, you'll find excellent beaches with broad swaths of white sand. The unique pink coral sand at Crane Beach and magnificent—and rather remote—Bottom Bay definitely lure romantics. Sand on the east-coast beaches is equally white, but the treacherous surf means you can only wade or stroll, not swim.

SOUTH COAST

A young, energetic crowd favors the south-coast beaches, which are broad and breezy, blessed with powdery white sand, and dotted with tall palms. The reef-protected areas with crystal clear water are safe for swimming and snorkeling. The surf is medium to high, and the waves get bigger and the winds stronger (windsurfers take note) the farther southeast you go.

Accra Beach. This popular beach, also known as Rockley Beach, is next to the Accra Beach Hotel. Look forward to gentle surf and a lifeguard, plenty of nearby restaurants for refreshments, a children's playground, and beach stalls for renting chairs and equipment for snorkeling and other water sports. Parking is available at an on-site lot. ✉ *Hwy. 7, Rockley, Christ Church.*

Bottom Bay. Popular for fashion and travel-industry photo shoots, Bottom Bay is the quintessential Caribbean beach. Surrounded by a coral cliff, studded with a stand of palms, and with an endless ocean view, this dreamy enclave is near the southeastern tip of the island. The waves can be too strong for swimming, but it's the picture-perfect place for a picnic lunch. Park at the top of the cliff and follow the steps down to the beach. ✉ *Dover, St. Philip.*

Word of Mouth. "[C]heck out Bottom Bay. There are limestone cliffs with a small field of palm trees and a natural looking gorgeous beach. It's featured in most of the promotional commercials for Barbados, and for a reason."—Blamona

Carlisle Bay. Adjacent to the Hilton Barbados just south of Bridgetown, this broad half circle of white sand is one of the island's best beaches—but it can become crowded on weekends and holidays. Park at Harbour Lights or at the Boatyard Bar and Bayshore Complex, both on Bay Street, where you can also rent umbrellas and beach chairs and buy refreshments. ✉ *Aquatic Gap, Needham's Point, St. Michael.*

Word of Mouth. "Carlisle bay is calm and has the most beautiful crystal clear aqua water."—nunnles

Casuarina Beach. Stretched in front of the Almond Casuarina Resort, where St. Lawrence Gap meets the Maxwell Coast Road, this broad strand of powdery white sand is great for both sunbathing and strolling, with the surf from low to medium. Find public access and parking on Maxwell Coast Road, near the Bougainvillea Resort. ✉ *Maxwell Coast Rd., Dover, Christ Church.*

Crane Beach. This exquisite crescent of pink sand on the southeast coast was named not for the elegant long-legged wading birds but for the crane used to haul and load cargo when this area was a busy port. Crane Beach usually has a steady breeze and lightly rolling surf

9

(opposite page) Miami Beach (this page) Mullins Beach

that is great for bodysurfing. A lifeguard is on duty. Changing rooms are available at the Crane resort for a small fee. Access is through the hotel and down to the beach via either a cliff-side elevator or 98 steps. ⊠ *Crane Bay, St. Philip.*

Word of Mouth. "[Crane Beach] has pink sand like baby powder. The cliffs are a sight, and you can jump off into the ocean."—kmw1211

Fodor's Choice ★ **Miami Beach.** Also called Enterprise Beach, this isolated spot on Enterprise Coast Road, just east of Oistins, is an underrated slice of pure white sand with cliffs on either side and crystal clear water. You can find a palm-shaded parking area, snack carts, and chair rentals. Bring a picnic or have lunch across the road at Café Luna in Little Arches Hotel. ⊠ *Enterprise Beach Rd., Enterprise, Christ Church.*

Sandy Beach. Next to the Sandy Bay Beach Resort, this beach has shallow, calm waters and a picturesque lagoon, making it an ideal location for families with small kids. Park right on the main road. You can rent beach chairs and umbrellas, and plenty of places

nearby sell food and drinks. ⊠ *Hwy. 7, Worthing, Christ Church.*

Silver Sands–Silver Rock Beach. Nestled between South Point, the southernmost tip of the island, and Inch Marlow Point, Silver Sands–Silver Rock is a beautiful strand of white sand that always has a stiff breeze. That makes this beach the best in Barbados for intermediate and advanced windsurfers and, more recently, kitesurfers. ⊠ *Off Hwy. 7, Christ Church.*

EAST COAST

Be cautioned: Swimming at east-coast beaches is treacherous, even for strong swimmers, and is *not* recommended. Waves are high, the bottom tends to be rocky, the currents are unpredictable, and the undertow is dangerously strong.

Barclays Park. Serious swimming is unwise at this beach, which follows the coastline in St. Andrew, but you can take a dip, wade, and play in the tide pools. A lovely shaded area with picnic tables is directly across the road. ⊠ *Ermy Bourne Hwy., north of Bathsheba, St. Andrew.*

Bathsheba/Cattlewash. Although it's not safe for swimming, the miles of untouched, windswept sand along the East Coast Road in St. Joseph Parish are great for beachcombing and wading. As you approach Bathsheba Soup Bowl, the southernmost stretch just below Tent Bay, the enormous mushroomlike boulders and rolling surf are uniquely impressive. This is also where expert surfers from around the world converge each November for the Independence Classic Surfing Championship. ⊠ *East Coast Rd., Bathsheba, St. Joseph.*

WEST COAST

Gentle Caribbean waves lap the west coast, and its stunning coves and sandy beaches are shaded by leafy mahogany trees. The water is perfect for swimming and water sports. An almost unbroken chain of beaches runs between Bridgetown and Speightstown. Elegant homes and luxury hotels face much of the beachfront property in this area, dubbed Barbados's "Platinum Coast."

West-coast beaches are considerably smaller and narrower than those on the south coast. Also, prolonged stormy weather in September and October may cause sand erosion, temporarily making the beach even narrower. Even so, west-coast beaches are seldom crowded. Vendors stroll by, selling handmade baskets, hats, dolls, jewelry, even original watercolors; owners of private boats offer waterskiing, parasailing, and snorkeling excursions. There are no concession stands, but hotels and beachside restaurants welcome nonguests for terrace lunches (wear a cover-up), and you can buy picnic items at supermarkets in Holetown.

Brighton Beach. Calm as a lake, this is where you can find locals taking a quick dip on hot days. Just north of Bridgetown, Brighton Beach is also home to the Malibu Beach Club. ⊠ *Spring Garden Hwy., Brighton, St. Michael.*

Fodor's Choice ★ **Mullins Beach.** This lovely beach just south of Speightstown is a perfect place to spend the day. The water is safe for swimming and snorkeling, there's easy parking on the main road, and Mullins Restaurant serves snacks, meals, and drinks—and rents chairs and umbrellas. ⊠ *Hwy. 1, Mullins Bay, St. Peter.*

Paynes Bay. The stretch of beach just south of Sandy Lane is lined with luxury hotels. It's a very pretty area, with plenty of beach to go around and good snorkeling. Public access is available at several locations along Highway 1; parking is limited. Grab liquid refreshments and a bite to eat at Bomba's Beach Bar. ⊠ *Hwy. 1, Paynes Bay, St. James.*

9

BONAIRE

Although most of Bonaire's charms are underwater there are a few excellent beaches. Even those beaches that are unsuitable for sunbathing can be worth a visit if only to view the intense turquoise waters that surround this little desert island.

(this page above) Boca Slagbaai Beach; (opposite page bottom) The coast of Klein Bonaire; (opposite page top) Grab a chair at Sorobon Beach

Don't expect long stretches of glorious powdery sand. Bonaire's beaches are small, and though the water is blue (several shades of it, in fact), the sand isn't always white. Bonaire's National Parks Foundation requires all nondivers to pay a $10 annual Nature Fee to enter the water anywhere around the island (divers pay $25). The fee can be paid at most dive shops, and the receipt will also allow access to Washington–Slagbaai Park.

SALT AND PEPPER

Sorobon Beach offers white powder. Many beaches have white sand but are also peppered with broken coral and rocks, which makes strolling difficult. At the rugged Washington Slagbaai Park you'll find the black sand of Boca Cocolishi, a testament to the island's past volcanic activity. Pink Beach near Kralendijk is popular with families but offers no facilities and no shade.

Boca Slagbaai. Inside Washington–Slagbaai Park is this beach of coral fossils and rocks with interesting offshore coral gardens that are good for snorkeling. Bring scuba boots or canvas sandals to walk into the water, because the beach is rough on bare feet. The gentle surf makes it an ideal place for swimming and picnicking. ⊠ *Off main park road, in Washington–Slagbaai National Park.*

Klein Bonaire. Just a water-taxi hop across from Kralendijk, this little island offers picture-perfect white-sand beaches. The area is protected, so absolutely no development has been allowed. Make sure to pack everything before heading to the island, including water and an umbrella to hide under, because there are no refreshment stands or changing facilities, and there's almost no shade to be found. Boats leave from the Town Pier, across from the City Café, and the round-trip water-taxi ride costs roughly $15 per person.

Lac Bay Beach. Known for its festive music on Sunday nights, this open bay area with pink-tinted sand is equally dazzling by day. It's a bumpy drive (10 to 15 minutes on a dirt road) to get here, but you'll be glad when you arrive. It's a good spot for diving, snorkeling, and kayaking (as long as you bring your own), and there are public restrooms

and a restaurant for your convenience. ⊠ *Off Kaminda Sorobon, Lac Cai.*

Playa Funchi. This Washington–Slagbaai National Park beach is notable for the lagoon on one side, where flamingos nest, and the superb snorkeling on the other, where iridescent green parrot fish swim right up to shore. ⊠ *Off main park road, in Washington–Slagbaai National Park.*

Sorobon Beach. This is *the* windsurfing beach on Bonaire and one of the most beautiful beaches on the island, with a wide swath of soft white sand sloping gently into the intense blue waters of the sheltered cove. You can find a restaurant-bar next to the resort and windsurfing outfitters on the beach. The public beach area has restrooms and huts for shade, as well as a direct line of sight to the nude section. Take the E.E.G. Boulevard south from Kralendijk to Kaya I.R. Randolf Statuuis Van Eps, and then follow this route straight on to Sorobon Beach. ⊠ *Kaya I.R. Randolf Statuuis Van Eps, Sorobon Beach.*

Windsock Beach *(Mangrove Beach)*. Near the airport (just off E.E.G. Boulevard), this pretty little spot looks out toward the north side of the island and has about 200 yards of white sand along a rocky shoreline. It's a popular dive site and swimming conditions are good. ⊠ *Off E.E.G. Blvd. near Flamingo Airport.*

9

CURAÇAO

Beautiful beaches are not hard to find on Curaçao. The island boasts more than three dozen beaches, with many of the best ones on the western side. The more popular beaches offer a wide range of facilities and excellent restaurants.

(this page above) Snorkeling Playa Knip; (opposite page bottom) Windsurfers on Seaquarium Beach; (opposite page top) Cas Abao Beach

Beaches in Curaçao range from small inlets shielded by craggy cliffs to longer expanses of sparkling sand. Beaches along the southeast coast tend to be rocky in the shallow water (wear reef shoes—some resorts lend them out for free); the west side has more stretches of smooth sand at the shoreline. Exploring the beaches away from the hotels is a perfect way to soak up the island's character. Whether you're seeking a lovers' hideaway, a special snorkeling adventure, or a great spot to wow the kids, you're not likely to be disappointed. There are snack bars and restrooms on many of the larger beaches, but it's at the smaller ones with no facilities where you might find utter tranquillity, especially during the week. Most spots with entry fees offer lounge chairs for rent at an additional cost, typically $2 to $3 per chair.

THE SCOOP

The most popular beaches on the west and south sides of the island have beautiful, powdery white sand. Those seeking solitude and inspiration can find beaches of all sizes on the north and east coasts. The rugged and windswept nature of these coasts means that the white sand will usually be liberally sprinkled with pebbles, which can make sunbathing uncomfortable and walking difficult.

EAST END

☾ **Seaquarium Beach**. This 1,600-foot stretch of sandy beach is divided into separate sections, each uniquely defined by a seaside resort or restaurant as its central draw. By day, no matter where you choose to enter the palm-shaded beach, you can find lounge chairs in the sand, thatched shelters, and restrooms. The sections at **Mambo** and **Kontiki** beaches also have showers. The island's largest water-sports center (Ocean Encounters at Lions Dive) caters to nearby hotel guests and walk-ins. Mambo Beach is always a hot spot and quite a scene on weekends, especially during the much-touted Sunday-night fiesta that's become a fixture of the island's nightlife. The ubiquitous beach mattress is also the preferred method of seating for the Tuesday-night movies at Mambo Beach (check the *K-Pasa* guide for listings—typically B-films or old classics—and reserve your spot with a shirt or a towel). At Kontiki Beach, you can find a spa, a hair braider, and a restaurant that serves refreshing piña colada ice cream. Unless you're a guest of a resort on the beach, the entrance fee to any section is $3 until 5 PM, then free. After 11 PM, you must be 18 or older to access the beach. ⊠ *Bapor Kibra z/n, about 1 mi (1.5 km) east of downtown Willemstad.*

WEST END

☾ **Cas Abao**. This white-sand gem has the brightest blue water in Curaçao, a treat for swimmers, snorkelers, and sunbathers alike. You can take respite beneath the hut-shaded snack bar. The restrooms and showers are immaculate. The only drawback is the weekend crowds, especially Sunday, when local families descend in droves; come on a weekday for more privacy. You can rent beach chairs, paddleboats, and snorkeling and diving gear. The entry fee is $3, and the beach is open from 8 to 6. Turn off Westpunt Highway at the junction onto Weg Naar Santa Cruz; follow until the turnoff for Cas Abao, and then drive along the winding country road for about 10 minutes to the beach. ⊠ *West of St. Willibrordus, about 3 mi (5 km) off Weg Naar Santa Cruz.*

Playa Jeremi. No snack bar, no dive shop, no facilities, no fee—in fact, there's nothing but sheer natural beauty. Though the beach is sandy, there are rocky patches, so barefoot visitors should exercise care. The parking area is offset from the beach and vehicle break-ins are common. Quite a bit of development is planned for this beach, so have a look before it's too late. ⊠ *Off Weg Naar Santa Cruz, west of Lagun.*

Playa Kalki. Noted for its spectacular snorkeling, this beach is at the western tip of the island. Sunbathers may find the narrow and rocky beach less than

9

(this page above) Playa Lagun (opposite page) Christoffel National Park

ideal. The Ocean Encounters dive shop is here. ✉ *Westpunt, near Jaanchi's.*

🐣 **Playa Knip.** Two protected coves offer crystal clear turquoise waters. Big (Groot) Knip is an expanse of alluring white sand, perfect for swimming and snorkeling. You can rent beach chairs and hang out under the *palapas* (thatch-roof shelters) or cool off with ice cream at the snack bar. There are restrooms here but no showers. It's particularly crowded on Sunday and school holidays. Just up the road, also in a protected cove, Little (Kleine) Knip is a charmer, too, with picnic tables and palapas. Steer clear of the poisonous manchineel trees. There's no fee for these beaches. ✉ *Banda Abou, just east of Westpunt.*

🐣 **Playa Lagun.** This northwestern cove is caught between gray cliffs, which dramatically frame the Caribbean blue. Cognoscenti know this as one of the best places to snorkel—even for kids—because of the calm, shallow water. It's also a haven for fishing boats and canoes. There's a small dive shop on the beach, a snack bar (open weekends), and restrooms, but there's no fee. ✉ *Banda Abou, west of Santa Cruz.*

🐣 **Playa Porto Mari.** Calm, clear water and a long stretch of white sand are the hallmarks of this beach. Without the commercial bustle of Seaquarium Beach, it's one of the best for all-around fun, and it therefore draws throngs of local families and tourists on the weekends. A decent bar and restaurant, well-kept showers, changing facilities, and restrooms are all on-site; a nature trail is nearby. The double coral reef—explore one, swim past it, explore another—is a special feature that makes this spot popular with snorkelers and divers. The entrance fee (including one free beverage) is $2 on weekdays, $3 on Sunday and holidays. From Willemstad, drive west on Westpunt Highway for 4 mi (7 km); turn left onto Willibrordus Road at the Porto Mari billboard, and then drive 3 mi (5 km) until you see a large church; follow signs on the winding dirt road to the beach. ✉ *Off Willibrordus Rd.*

GRENADA AND CARRIACOU

Grenada's best beaches are found all along the island's southwest coastline, which is also where you'll find most of the tourist facilities. Carriacou has lovely beaches that are an easy walk for day-trippers who arrive by ferry, but the deserted islands just offshore are the most memorable.

(this page above) Grande Anse Beach; (opposite page bottom) La Sagesse Beach; (opposite page top) Sandy Island

Grenada has some 80 mi (130 km) of coastline, 65 bays, and 45 beaches—many in little coves. The best beaches are just south of St. George's, facing the Caribbean, where most resorts are also clustered. Nude or topless bathing is against the law if you are in view of others.

On Carriacou, you'll find beaches within walking distance of the ferry jetty in Hillsborough—miles of soft, white sand that slope gently down to the warm (average 83°F), calm sea. Carriacou's best beach experience, though, is a day spent swimming, snorkeling, and picnicking on one of the otherwise uninhabited islands just offshore.

WHITE OR BLACK?

Grenada primarily has white-sand stretches with a few black-sand beaches. Grand Anse Beach has 2 mi (3 km) of white sand. Morne Rouge, nearby, is a perfect semicircle of white sand.

Paradise Beach on Carriacou has lovely white sand. Sandy Island or White Island require a water taxi from Hillsborough, but the powdery sand and crystal clear water make the effort worthwhile.

GRENADA

Bathway Beach. A broad strip of sand with a natural reef that protects swimmers from the rough Atlantic surf on Grenada's far northern shore, this Levera National Park beach has changing rooms at the park headquarters. ✉ *Levera, St. Patrick.*

Fodor's Choice ★ **Grand Anse Beach**. In the southwest, about 3 mi (5 km) south of St. George's, Grenada's loveliest and most popular beach is a gleaming 2-mi (3-km) semicircle of white sand lapped by clear, gentle surf. Sea grape trees and coconut palms provide shady escapes from the sun. Brilliant rainbows frequently spill into the sea from the high green mountains that frame St. George's Harbour to the north. The Grand Anse Craft & Spice Market is at the midpoint of the beach. ✉ *Grand Anse, St. George.*

La Sagesse Beach. Along the southeast coast, at La Sagesse Nature Centre, this is a lovely, quiet refuge with a strip of powdery white sand. Plan a full day of nature walks, with lunch at the small inn adjacent to the beach. ✉ *La Sagesse, St. David.*

Morne Rouge Beach. One mile (1½ km) south of Grand Anse Bay, this ½-mi-long (¾-km-long) sheltered crescent has a gentle surf, excellent for swimming. Light meals are available nearby. ✉ *Morne Rouge, St. George.*

CARRIACOU

Anse La Roche. About a 15-minute hike from the village of Prospect, in the north, this beach has white sand, sparkling clear water, and abundant marine life for snorkelers. And it's never crowded. ✉ *Windward.*

Paradise Beach. This long, narrow stretch between Hillsborough and Tyrrel Bay has calm, clear, inviting water and a snack bar, but no changing facilities. ✉ *L'Esterre.*

Sandy Island. This is a truly deserted island off Hillsborough—just a ring of white sand with a few young palm trees. Arrange transportation from the jetty at Hillsborough or the restaurant at Paradise Beach for $25 to $30 (EC$70) round-trip. Bring your snorkeling gear and, if you want, a picnic. ✉ *Hillsborough Bay, Hillsborough.*

White Island. On this deserted island off Carriacou's southern coast, a beautiful white sandy beach and calm Caribbean waters await you, your snorkeling gear, and your picnic lunch. Arrange transportation from Belmont, on the south shore, for about $25 to $30 (EC$70) round-trip. ✉ *Manchineel Bay.*

9

ST. LUCIA

Don't come to St. Lucia for powdery-white sand; you won't find it, but the island has some of the best off-the-beach snorkeling in the Caribbean, especially in the southwest.

(this page above) Reduit Beach in Rodney Bay; (opposite page bottom) Anse des Pitons in Jalousie Bay; (opposite page top) Marigot Bay

St. Lucia's longest, broadest, and most popular beaches are in the north, which is also the flattest part of this mountainous island and the location of most resorts, restaurants, and nightlife. Most of the island's biggest resorts front one of the beaches in the Rodney Bay area north to Cap Estate. Elsewhere, tiny coves with inviting crescents of sand offer great swimming and snorkeling opportunities. Beaches are all public, but many along the northwest coast are flanked by hotels. A few secluded stretches of beach on the west coast south of Marigot Bay are accessible primarily by boat and are popular swimming and snorkeling stops on catamaran or powerboat sightseeing trips. Don't swim along the windward (east) coast; the Atlantic Ocean is too rough—but the views are spectacular. There's only one resort facing the Atlantic at this writing: the Coconut Bay Resort, which is next to Hewanorra Airport. Although it has a beautiful beach, the surf is really too rough for swimming.

GOLDEN SAND

Reduit Beach at Rodney Bay Village is considered St. Lucia's finest, with golden sand and lots of water sports. Farther south, tiny beaches have sand ranging in color from gold to gray, becoming darker as you head south, and one, magnificently located right between the Pitons, with imported white sand on top of the natural black. Marigot Bay, a little peninsula of golden sand studded with palm trees, is particularly lovely.

Anse Chastanet. In front of the resort of the same name, just north of the city of Soufrière, this palm-studded dark-sand beach has a backdrop of green hills, brightly painted fishing skiffs bobbing at anchor, and the island's best reefs for snorkeling and diving. The resort's gazebos are nestled among the palms; its dive shop, restaurant, and bar are on the beach and open to the public. ⊠ *1 mi (1½ km) north of Soufrière.*

Anse Cochon. This remote dark-sand beach is reached only by boat or via Ti Kaye Village's mile-long access road. The water and adjacent reef are superb for swimming, diving, and snorkeling. Moorings are free, and boaters can enjoy refreshments at Ti Kaye's beach bar. ⊠ *3 mi (5 km) south of Marigot Bay.*

Anse des Pitons (*Jalousie Beach*). The white sand on this crescent beach, snuggled between the Pitons, was imported and spread over the natural black sand. Accessible through the Jalousie Plantation resort property, which will be rebranded as The Tides at Sugar Beach in 2011, or by boat, the beach offers good snorkeling, diving, and breathtaking scenery. ⊠ *1 mi (1½ km) south of Soufrière.*

Marigot Beach (*Labas Beach*). Calm waters rippled only by passing yachts lap a sliver of sand studded with palm trees on the north side of Marigot Bay. The beach is accessible by a ferry that

operates continually from one side of the bay to the other, and you can find refreshments at adjacent restaurants. ⊠ *Marigot Bay.*

Pigeon Point. At this small beach within Pigeon Island National Park, on the northwestern tip of St. Lucia, a restaurant serves snacks and drinks, but this is also a perfect spot for picnicking. ⊠ *Pigeon Island.*

Fodor's Choice ★ **Reduit Beach.** This long stretch of golden sand frames Rodney Bay and is within walking distance of many hotels and restaurants in Rodney Bay Village. The Rex St. Lucian hotel, which faces the beach, has a watersports center, where you can rent sports equipment and beach chairs and take windsurfing or waterskiing lessons. Many feel that Reduit (pronounced red-wee) is the island's finest beach. ⊠ *Rodney Bay.*

Vigie Beach. This 2-mi (3-km) strand runs parallel to the George F. L. Charles Airport runway in Castries and continues on to become Malabar Beach, the beachfront in front of the Rendezvous resort. ⊠ *Castries, next to airport.*

9

ST. VINCENT AND THE GRENADINES

St. Vincent has a dramatic coastline with pretty coves, but its beaches, by and large, are not the primary reason to visit this interesting volcanic island. On the other hand, the Grenadines— all of them—boast some of the most stunning beaches you'll find in the Caribbean.

(this page above) A fence-through view of Friendship Bay, Bequia; (opposite page bottom) A sandbar in the Tobago Cays; (opposite page top) Macaroni Beach, Mustique

Although you'll find some of the most exclusive and expensive resorts in the Caribbean in the Grenadines, most of the island chain is relatively untouched and undeveloped. Many beaches on larger islands such as St. Vincent and Bequia are completely wild and rarely visited. Other beaches, such as the dozens of sugar-white sandy beaches on Mustique and those on Canouan, Palm Island and Petit St. Vincent, look as if they stepped right out of the pages of a fashion magazine photo shoot—and in some cases they have. But the Grenadines also include the chain of uninhabited, completely undeveloped islands known as the Tobago Cays, five islands that make up the Tobago Cays Marine Park, each with a pristine beach. Not all the beaches in the Grenadines are equally beautiful, but none is crowded.

VOLCANIC SAND

St. Vincent's origin is volcanic, so the sand on its beaches—the remnants of past volcanic eruptions— ranges in color from golden brown to black. On the windward coast, near Argyle, rolling surf breaks onto a broad expanse of black-sand beach—a beautiful view but dangerous for swimming. Indian Bay Beach has fairly light sand and is best for swimming.

ST. VINCENT

Aside from the beach on the private **Young Island,** all beaches on St. Vincent are public. **Indian Bay** is a popular bathing and snorkeling spot. **Villa Beach,** on the mainland opposite Young Island, is really more of a waterfront area than a beach. The strip of sand is sometimes so narrow it becomes nonexistent; nevertheless, boats bob at anchor in the channel, and dive shops, inns, and restaurants line the shore, making this an interesting place to be. On the windward coast, dramatic swaths of broad black sand are strewn with huge black boulders, but the water is rough and unpredictable. On the leeward coast, swimming is recommended only in the lagoons, rivers, and bays.

BEQUIA

Bequia has clean, uncrowded white-sand beaches. Some are a healthy trek by foot or a short water-taxi ride from the jetty at Port Elizabeth; others require land transportation.

CANOUAN

Though only 3½ mi long, Canouan faces a mile-long coral reef—one of the longer barrier reefs in the Caribbean—that offers excellent diving and snorkeling opportunities. In addition, the island also has four exquisite white-sand beaches. Two-thirds of the island is set aside for a luxury resort and golf club. Its proximity to several of the other Grenadines (Mayreau and the Tobago Cays in particular), make excursions to other beautiful beaches easy.

MAYREAU

Mayreau's primary beach, **Saltwhistle Bay,** is unique because on one side is the calm water of the Caribbean while on the other side is the more powerful Atlantic surf, and this narrow strip of white beach is all that separates them.

MUSTIQUE

For a relatively small island, Mustique has a large number of beautiful white-sand beaches at the foot of each of its lovely green valleys, perhaps one reason for its appeal to the private-jet set. Villas are strung out along the northern half of the island, but the best beach, picture-perfect **Macaroni Beach,** is on the south side.

PALM ISLAND

The beach on tiny Palm Island is beautiful, white, and powdery. Offshore, between Palm Island and its neighbor Petit St. Vincent is a sandbar with a single palapa that offers an isolated spot in mid-ocean for a beach picnic.

Word of Mouth. "Palm Island has the most beautiful water and beach. It provides enormous seclusion."—Knowing

PETIT ST. VINCENT

This tiny private resort has beautiful white-sand beaches on its western end; the sand there is particularly soft and

9

(this page above) Macaroni Bay, Mustique; (opposite page) A young sailor off Union Island

free of most rocks, but there's a drop-off. The beaches on the north shore, while beautiful, are fairly rocky. There's also a small, rocky beach on the south shore. Since the island is private, there are never any crowds.

TOBAGO CAYS

The five uninhabited Tobago Cays are known for their colorful reefs full of tropical fish and many green sea turtles, which can be spotted on almost any visit. Four of the five islands—Petit Rameau, Petit Bateau, Jamesby, and Baradal—are enclosed within Horseshoe Reef; the fifth, Petit Tabac, stands separate to the east. All of the islands have gorgeous white-sand beaches that are the most pristine in the Grenadines since they are completely unmarred by development (the Tobago Cays make up a marine sanctuary). A wreck just off the tip of Baradal offers good snorkeling. The cays are one of the top snorkeling destinations in the Caribbean.

Word of Mouth. "It was a great trip [to the Tobago Cays] . . . we swam with turtles and saw stingrays, blue tang, angelfish and lots of other smaller fish."—ChrisAroundtheWorld

UNION ISLAND

Although it's an important hub for travelers heading to some of the smaller islands in the Grenadines (especially the private retreats like Petit St. Vincent and Palm Island and also Mayreau, which does not have an airstrip), Union isn't a very popular destination in its own right. The hilly, volcanic island doesn't have beaches that compare in any way with those on its closest neighbors. The best beach, **Bigsand Beach,** is on the north shore, though, and has powdery white sand.

TRINIDAD AND TOBAGO

Trinidad and Tobago offer two completely different beach experiences. Tobago attracts thousands of international visitors with a choice of white or honey-colored beaches. Big sister Trinidad has a few good beaches on the north coast and sightseeing on the island's east coast.

(this page above) Sarongs for sale on Turtle Beach, Tobago; (opposite page bottom) Manzanilla Beach, Trinidad; (opposite page top) A lifeguard tower at Maracas Bay, Trinidad

Trinidad has some good beaches for swimming and sunning, though none as picture-perfect as those in Tobago. Although popular with some locals, the beaches of the western peninsula (such as Maqueripe) are not particularly attractive, and the water in this area is often polluted by sewage. All beaches on Trinidad are free and open to the public. Many locals are fond of playing loud music wherever they go, and even the most serene beach may suddenly turn into a seaside disco.

You won't find manicured country-club sand in Tobago. But those who enjoy feeling as though they've landed on a desert island will relish the untouched quality of these shores.

BAKE AND SHARK

Maracas Bay in Trinidad is famous for its bake and shark (about $5), a deep-fried piece of shark stuffed into fried batter. To this, you can add any of dozens of toppings, such as tamarind sauce and coleslaw. There are dozens of beach huts serving the specialty, as well as stands in the nearby parking lot (Richard's is by far the most popular).

TRINIDAD

Balandra Bay. On the northeast coast, the beige-sand beach—popular with locals on weekends—is sheltered by a rocky outcropping and is a favorite of body-surfers. Much of this beach is suitable for swimming. The noise level on weekends can be a problem for those seeking solace. Take the Toco Main Road from the Valencia Road, and turn off at the signs indicating Balandra (just after Salybia). ✉ *Off Valencia Rd. near Salybia.*

Blanchisseuse Bay. On North Coast Road you can find this narrow, palm-fringed beach. Facilities are nonexistent, but it's an ideal spot for a romantic picnic. A lagoon and river at the east end of the beach allow you to swim in freshwater, but beware of floating logs in the river, as they sometimes contain mites that can cause a body rash (called *bete rouge* locally). You can haggle with local fishermen to take you out in their boats to explore the coast. This beach is about 14 mi (23 km) after Maracas; just keep driving along the road until you pass the Arima turnoff. The coastal and rain-forest views here are spectacular. ✉ *North Coast Rd. just beyond Arima turnoff.*

Grande Riviere. On Trinidad's rugged northeast coast, Grande Riviere is well worth the drive. Swimming is good, and there are several guesthouses nearby for refreshments, but the main attractions here are turtles. Every year up to 500 giant leatherback turtles come onto the beach to lay their eggs. If you're here at night, run your hand through the black sand to make it glow—a phenomenon caused by plankton. ✉ *Toco Main Rd. at end of road.*

Las Cuevas Bay. This narrow, picturesque strip on North Coast Road is named for the series of partially submerged and explorable caves that ring the beach. A food stand offers tasty snacks, and vendors hawk fresh fruit across the road. You can also buy fresh fish and lobster from the fishing depot near the beach. You have to park your car in the small parking lot and walk down a few steps to get to the beach, so be sure to take everything from the car (which is out of sight once you are on the beach). There are basic changing and toilet facilities. It's less crowded here than at nearby **Maracas Bay** and seemingly serene, although, as at Maracas, the current can be treacherous. ✉ *North Coast Rd., 7 mi (11 km) east of Maracas Bay.*

Manzanilla Beach. You can find picnic facilities and a pretty view of the Atlantic here, though the water is occasionally muddied by Venezuela's Orinoco River. The Cocal Road running the length of this beautiful beach is lined with stately palms, whose fronds vault like the arches at Chartres. This is where many well-heeled Trinis have vacation homes. The Nariva River, which enters the sea just south of this beach and the

9

(opposite page) Trutle Beach, Tobago (this page) Pigeon Point, Tobago

surrounding Nariva Swamp, is home to the protected manatee and many other rare species, including the much-maligned anaconda. To get to this beach take the Mayaro turnoff at the town of Sangre Grande. Manzanilla is where this road first meets the coast. ⊠ *Southeast of Sangre Grande.*

Maracas Bay. This long stretch of sand has a cove and a fishing village at one end. It's *the* local favorite, so it can get crowded on weekends. Lifeguards will guide you away from strong currents. Parking sites are ample, and there are snack bars (selling the famous bake and shark) and restrooms. Take the winding North Coast Road from Maraval (it intersects with Long Circular Road right next to KFC Maraval) over the Northern Range; the beach is about 7 mi (11 km) from Maraval. ⊠ *North Coast Rd.*

Salibea Bay *(Salybia Bay).* This gentle beach has shallows and plenty of shade—perfect for swimming. Snack vendors abound in the vicinity. Like many of the beaches on the northeast coast, this one is packed with people and music trucks blaring soca and reggae on weekends. It's off the Toco Main

Road, just after the town of Matura. ⊠ *Off Toco Main Rd. south of Toco.*

TOBAGO

Bacolet Beach. This dark-sand beach was the setting for the films *Swiss Family Robinson* and *Heaven Knows, Mr. Allison.* Though used by the Blue Haven Hotel, like all local beaches it's open to the public. If you are not a guest at the hotel, access to the beach is down a track next door to the hotel. The bathroom and changing facilities on the beach are for hotel guests only. ⊠ *Windward Rd. east of Scarborough.*

Great Courland Bay. Near Ft. Bennett, the bay has clear, tranquil waters. Along the sandy beach—one of Tobago's longest—you can find several glitzy hotels. A marina attracts the yachting crowd. ⊠ *Leeward Rd. northeast of Black Rock, Courland.*

King's Bay. Surrounded by steep green hills, this is the most visually satisfying of the swimming sites off the road from Scarborough to Speyside—the bay hooks around so severely, you can feel like you're in a lake. The crescent-shape beach is easy to find because it's marked by a sign about halfway between the two towns. Just before you reach the bay, there's a bridge with an unmarked turnoff that leads to a gravel parking lot; beyond that, a landscaped path leads to a waterfall with a rocky pool. You'll likely meet locals who can offer to guide you to the top of the falls; however, you may find the climb not worth the effort. ⊠ *Delaford.*

Lovers Beach. So called because of its pink sand and its seclusion—you have to hire a local to bring you here by boat—it's an isolated and quiet retreat. Ask one of the fishermen in Charlotteville to arrange a ride for you, but be sure to haggle. It should cost you no more than $25 a person for a return ride (considerably less sometimes). ⊠ *North coast, reachable only by boat from Charlotteville.*

Mt. Irvine Beach. Across the street from the Mt. Irvine Bay Hotel is this unremarkable beach, but it has great surfing in July and August; the snorkeling is excellent, too. It's also ideal for windsurfing in January and April. There are picnic tables surrounded by painted concrete pagodas, and there's a snack bar. ⊠ *Shirvan Rd., Mt. Irvine.*

Parlatuvier. On the north side of the island, the beach is best approached via the road from Roxborough. It's a classic Caribbean crescent, a scene peopled by villagers and fishermen. ⊠ *Parlatuvier.*

Pigeon Point Beach. This stunning locale is often displayed on Tobago travel brochures. The white-sand beach is lined with swaying coconut trees, and there are changing facilities and food stalls nearby. Although the beach is public, it abuts part of what was once a large coconut estate, and you must pay a token admission (about TT$18) to enter the grounds and use the facilities. ⊠ *Pigeon Point.*

Sandy Point Beach. Situated at the end of the Crown Point Airport runway, this beach is abutted by several hotels, so you won't lack for amenities around

here. The beach is accessible by walking around the airport fence to the hotel area. ⊠ *At Crown Point Airport.*

Stone Haven Bay. A gorgeous stretch of sand is across the street from the Grafton Beach Resort. ⊠ *Shirvan Rd., Black Rock.*

Store Bay. The beach, where boats depart for Buccoo Reef, is little more than a small sandy cove between two rocky breakwaters, but the food stands here are divine: several huts licensed by the tourist board to local ladies who sell roti, *pelau* (meat stewed in coconut milk with peas and rice), and the world's messiest dish—crab and dumplings. Near the airport, just walk around the Crown Point Hotel to the beach entrance. ⊠ *Crown Point.*

Turtle Beach. Named for the leatherback turtles that lay their eggs here at night between February and June, it's on Great Courland Bay. (If you're very quiet, you can watch; the turtles don't seem to mind.) It's 8 mi (13 km) from the airport between Black Rock and Plymouth. ⊠ *Southern end of Great Courland Bay between Black Rock and Plymouth.*

9

CARNIVAL IN TRINIDAD

Vernon O'Reilly Ramesar

The "Greatest Show on Earth" is also the best party in the Caribbean, and it's not brought to you by Barnum & Bailey but by the people of Trinidad. The island's pre-Lenten Carnival is rooted in Trinidad's African and French-Creole cultures and is more spontaneous than similar celebrations in Latin America; its influence reaches as far as Miami, Toronto, and London.

Trinidad's celebration has evolved through the years. What was once a two-day affair has turned into a lengthy party season starting in early January and lasting until Ash Wednesday. The biggest and best parties are held in and around Port of Spain, where locals max out their credit cards and even take out bank loans to finance their costumes and attend as many parties as possible.

On Carnival Monday and Tuesday the traffic lights of Port of Spain are turned off and the streets are turned over to a human traffic jam of costumed revelers.

They jump and dance to the pounding sound of music trucks—featuring huge speakers and either live music or a DJ—and turn Port of Spain into a pulsing celebration of island life that they call the *mas*.

Mas bands—some with thousands of members, others with a mere handful—must follow a route and pass judging points to win a prize, but increasingly, they simply don't bother. They're in it for the fun. To grease the wheels, makeshift bars are set up along all the city's streets.

(opposite) Carnival in Trinidad brings out colorful costumes, (top) Children stiltwalkers in colorful Carnival costumes, Queens Park Savannah, Port of Spain.

CARNIVAL 101

THE FETE

Huge outdoor parties (called *fêtes*) are held in the months before Carnival; during the final week, there are usually several fêtes every day. You can get tickets for many of them through the major hotels, but some exclusive fêtes may require an invitation from a well-connected Trinidadian.

THE PANORAMA

While fêtes are important to Carnival, the Panorama Steelpan Preliminaries and finals are essential. Two weeks before Carnival, the "Prelims" are held, when dozens of steel drum orchestras compete for a place in the finals held on Carnival Saturday. Music lovers go to hear the throbbing sound of hundreds of steelpans beating out a syncopated rhythm, and the rum-fueled party often rivals even the best fêtes.

DIMANCHE GRAS

On Carnival Sunday, top calypsonians compete to be Calypso Monarch, and this offers you an especially good opportunity to experience Carnival in one easy shot. The show was once held in Queen's Park Savannah, but the location now varies.

THE COSTUMES

To be a true part of Carnival, you need a costume. Every mas band has its own costumes, which must be reserved months in advance (these days online). You pick up yours at the band's mas "camp" and find out where and when to meet your band. Then all you have to do is jump, walk, or wave in the Carnival procession as the spirit moves you. Drinks and food may be included.

(top) Trinidad Carnival celebrations during Junior Parade of the Bands, (bottom) masquerader in a colorful costume.

MUSIC

Carnival is powered by music, and though the steelpan still plays a big part, it is the *soca* performers who draw the biggest crowds. Some of the big names include Machel Montano, Shurwayne Winchester, and Allyson Hinds. You can hear the most popular performers at the bigger fêtes and at the Soca Monarch competition held on Carnival Friday before the more prestigious Calypso Monarch contest.

THE MAS BANDS

Trinis are passionate about their favorite mas band. The most popular have costumes largely comprised of beaded bikinis and feathered headdresses and are called "pretty mas." Very large bands such as Tribe, Island People, and Hart's fall into this category. If you're not willing to show that much skin or want more theater, then choose a band like MacFarlane, which offers more elaborate costumes with a thematic story. As has always been the case, women greatly outnumber men in the bands.

Carnival costumes are usually colorful—and skimpy.

TOP FÊTES

Safety is an increasing concern in Trinidad, especially at Carnival time. Fêtes that attract a better heeled crowd offer more security and sufficient bars to cater to the thousands of revelers who attend. They usually command higher prices but are worth the cost.

Kama Sutra is held at the Trinidad Country Club on the Saturday before Carnival weekend. It is all-inclusive and features a good selection of food and premium drinks.

Eyes Wide Shut is held at The Oval (home of Trinidad cricket) and tends to attract a younger crowd.

Insomnia is an overnight fete held in Chaguaramas, just West of Port of Spain, on Carnival Saturday, and the partying doesn't stop till sunrise.

The Brian Lara and Moka all-inclusive fêtes are both held on the afternoon of Carnival Sunday. Tickets for both are highly sought. Brian Lara is considered the most exclusive of all fêtes and is the most expensive.

Best Beaches in Mexico

WHAT'S WHERE

1 Oaxaca Coast. The coast is fairly remote, and it is strikingly exquisite. Puerto Escondido is surfer territory, though fancier digs are starting to pop up. Bahías de Huatulco is mostly a nature reserve, though the government is trying to transform the rest of the Oaxaca coast into another Cancún. Midway between the two are a few tiny beach villages, including the up-and-coming paradises of Zipolite, Mazunte, and San Agustinillo.

2 Los Cabos. There are two Bajas, literally and figuratively. Baja Norte is still slightly rugged, with boulder-strewn deserts, mountain ranges, and long beaches. Baja Sur has Los Cabos and expensive spa-resorts and the best beaches.

3 Puerto Vallarta. Ever-popular Puerto Vallarta (PV) fronts the big, blue Bahía de Banderas and is backed by foothills covered in tropical forest. Ecotour opportunities abound, but most people come to party—outside of Acapulco, PV has the coast's most sophisticated nightlife.

4 Pacific Coast Resorts. North of Puerto Vallarta is Mazatlán, a former spring-break spot that now attracts families and retirees. South of PV are miles of untouched beaches reached by dirt roads and linked by the port town of Manzanillo and the twin resorts of Ixtapa and Zihuatanejo.

5 Acapulco. This city has many draws: an undeniably gorgeous bay, great restaurants, sizzling nightlife.

6 Cancún. The "7"-shape barrier island is blessed on both sides by soft white sands. Cancún's beachfront high-rises offer loads of creature comforts and nonstop water sports; hotels inland are more reasonably priced and let you enjoy a more authentic Mexican experience.

7 Cozumel. The island is hugely popular with divers and snorkelers, who come to admire the underwater reefs and abundant fish. Onshore, beaches are not quite as nice as those in Cancún, but the island is much mellower (at least when cruise ships are not in port).

8 The Riviera Maya. The dazzling white sands and glittering blue-green waters of the Riviera Maya beckon to sun worshippers and spa-goers as well as snorkelers, divers, and bird-watchers. Although sugary beaches are the principal draw here, the seaside ruins of Tulum, jungle-clad pyramids at Cobá, and several other Mayan sites are all nearby.

San Diego
CA
AZ
3
5
1
2
15
Hermosillo
15
Golfo de California
1   La Paz
2   San José del Cabo
LOS CABOS
Cabo San Lucas

P A C I F I C

THE OAXACA COAST

Oaxaca's 520-km (322-mi) coastline is one of Mexico's last Pacific frontiers. It's the least explored and least developed shoreline in the country. Friendly locals, superb vistas, and first-rate beaches combine to make Oaxaca's coast a stunner.

(this page above) Puerto Angel; (opposite page upper right) Playa Mazunte, Zipolite; (opposite page lower left) Lifeguard tower, Puerto Escondido

No matter where you hole up along Mexico's southern Pacific Coast, you'll find that it's all about the beach, the water, and the waves. Surfers and bodysurfers whoop it up at famous and less famous breaks; snorkelers hug rocky coves in search of unusual specimens; and divers share the depths with dolphins, rays, eels, and schools of fish instead of shoals of other humans. The town of Puerto Escondido has long been prime territory for international surfers. Tiny Puerto Angel has a limited selection of unpolished hotels and funky bungalows tucked into the hills. The Huatulco area covers 51,900 acres, 40,000 of which are dedicated as a nature reserve, and has the most development. Its string of nine sheltered bays stretch across 35 km (22 mi) of stunning coast.

TURTLES

The local economy in much of coastal Oaxaca (where four species of turtles lay their eggs) was based on catching the *golfina* (olive ridley) turtle until the government put a ban on turtle hunting in 1990. The **Centro Mexicano de la Tortuga** (⊠ *Carretera Puerto Angel–San Antonio Mazunte Km 10, Zipolite*) is now devoted to protecting the species and teaching about turtles.

PUERTO ESCONDIDO

Playa Carrizalillo. In a region full of beautiful beaches, Playa Carrizalillo can still take your breath away. The high cliffs that surround it ensure that it's never too crowded. The aquamarine water here is clean, clear, and shallow—perfect for swimming and snorkeling, especially around the rocks that frame the beautiful cove. It's a 2-minute drive or 35-minute walk from the center of town.

Playa Manzanillo. Of Puerto Escondido's seven beaches, Playa Manzanillo is one of the safest for swimming. It's also one of the best for snorkeling, with a sandy ocean floor, some rock and coral formations, and calm, clear water. You can reach this beach on foot (a 15-minute walk west of town), by taxi (less than $2 per ride), or by boat ($3 per person one-way) from **Playa Marinero.**

Playa Zicatela. One of the world's top surfing beaches, Zicatela has cream-color sand that is battered by the mighty Mexican Pipeline. In the third week of November, international surfing championships are held here. But the beach is just about always filled with sun-bleached aficionados of serious surfing.

ZIPOLITE

Playa Mazunte. Eight kilometers (5 mi) west of Zipolite, Mazunte is a stunning stretch of soft sand with a few simple seafood restaurants and low-key accommodations (though there are fewer

than at Zipolite). The surf is rough and attracts body boarders.

PUERTO ANGEL

Playa La Boquilla. About 2 km (1½ mi) east of Puerto Angel, 400-foot-long La Boquilla can be reached by a dirt road from Highway 200, but it's better to come by boat from Puerto Angel. The ride is about 20 minutes. Shallow and clear water make this a good spot for snorkeling as well as swimming.

HUATULCO

Bahía Santa Cruz. This bay was once home to a 30-family fishing community until development forced everyone to move elsewhere. Today the bay is a nice spot for swimming and snorkeling, although Jet Skis make a lot of noise on busy weekends and holidays.

Bahía Tangolunda. The Huatulco of the future is most evident here, where the poshest hotels are in full swing and the sea—in high season—is abob with sightseeing *lanchas* (small motorboats), kayaks, and sailboats.

Playa Entrega. If you're looking for the best fishing and water sports in the area, head to this beach, west of Bahía Santa Cruz, where dozens of fishermen aren't shy about offering their services from the moment you set foot in the sand. It's a great place to go out on a fishing boat in the early morning; snorkeling and kayaking are also options.

10

LOS CABOS

Along the rocky cliffs of the Pacific Ocean and the Sea of Cortez lie many bays, coves, and some 50-odd mi (80-odd km) of sandy beaches with waters from translucent green to deep navy.

(this page above) Lover's Beach; (opposite page upper right) Playa Palmilla; (opposite page lower left) Bahía Santa Maria

Playa Médano, in Cabo San Lucas, is the most visited and active stretch of sand. Gorgeous and somewhat secluded, but by no means free of people, Playa del Amor (Lover's Beach) is five minutes across the bay by speedboat. Just southwest of San José, the most popular beaches are Costa Azul and Playa Palmilla. Most beaches in the area are seldom crowded, with the one major exception being the 2-mi (3-km) Playa Médano in Cabo San Lucas. No other beaches are within walking distance of either Cabo San Lucas or San José del Cabo; some can be accessed by boat, but most require a car ride (unless you're staying at a Corridor hotel nearby). You can reach nearly all the beaches by bus, which is safe and affordable, but it takes time and requires you to take along extra water, especially in the searing summer months.

GOLF

Los Cabos has become one of the world's top golf destinations, with championship courses that combine lush greens and desert terrain. Greens fees are exorbitant—more than $350 in winter and $220 in summer. But the courses themselves are spectacular and very busy. One of the best courses is the 27-hole Jack Nicklaus–designed course at the One & Only Hotel Palmilla.

CABO SAN LUCAS

Playa del Amor. Lovers have little chance of finding romantic solitude at Lover's Beach, reachable by water taxi or kayak. The azure cove on the Sea of Cortez at the tip of the peninsula may well be the area's most frequently photographed patch of sand. It's a must-see on every first-timer's list. Seals hang out on the rocks at the base of the arch. Walk along the sand to the Pacific side to see pounding white surf; just don't dive in.

Playa Médano. Foamy plumes of water shoot from Jet Skis and WaveRunners buzzing through the water off Médano, a 2-mi (3-km) span of grainy tan sand that's always crowded. When cruise ships are in town it's mobbed. Swimming areas are roped off to prevent accidents, and the water is calm enough for toddlers.

THE CORRIDOR

Bahía Chileno. A private enclave with golf courses and residences is being developed at Bahía Chileno, roughly midway between San José and San Lucas. The beach skirts a small cove with aquamarine waters that are perfect for snorkeling.

Bahía Santa María. Sometimes it feels like the vultures overhead are just waiting for your parched body to drop during the 10-minute walk from the parking lot to Bahía Santa María, a turquoise bay backed by cliffs and lined by a wide, sloping beach. Shade is nonexistent except in the shadows at the base of the cliffs. The bay, part of an underwater reserve, is a great place to snorkel: brightly colored fish swarm through chunks of white coral and golden sea fans.

Playa Costa Azul. Cabo's best surfing beach runs 2 mi (3 km) south from San José's hotel zone along Highway 1. Its Zippers and La Roca breaks (the point where the wave crests and breaks) are world famous. Surfers gather here year-round, but most come in summer, when waves are largest. Swimming isn't advised unless the waves are small and you're a good swimmer.

Playa Palmilla. This is the best swimming beach near San José. The entrance is from the side road through the ritzy Palmilla development; turn off before you reach the guardhouse at the star-studded One & Only Hotel Palmilla. The beach is protected by a grouping of rocks, and the water is almost always calm.

LA PAZ

Playa Balandra. A rocky point shelters a clear, warm bay at Playa Balandra, 13 mi (21 km) north of La Paz. Several small coves and pristine beaches appear and disappear with the tides, but there's always a calm area where you can wade and swim. Snorkeling is fair around Balandra's south end where there's a coral reef.

10

A WHALE'S TALE by Kelly Lack and Larry Dunmire

Seeing the gray whales off Baja's western coast needs to be on your list of things to do before you die. "But I've *gone* whale watching," you say. Chances are, though, that you were in a big boat and might have spotted the flip of a tail 100 yards out. In Baja your vessel will be a tiny panga, smaller than the whales themselves; they'll swim up, mamas with their babies, coming so close that you can smell the fishiness of their spouts.

(opposite) Baja California, a humpback whale in the Sea of Cortez, (top) Gray whales, Guerrero Negro.

WHEN TO GO

Gray whales and tourists both head south to Baja around December—the whales in pods, the snowbirds in RV caravans—staying put through to April to shake off the chill of winter. So the beaches, hotels, restaurants, and bars during whale-watching season will be bustling. Book your room five to six months ahead to ensure a place to stay. The intense experience that awaits you at Magdalena Bay, San Ignacio, or Scammion's Lagoon is worth traveling in high season.

Though the average life span of a gray whale is 50 years, one individual was reported to reach 77 years of age—a real old-timer.

THE GRAY WHALE:
Migrating Leviathan

Yearly, gray whales endure the longest migration of any mammal on earth—some travel 5,000 miles one way between their feeding grounds in Alaska's frigid Bering Sea and their mating/birthing lagoons in sunny Baja California. The whales are bottom-feeders, unique among cetaceans, and stir up sediment on the sea floor, then use their baleen—long, stiff plates covered with hair-like fibers inside their mouths—to filter out the sediment and trap small marine creatures such as crustaceanlike Gammarid amphipods.

DID YOU KNOW?

Gray whales' easygoing demeanor and predilection for near-shore regions makes for frequent, friendly human/whale interactions. Whalers, however, would disagree. They dubbed mother grays "devilfish" for the fierce manner in which they protect their young.

WHALE ADVENTURES

Cabo Expeditions (*www.caboexpeditions. com.mx*) was the first with whale watching tours more than a dozen years ago. The staff is well-trained, and owner Oscar Ortiz believes not only in seeing the whales, but also saving them. Last year his Zodiacs rescued two grays from entanglement in giant fishing nets. Boats depart from the Cabo San Lucas Marina, near Dock M.

You've seen whales, but how about swimming with them? **Baja AirVentures** (*www. bajaairventures.com*) arranges weeklong trips to Bahia de los Angeles where you can swim with whale sharks daily. (Don't worry—the toothless plankton eaters are much more like whales than sharks.)

You fly from San Diego to the secluded Sea of Cortez fishing village, then take pangas out to Las Animas Wilderness Lodge, where you stay in spacious, comfortable yurts.

WHALE NURSERIES: THE BEST SPOTS FOR VIEWING

If you want an up-close encounter, head to one of these three protected spots where the whales gather to mate or give birth; the lagoons are like training wheels to prep the youngsters for the open ocean.

Laguna Ojo de Liebre (Scammon's Lagoon). Near Guerrero Negro, this lagoon is an L-shaped cut out of Baja's landmass, protected to the west by the jut of a peninsula.

Laguna San Ignacio. To reach the San Ignacio Lagoon, farther south than Scammon's, base yourself in the charming town of San Ignacio, 35 miles away. This lagoon is the smallest of the three, and along with Scammon's, has been designated a U.N. World Heritage site.

Bahía de Magdalena. This stretch of ocean, the farthest south, is kept calm by small, low-lying islands (really just humps of sand) that take the brunt of the ocean's waves. Very few people overnight in nearby San Carlos; most day-trip in from La Paz or Loreto.

WHAT TO EXPECT

The experience at the three lagoons is pretty standard: tours push off in the mornings, in *pangas* (tiny, low-lying skiffs) that seat about eight. Wear a water-resistant windbreaker—it will be a little chilly, and you're bound to be splashed once or twice.

The captain will drive around slowly, cutting the motor if he nears a whale (they'll never chase whales). Often the whales will approach you, sometimes showing off their babies. They'll gently nudge the boat, at times sinking completely under it and then raising it up a bit to get a good, long scratch.

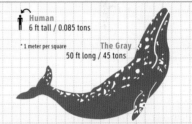

Human
6 ft tall / 0.085 tons

* 1 meter per square

The Gray
50 ft long / 45 tons

Baja whale watching, gray whale

IN FOCUS A WHALE'S TALE

10

PUERTO VALLARTA

Puerto Vallarta sits smack dab at the center of a 26-mi-long (42-km-long) bay, Bahía de Banderas (Banderas, or Flags, Bay), Mexico's largest. The city and region have many popular beaches that have drawn tourists since the 1950s.

(this page above) Playa de Sayulita; (opposite page upper right, and opposite page lower left) Playa Mismaloya

Though tropical, the waters around PV are not as clear as those around the Yucatán Peninsula. Its Zona Romántica borders Los Muertos Beach and has the most restaurants and shops. Part of what's now called the Riviera Nayarit, the beach towns north of Nuevo Vallarta are steadily gaining in popularity and tourist infrastructure. Once the private stomping grounds of local fishermen and surfers, Punta de Mita is now a super-exclusive gated community, but a sliver of paradise is still accessible to the hoi polloi. Bucerías, Sayulita, and other small communities are attracting more and more travelers while retaining their small-town appeal. South of PV to Mismaloya, the condos and hotels of the Zona Hotelera Sur straddle the beach or overlook it from cliff-side aeries.

LOS ARCOS

Protected area Los Arcos is an offshore group of giant rocks rising some 65 feet above the water, making the area great for snorkeling and diving. For reasonable fees, local men along the road to Mismaloya Beach run diving, snorkeling, fishing, and boat trips here and as far north as Punta Mita and Las Marietas or the beach villages of Cabo Corrientes.

PUERTO VALLARTA

Playa los Muertos. PV's original happenin' beach isn't particularly stunning, but it is engaging. Facing Vallarta's South Side (south of the Río Cuale), this flat beach hugs the Zona Romántica. The surf ranges from mild to choppy with an undertow.

NAYARIT

Bucerías. Five miles (8 km) north of Nuevo Vallarta, the substantial town of Bucerías attracts flocks of snowbirds. The beach here is endless: you could easily walk along its medium-coarse beige sands all the way south to Nuevo Vallarta. The surf is gentle enough for swimming but also has body-surfable waves, and beginning surfers occasionally arrive with their longboards.

El Anclote. The most accessible beach at Punta Mita is considered to be surf central. Just a few minutes past the gated entrance to the tony Four Seasons and St. Regis hotels, the popular beach has a string of restaurants and is a primo spot for viewing a sunset. It's also a good spot for children and average to not-strong swimmers.

Playa de Sayulita. The increasingly popular town and beach of Sayulita is about 45 minutes north of PV on Carretera 200. Despite the growth, this small town is still laid-back and retains its surfer-friendly vibe. Fringed in lanky palms, Sayulita's heavenly beach curves along

its small bay. A decent shore break here is good for beginning or novice surfers.

SOUTH OF PUERTO VALLARTA

Playa Conchas Chinas. Frequented mainly by visitors staying in the area, this beach is a series of rocky coves with crystal-line water. Millions of tiny white shells, broken and polished by the waves, form the sand while rock formations separate one patch of beach from the next. These individual coves are perfect for reclusive sunbathing and, when the surf is mild, for snorkeling.

Playa las Ánimas. There's lots to do besides sunbathe at this beach and town 15 minutes south of Boca de Tomatlán. Framing the ½-mi-long (1-km-long) beach are piles of smooth, strange rocks. Because of its very shallow waters, it tends to fill up with families on weekends and holidays.

Playa Mismaloya. Despite some hurricane damage and development, this beach retains a certain cachet. Sun-seekers kick back in wooden beach chairs, waiters serve up food and drink on the sand, massage techs offer their (so-so) services alfresco.

Yelapa. This secluded village and ¼-mi-long (½-km-long) beach is about an hour southeast of downtown PV and a half hour from Boca de Tomatlán—by boat, of course. The clean, grainy beach slopes down to the water, and small waves break right on the shore.

10

PACIFIC COAST RESORTS

Mexico's Pacific Coast is 1,000 mi (1,609 km) of lovely real estate that spans no fewer than six states. Though there are four major resorts, the region still has miles of deserted beaches.

(this page above) Cliff diver in Mazatlán; (opposite page upper right) Fishing Boat, Ixtapa; (opposite page lower left) Playa Las Gatas

The so-called "Mexican Riviera" along the Pacific Ocean has four developed resort areas: Mazatlán, Puerto Vallarta, Manzanillo, and Ixtapa/Zihuatanejo. At the northern end is Mazatlán, about 750 mi (1,207 km) from the U.S. border; at the southern end is Zihuatanejo, 152 mi (245 km) north of Acapulco. Puerto Vallarta is more or less in the middle. Many are content to party in Mazatlán's highly developed hotel zone (Zona Dorada); the beaches here aren't the best, but there's some decent snorkeling. The twin bays of Manzanillo and Santiago—collectively called Manzanillo—are popular with Mexican families and snowbirds; sailfishing is a big sport here, and in-town beaches are nice. Both Ixtapa and Zihuatanejo have lovely bays and beaches. But Ixta, a resort created by the Mexican government, has less personality than Zihua—a more authentic place. Cruise ships ply these waters with great frequency, so beaches can be especially busy depending on which ships are in port.

FISHING

Anglers revel in the profusion of sailfish (November through March), black and blue marlin (May through January), yellowfin tuna (November through June), and mahimahi (November through January). Light-tackle fishing in the lagoons and just off the beach for *huachinango* (red snapper) is also popular. Fishing outfitters abound in all the resort destinations along the Pacific Coast.

MAZATLÁN

Playa Camarón Sábalo. This beach is just north of Playa las Gaviotas on the map but a couple of notches lower on the energy scale. Although hotels and sports concessions back both stretches, there's more room to spread out on this beach. It's also well protected from heavy surf.

Playa Isla de la Piedra. Stone Island is really a long peninsula and has 10 mi (16 km) of unspoiled sand fronting a coconut plantation and an adjacent village. There's plenty of space, but the northern end is most popular.

Playa Isla de los Venados. It's a 20-minute boat ride to Deer Island from Mazatlán. The beach is lovely and clean. Small, secluded coves offer the best snorkeling.

MANZANILLO

Playa la Audiencia. On the west side of the Península de Santiago, below the Gran Costa Real Resort & Spa and between two rock outcroppings, Playa la Audiencia is small but inviting, with calm water. This is a good spot for snorkeling, and it has several good dive spots as well.

Playa la Boquita. A little corner of serenity at the far west end of Bahía de Santiago, this beach offers the shade of palm-frond palapas, where you can order seafood or iced coconuts from the informal restaurants. The calm water is

Manzanillo's safest for kids, perfect for swimming and snorkeling, and an offshore wreck is a good spot for diving.

IXTAPA

Isla Ixtapa. The most popular spot on Isla Ixtapa (and the one closest to the boat dock) is **Playa Cuachalalate.** An excellent swimming beach, it was named for a local tree. A short walk across the island, **Playa Varadero** hugs a rocky cove. Just behind is **Playa Coral**, whose calmer, crystal-clear water is more conducive to swimming.

ZIHUATANEJO

Playa la Ropa. The area's most magnificent beach is a 20-minute walk from Playa la Madera and a five-minute taxi ride from town. Up and down the beach are open-air restaurants—some with hammocks for post-meal siestas—and a handful of hotels. Kids can splash in the calm, aquamarine water or play on the shore—but the little stream at the southern end is a crocodile refuge!

Playa las Gatas. Named for the *gatas* (nurse sharks) that once lingered here, this beach is bordered by a long breakwater. Snorkelers scope out the rocky coves, and surfers spring to life with the arrival of small but fun summer swells. The beach is lined with simple seafood eateries that provide lounge chairs for sunning, as well as kayak and snorkeling-gear rentals, and guiding services.

10

ACAPULCO

Acapulco is the world's largest U-shape outdoor amphitheater, and the Bahía de Acapulco is center stage. East of Acapulco Bay, Acapulco Diamante includes the smaller bay of Puerto Marqués and the long wide beaches of Revolcadero.

(this page above) Bahía de Acapulco; (opposite page upper right) Pie de la Cuesta; (opposite page lower left) Playa Caletilla

The city of Acapulco is on the Pacific Coast 268 mi (433 km) south of Mexico City. Warm water, nearly constant sunshine, and balmy year-round temperatures let you plan your day around the beach—whether you want to lounge in a hammock or go snorkeling, parasailing, fishing, or waterskiing. Attractions to lure you away from the sands include crafts markets, cultural institutions, and the amazing cliff divers at La Quebrada. In the past few years city officials made a great effort to clean up the Bahía de Acapulco, and maintaining it is a priority. Vending on the beach has been outlawed, but you'll probably still be approached. In Acapulco Bay watch for a strong shore break that can knock you off your feet in knee-deep water. It is wise to observe the waves for a few minutes before entering the water.

SAFETY FIRST

Acapulco Bay is fairly well protected from the rough Pacific surf, but steep offshore drop-offs can produce waves large enough to knock you off your feet. Some beaches, mostly those outside the bay such as Revolcadero and Pie de la Cuesta, have a strong surf and some have a rip current, so be careful.

PIE DE LA CUESTA

This quiet spot is about a 25-minute drive west of downtown. The bus runs every 15 minutes past the zocalo along the Costera, the last one at 8 PM. Simple, thatch-roof restaurants and small, rustic inns border the wide beach, with straw palapas providing shade. What attracts people to **Pie de la Cuesta**, besides the long expanse of beach and spectacular sunsets, is excellent **Laguna Coyuca**, a favorite spot for waterskiing, freshwater fishing, and boat rides.

PLAYA CALETA

On the southern peninsula in Old Acapulco, this beach and smaller **Playa Caletilla** (Little Caleta) to the south once rivaled **La Quebrada** as the main tourist area, and were quite popular with the early Hollywood crowd. Today their snug little bays and calm waters make them a favorite with Mexican families. Caleta has the Mágico Mundo Marino entertainment center for children and a large seafood restaurant. Small family-run restaurants serve good, cheap food. On both beaches vendors sell everything from seashells to peeled mangos; boats depart from both to Isla de Roqueta.

PLAYA CONDESA

Referred to as "the Strip," **Playa Condesa**, which faces the middle of Bahía de Acapulco, has more than its share of visitors, especially singles. It's lined with lively restaurants and rockin' bars.

PLAYA HORNITOS

Running from the Avalon Excalibur west to Las Hamacas, **Playa Hornitos** (Little Hornos) and adjacent **Playa Hornos** are shoulder-to-shoulder with locals and visitors on weekends. Graceful palms shade the sand, and there are scads of casual eateries on the beach, especially on Playa Hornos. A slice of Playa Hornos and Playa Hornitos marks the beginning of the hotel zone to the east. The swimming is generally really safe in this area.

PLAYA ICACOS

Stretching from the naval base to El Presidente hotel, away from the famous Strip, **Playa Icacos** is less populated than others on the Costera. The morning surf is especially calm.

PLAYA PUERTO MARQUÉS

Tucked below the airport highway, the protected strand **Playa Puerto Marqués** is popular with Mexican tourists, so it tends to get crowded on weekends. Beach shacks here sell fresh fish, and vendors sell silver and other wares.

PLAYA REVOLCADERO

Sprawling **Playa Revolcadero** fronts the two Fairmont hotels. People come here to surf and ride horses. The water is shallow, but the waves can be rough, and the rip current can be strong, so be careful while swimming.

10

CANCÚN

Offering 23 km (14 mi) of accessible coastline, Cancún is riddled with postcard-worthy beaches that beckon outdoor enthusiasts of every ilk. Cancún's turquoise waters and white-sandy beaches are the perfect place to leave your cares behind.

(this page above) Playa Graviota Azul; (opposite page upper right) Playa Delfines; (opposite page lower left) Playa Tortugas

Cancún Island is one long continuous beach shaped like the number "7." It's virtually impossible to find a bad beach in here; they all have turquoise waters and powdery white sand. In general, beaches on the northwestern side tend to have calmer waters and softer sand than those facing the Caribbean. The light and fluffy sand stays cool underfoot, even when the sun is beating down during prime tanning hours. By law, the entire coast of Mexico is federal property and open to the public. Everyone is welcome to walk along the beach as long as you enter and exit from one of the public points—the problem is that these points are often miles apart. One way around the situation is to find a hotel open to the public, go into the lobby bar for a drink or snack, and afterward head to the beach for a swim.

SAFETY FIRST

Most hotel beaches have lifeguards, but as with all ocean swimming, use common sense. Overall, the beaches facing the Bahía de Mujeres are best for swimming. Farther out, the undertow can be tricky. Some beaches facing the Caribbean have riptides and currents, especially when the surf is high. In December, strong north winds can bring some stronger currents and waves here.

PLAYA DELFINES (DOLPHIN BEACH)

Playa Delfines is easy to locate, since it is the only one that has yet to be blocked by resorts. The white sand and water in four shades of turquoise will often bring cars to a halt on Boulevard Kukulcan. Families and locals are drawn to this wide-open stretch of sand, where kites and beach supplies are sold. The strong currents and high winds make this a better place to catch some rays than to snorkel or swim. Playa Delfines is the only beach in Cancún with its own parking lot.

PLAYA GAVIOTA AZUL (BLUE SEAGULL BEACH)

As the most northern beach on the Caribbean side, the waves at **Playa Graviota Azul** pick up wind swell, making it one of the few spots in Cancún where surfing is possible. During hurricane season, waves can reach up to 6 feet; all other times of year the waters are great for a playful day in the surf. Adding to the lure of this beach is its proximity to shops, restaurants, and Playa Cabana Beach Club, where you can rent a beach bed and eat fresh sushi.

PLAYA LANGOSTA (LOBSTER BEACH)

The calm waters and designated swimming area make **Playa Langosta** Cancún's most child-friendly beach. Facing Bahía de Mujeres at the top of the "7," this stretch of sand is protected from high winds and is less crowded than those

on the Caribbean side. Families can take a break from the sun and head to the neighboring ice-cream shop or Dolphin Discovery Center.

PLAYA PUNTA NIZUC

Located at the southern tip of Boulevard Kukulcan, **Playa Punta Nizuc** is so secluded that you may think you're on a deserted island. Since there are no amenities, few travelers visit this stretch of pristine coastline. The water is placid and the beaches are well manicured by the neighboring Camino Real Hotel. Parking, crowds, and noise are never an issue, and it's most likely the only Cancún beach you'll have entirely to yourself.

PLAYA TORTUGAS (TURTLE BEACH)

Snorkeling, sailing, kayaking, swimming—**Playa Tortugas** is an aquatic playground for active travelers. The deep waters and wide sandbanks also make it an ideal launching point for paragliding and jet skiing. If water sports are not your thing, purchase a blow-up raft from one of the beach vendors, and float the day away. There are also plenty of snack shops to keep your tummy happy.

10

COZUMEL

Cozumel's aquamarine sea is irresistible and easily accessed from most of the coastline. Beaches have soft sand and calm water; tropical fish swim right beside limestone shelves, and white anemones wave with the currents in tide pools.

(this page above, and opposite page upper right) Punta Sur; (opposite page lower left) Playa Palancar

At some spots you can see fish swimming in the crystal clear water close to shore without ever getting a toe wet. But it would be a shame to visit the island and skip seeing the endless array of sea life along the coral reefs. Most swimmers don masks and snorkels even if they're just paddling about beside the beach at their hotel. Cozumel lacks the long, broad beaches you find in Cancún or the Riviera Maya. Instead, pockets of sand form between sections of brittle limestone. The best sandy beaches are located along the island's southern shores, where sea grass mars the underwater scenery. Gorgeous, isolated beaches stretch along portions of the windward coast, where rough tides can make swimming dangerous. Fortunately, the hotels and beach clubs make the most of what they have.

SAFETY FIRST

If you're snorkeling or swimming from shore, swim shoes will protect your feet from coral and rocks. The water is typically shallow close to shore, though currents can be strong if you swim out several yards. It's best to swim against the current first then float back with it to your starting point. The sun is strong even on cloudy days.

PLAYA SANTA PILAR

Playa Santa Pilar runs along the northern hotel strip and ends at Punta Norte on the leeward side of the island. Long stretches of sand and shallow water encourage leisurely swims. The privacy diminishes as you swim south past hotels and condos.

PLAYA SAN JUAN

South of Playa Santa Pilar, **Playa San Juan** has a rocky shore with no easy ocean access. It's usually crowded with guests from nearby hotels. The wind can be strong here, which makes it popular with windsurfers.

PLAYA SAN MARTIN

The water is usually calm at windward-side **Playa San Martin**, making it a great place to enjoy the island's wild side without worrying about rough waves. Bring your own beach blanket, towels, and drinking water and enjoy the solitude.

PLAYA PALANCAR

There's nothing fancy or phony about simple **Playa Palancar**—just the aroma of fish grilled with garlic, the sounds of the sea, and the sensation of swinging in a hammock lazily. Even the sign is simple. Look for it between **Playa San Francisco** and Faro Celarain Eco Park.

PUNTA CHIQUEROS

A half-moon-shaped cove is sheltered by an offshore reef, the first popular

swimming area as you drive north on the coastal road (it's about 8 mi [12 km] north of Parque Punta Sur). Part of a longer beach that some locals call Playa Bonita, **Punta Ciqueros** has fine sand, clear water, and moderate waves. This is a great place to swim, watch the sunset, and eat fresh fish.

PUNTA MORENA

Surfers and boogie boarders have adopted **Punta Morena**, a short drive north of Ventanas al Mar, as their official hangout. The pounding surf creates great waves, and the local restaurant serves typical surfer food (hamburgers, hot dogs, and french fries). Vendors sell hammocks by the side of the road. The owners allow camping here.

ISLA PASIÓN

If your idea of paradise is a tranquil island with beaches stretching toward the horizon beside still, clear waters, you'll absolutely love **Isla Pasión**, a patch of sand and palms off Cozumel's northwest point. When cruise passengers depart, you'll feel delightfully isolated (with plenty of fresh water, food, and cervezas close at hand).

PUNTA SUR

Faro Celarain Eco Park at Cozumel's southern tip claims some of the island's most gorgeous white-sand beaches with calm water and excellent snorkeling. It's worth the park's admission fee to spend hours lingering at **Punta Sur**.

10

THE RIVIERA MAYA

Turquoise waters, sugary sand, arching palms—this postcard perfection is about as ideal as it gets, and it aptly describes the stretch of coastline from Cancún to Tulum, which is popularly known as the Riviera Maya.

(this page above, and opposite page upper right) Tulum Beach; (opposite page lower left) Playa del Secreto

Beaches along the Riviera Maya are regularly groomed by adjacent resorts. Unfortunately, many beaches are inaccessible from Carretera 307 as security gates block such properties. The best way to reach the water is by taking one of the public roads that run between resorts, or by purchasing a drink in a hotel lobby before hitting the beach. The Caribbean's crystal clear waters are also great for diving at Banco Chichorro and the Great Maya Reef, the largest in the northern hemisphere. Far south, world-class fishing and secluded coastline can be found in the charming towns of Mahahual and Xcalak. If you're looking for lively and populated beaches, head to one of the beach clubs that parallel Playa del Carmen's 5th Avenue. Although Playa's beaches (as well as those in Tulum) lack protective outer reefs, the strong wind and waves make these areas great for kitesurfing, boogie-boarding, and playing in the surf.

SAFETY FIRST

Empty coastlines can be susceptible to car break-ins and theft. Most hotel beaches have lifeguards, but as with all ocean swimming, use common sense. Even the calmest-looking waters can have currents and riptides. If visiting isolated beaches, bring sunscreen and drinking water to avoid overexposure and dehydration. Waves (and currents) are most powerful and least conducive to swimming) in December.

PLAYA DEL SECRETO (NORTH OF PUNTA MAROMA)

Provided you like turquoise and emerald, the water at **Playa del Secreto** in Punta Maroma is as beautiful as it gets. Like fine powdered crystals, the soft white sand sparkles under the sun, and the beaches are kept spotless by neighboring resorts that groom them daily. And there are no sudden drop-offs or rocks in sight. Although not completely calm, surf is never too rough to keep you from swimming. Farther north of here is a stretch of coastline where clothing is optional.

XCACEL

The deep sand, outer reef, and isolated beaches make **Playa Xcacael** a haven for sea turtles that nest here between May and November. If you plan on visiting during turtle season, do not disturb the raised mounds of sand and avoid any turtles you see on shore. What makes this beach so appealing is the natural setting, completely void of resorts and amenities. Snorkeling is best toward the north end of the beach, and since the waters are protected by the outer reef, wind and waves are seldom a problem here. To reach Playa Xcacel, turn onto the dirt road between Chemuyil and Xel-Ha off Carretera 307. Since this beach is desolate, make sure you do not leave any valuables in your car.

TANKAH

Overshadowed by the southern beaches of Tulum, wide **Tankah Bay** is protected by an outer reef that blocks the wind and waves. The bay itself offers excellent snorkeling and kayaking, but you'll want to avoid swimming since a few rocks line the shore. Throw down a towel and sink into the sugary white sand or head to the neighboring Manatee Cenote for an underwater adventure. Surrounded by mangroves, this freshwater pool is rich with abundant sea life and spills directly into the bay. You'll find wonderful restaurants nearby at Blue Sky Hotel and Casa Cenote (but none directly on the beach).

TULUM

Tulum Beach is surrounded by ancient Mayan ruins, not to mention some of the softest sand on the coast, with water that illuminates four shades of turquoise. The small cove at the base of the ruins is accessible by way of a long wooden staircase. You'll have to pay the park entrance fee to get to the sand. This is by far the most picturesque of Tulum's beaches, but not the biggest. Head farther south, along the road to Boca Paila, for endless beach options. Wind and waves are common here, making Tulum one of the area's best spots for kitesurfing. For spectacular views, head to Punta Piedra (Rock Point) at Km 5 and grab a bite at Zamas.

10

RIVIERA MAYA SPAS

by Marlise Kast

This area offers plenty of pampering, be it footbaths or facials, manicures or massages. Whether in a spa pavilion, on a soft white beach, or in a palapa nestled in the jungle, you'll experience the ultimate in relaxation of body, mind, and spirit.

Most spas in the region also have heated pools, steam rooms, beachside massages, and fitness facilities. Some even offer beauty salons, personal consultants, organic cafés, and natural cenotes.

A visit to the region is not complete without participating in a temazcal ritual based on traditional Mayan healing methods. Temazcal is a type of sweat lodge that's used to purify the body and cleanse mind and spirit. You can also indulge in one of the other Mayan-inspired spa remedies like chaya detoxification, chocolate body wraps, or ground corn and honey exfoliation. Most resorts also offer treatments from around the globe. Japanese shiatsu,

Swedish massage, and deep-tissue Thai massage are just a few of the ways to rejuvenate your body.

There's a package for just about everyone: for men, for golfers, for expectant mothers. Send the kids to the teen spa for a Peppermint Patty foot massage or an ice cream pedicure. Newlyweds can indulge in candlelit massages for two or aroma baths brimming with floating petals.

Most spas are open to the public, but appointments are mandatory since walk-ins aren't the norm. Be sure to set aside extra time before or after your treatment and take advantage of all the facility has to offer.

Resort/ Spa name	Body Treatments	Facials	Outdoor Treatments	Couples Treatments	Fitness Day Pass	Sauna	Steam Room
Rosewood	$85–$195	$165–$255	Lagoon	yes	Free	yes	yes
Mandarin Oriental	$145–$205	$205	Garden	yes	Free	yes	yes
JW Marriott	$60–$270	$75–$155	Pool	yes	no	yes	yes
Banyan Tree	$90–$210	$180–$190	Lagoon	yes	no	yes	yes
The Tides	$70–$240	$85–$180	Jungle or Ocean	yes	no	yes	yes
Fairmont	$129–$499	$129–$229	Jungle	yes	$25	yes	yes
Azulik	$73–$165	$66–$90	Ocean	no	no	no	no
Maroma	$125–$215	$125–$210	Garden	yes	Free	yes	yes
Zoëtry Paraiso	$129–$220	$129–$250	Ocean	yes	Resort guests only	yes	yes
Hilton	$109–$199	$119–$179	Ocean	yes	$15	yes	no

10

TOP SPOTS

Banyan Tree Spa

Rosewood Mayakoba

BANYAN TREE SPA, MAYAKOBA

Built over freshwater lagoons, the Banyan Tree Spa draws on centuries old Asian traditions. The therapists (80% of whom are from Thailand) begin with a heavenly footbath, followed by your choice of the healing treatments. Unique to Banyan Tree is its signature Rainmist Steam Bath and the 12-step Rainforest Experience that combines hydrotherapy with infrared light to release tension and revitalize the body.

BODY TREATMENTS. Massage: Sukhothai, Balinese, Swedish, Thai, Chinese footwork, lomi lomi, Indian head massage. **Wraps/Baths:** Tumeric and lemongrass scrub, green tea scrub, lulur scrub, yogurt splash, fresh milk bath, sandalwood and ginger scrub, marigold and honey scrub, footbath. **Other:** Rainmist Steam Bath, detox mud wrap, rain shower, 12-step Rainforest, Thai herbal compress, yoga lessons, men's treatments

BEAUTY TREATMENTS. Facials, hair/scalp conditioning, manicures, pedicures, waxing, makeovers

PRICES. Body Treatments: $90–$210. Facials: $180–$190. Hair: $50–$90. Manicure/Pedicure: $70–$90.

Banyan Tree Spa. ⊠ *Carretera 307, Km 298. Mayakoba.* ☎ *984/877–3688* ⊕ *www. banyantree.com/mayakoba. Parking: Valet* ▭ *AE, MC, V*

SENSE, ROSEWOOD MAYAKOBA

Rosewood's 17,000-sq-ft spa is in a jungle on its very own island. Wooden walkways lead to a swimming pool and limestone cenote, which is fed by subterranean springs. Many treatments, such as the temazcal ritual and the Mayakoba ancient massage, incorporate the Mayan tradition of aligning the energies of the body in rhythmic harmony. Leave time to enjoy the spa facilities, including the gym, sauna, Jacuzzi, plunge pool and eucalyptus steam room.

BODY TREATMENTS. Massage: Swedish, deep tissue, hot stone, aromatherapy, reflexology, Asian. **Wraps/Baths:** Hydrating, chocolate, detox, revitalization, toning. **Other:** Natural cenote, temazcal ritual, 12 lagoon-side treatment rooms, 8 spa suites, Itzamná café, private yoga lessons, treatments for pregnant women.

BEAUTY TREATMENTS. Facials, hair cuts/style, manicures, pedicures, waxing, makeovers

PRICES. Body Treatments: $85–$195. Facials: $165–$255. Hair: $65–$85. Manicure/Pedicure: $75–$85.

Sense, Rosewood Spas. ⊠ *Carretera 307, Km 298. Mayakoba* ☎ *984/875–8000* ⊕ *www.rosewoodmayakoba.com. Parking: Valet* ▭ *AE, MC, V*

The Tides

Mandarin Oriental

THE TIDES, PUNTA BETE

Although not as grandiose as most spas in the area, the Tides is unique in its use of indigenous materials and local ingredients, such as chocolate, seaweed, aloe vera, and heated lava shells. It also offers a series of unusual treatments, like the Hammock Massage that allows the therapist to knead you through a hammock. Another massage uses a *manteada* (blanket stretch) to adjust posture and elongate muscles. The Sweet Honey and Rain Massage combine herbal bouquets, wild honey, and drops of water.

BODY TREATMENTS. Massage: Deep tissue, Thai, jantzu water massage, hot stone, reflexology, lunar, hammock. **Wraps/Baths:** Red seaweed wrap, aloe vera bath, mud wrap, Mayan bath. **Other:** Oceanfront yoga and Pilates, aromatherapy, fertility ceremony, temazcal ritual, men's treatments.

BEAUTY TREATMENTS. Facials, manicures, pedicures, waxing

PRICES. Body Treatments: $70–$240. Facials: $85–$180. Manicure/Pedicure: $85–$95.

The Tides. ⊠ *Playa Xcalacoco Frac 7, Punta Bete* ☎ *984/877-3000* ⊕ *www. tidesrivieramaya.com. Parking: Valet* ⊟ *AE, MC, V*

MANDARIN ORIENTAL

Both the design and philosophy of the spa are inspired by the Mayan healing elements of water, air, fire, and earth. Signature treatments include Oriental Harmony (four-hands massage), temazcal ceremony (guided by a Mayan shaman), and the Mayan Na Lu'Um massage (which opens blocked energy paths). For travelers who have spent too many days basking in the sun, the soothing Kinich Ahau program includes a sunburn remedy wrap, hair treatment, and hydrating facial.

BODY TREATMENTS. Massage: Shiatsu, hot stone, Thai, Oriental foot therapy, Swedish, deep tissue. **Wraps/Baths:** Yucatan mud wrap, Oriental salt scrub, herbal wrap, watsu pool, chocolate body treatment. **Other:** Aromatherapy, Kinesis fitness studio, yoga/pilates/meditation classes, temazcal, ice fountains.

BEAUTY TREATMENTS. Facials, manicures, pedicures

PRICES. Body Treatments: $145–$315. Facials: $205. Hair: $65–$85. Manicure/Pedicure: $80–$95.

The Spa at Mandarin Oriental. ⊠ *Carretera 307, Km 298.8* ☎ *984/877-3888* ⊕ *www. mandarinoriental.com/rivieramaya Parking: Valet* ⊟ *AE, MC, V*

10

HONORABLE MENTIONS

Fairmont Mayakoba

ZOËTRY PARAISO DE LA BONITA, PUNTA TANCHACTE

It's the only certified Thalassotherapy Spa and Anti-Aging Center in Riviera Maya, meaning many of it's treatments incorporate seawater. The extensive menu features body wraps, holistic treatments, saltwater hydrotherapy, and temazcal rituals. Although most treatments involve getting wet, you'll also find healing dry remedies like wraps, facials, massages, and acupuncture. To eliminate toxins, sea kelp and marine mud are infused into spa products.

Within the 22,000 sq-ft spa are facilities for yoga, Tai-Chi, acupuncture and Chinese medicine.

BODY TREATMENTS. Massage: Mayan, reflexology, pressotheraphy, Swedish, Thai, hot stone, therapeutic, regenerative, marine affusion shower massage, janzu massage. **Wraps/Baths:** Seaweed wrap, mud wrap, balneotherapy. **Other:** Temazcal, hydrotherapy, private yoga, Tai Chi, acupunture, Kinesiology, saltwater pool, fitness center, men's treatments.

BEAUTY TREATMENTS. Facials, manicures, pedicures, waxing, hair cut/style

PRICES. Body Treatments: $129–$220. Facials: $129–$250. Manicure/Pedicure: $55–$110.

Zoëtry Paraiso de la Bonia. ⊠ Carretera 307, Km 328 ☎ 984/872–8300 ⊕ www.zoetryparaisodelabonita.com/Paraiso. Parking: Valet ▭ AE, MC, V

WILLOW STREAM, FAIRMONT MAYAKOBA

It's easy to loose yourself (literally) within the enormous 37,000 sq-ft spa. Favorite treatments are the Mexican stone massage, the Cha Chac Rain Ritual (a massage that takes place on a seven-jet Vichy table), and Honey in the Heart (honey body mask and massage). Weary travelers will want to try the Jet Lag Recovery, an aromatherapy bath and massage that reverses the negative effects of flying and time zone changes. After a gym workout, ease your muscles in the rooftop vitality pool.

BODY TREATMENTS. Massage: hot stone, reflexology, aromatheraphy, deep tissue. **Wraps/Baths:** Seaweed bath, thermal mineral bath, chocolate wrap, rose bath, Mayan bath, clay purification. **Other:** Vichy shower, saltwater pool, fitness center, specialized wedding menu, men's treatments.

BEAUTY TREATMENTS. Facials, manicures, pedicures, waxing, hair cut/color/style, make-up application

PRICES. Body Treatments: $129–$499. Facials: $129–$229. Manicure/Pedicure: $59–$89.

Willow Stream at Fairmont Mayakoba. ⊠ Carretera 307, Km 298 ☎ 984/206–3039 ⊕ www.willowstream.com. Parking: Valet ▭ AE, MC, V

JW Marriott   Aventura Spa Palace

JW MARRIOTT, CANCUN

Located in Cancun proper, this 35,000 sq-ft spa should be included as one of the area's best. Choose from one of 13 invigorating facials including the pumpkin enzyme treatment or the cucumber green-tea facial. Women will enjoy Precious Stones and Flowers which begins with a detoxifying marine mask followed by flower petals and crystals placed over energy points to bring balance and harmony to the body. The JW Spa even offers specialized treatments for men, golfers, couples, and teens. For the ultimate Caribbean experience, take a dip in the ocean followed by a beachside massage.

BODY TREATMENTS. Massage: Swedish, Oriental, lomi lomi, deep tissue, shiatsu, hot stone. **Wraps/Baths:** Mayan herbal bath, chocolate body scrub. **Other:** Vichy shower, indoor/outdoor pool, fitness center, temezcal, teen spa menu (ages 6–17), men's treatments.

BEAUTY TREATMENTS. Facials, manicures, pedicures, waxing, hair cut/color/style, make-up application

PRICES. Body Treatments: $60–$270. Facials: $75–$155. Manicure/Pedicure: $10–$70.

JW Marriott Cancun Resort & Spa. ⊠ *Blvd Kukulcan Km 14.5, Zona Hotelera, Cancun* ⌂ *998/848–9700 Parking: Valet* ▭ *AE, MC, V*

ALSO WORTH NOTING

Several other Riviera Maya spas are also worth mentioning. The **Kinan Spa at Maroma Resort** (⊠ *Carretera 307, Km 51* ☎ *998/872–8200* ⊕ *www.maromahotel. com*), has treatments based on ancient Mayan healing. **Aventura Spa Palace** (⊠ *Carretera 307, Km 72, Puerto Aventuras* ☎ *984/875–1100* ⊕ *www.palaceresorts. com*) is known for its excellent hydrotherapy facilities. For treatments with a view, head to **Azulik Eco-Resort** in Tulum (⊠ *Carretera Tulum Ruinas Km 5* ☎ *800/123–3278* ⊕ *www.azulik.com*).

Located in Cancun's Zona Hotelera, this impressive spa at **The Hilton** (⊠ *Blvd. Kukulcan, Km 17, Zona Hotelera, Cancun* ☎ *998/881–8000* ⊕ *www.hiltoncancun. com*) has a Zen garden, relaxation lounge and treatments on the beach for men and women.

Also located in Cancun is the **Kayantá Spa at The Rtiz Carlton** (⊠ *Blvd. Kukulcan, Km 14, Zona Hotelera, Cancun* ☎ *998/881–0808* ⊕ *www.ritzcarlton.com*) where you can experience the "Deep Blue Peel." This massage and body-scrub combo consists of marine extracts, seaweed, bergamot and jojoba oil. The avocado and yogurt wrap will leave your skin feeling silky smooth.

At the **Ceiba del Mar Spa** (⊠ *Costera Norte, Puerto Morelos* ☎ *998/872–8063* ⊕ *www. ceibadelmar.com*) you can begin with a biotensor rod for testing vital energy. Based on the findings, specific treatments are then selected to help restore energy levels.

GLOSSARY

acupuncture. Painless Chinese medicine in which needles are inserted into key spots on the body to restore the flow of qi and allow the body to heal itself.

aromatherapy. Massage and other treatments using plant-derived essential oils intended to relax the skin's connective tissues and stimulate the flow of lymph fluid.

balneotherapy. Theraputic hot baths and natural vapor baths.

body brushing. Drybrushing of the skin to remove dead cells and stimulate circulation. Also called body scrub; see also salt glow.

body polish. Use of scrubs, loofahs, and other exfoliants to remove dead skin cells.

janzu. An aquatic therapeutic technique that unblocks physical, emotional, and mental energy by movement in the water.

hot-stone massage. Massage using smooth stones heated in water and applied to the skin with pressure or

strokes or simply rested on the body.

hydrotherapy. Underwater massage, alternating hot and cold showers, and other water-oriented treatments.

lomi lomi. A type of massage that imposes a rhythmic rocking sensation, while stimulating the circulatory system.

pressotheraphy. Compression technique to help improve circulation and tone the circulatory system.

Reiki. A Japanese healing method involving universal life energy, the laying on of hands, and mental and spiritual balancing. It's intended to relieve acute emotional and physical conditions. Also called adiance technique.

salt glow. Rubbing the body with coarse salt to remove dead skin.

shiatsu. Japanese massage that uses pressure applied with fingers, hands, elbows, and feet.

shirodhara. Ayurvedic massage in which warm herbal-

ized oil is trickled onto the center of the forehead, then gently rubbed into the hair and scalp.

Swiss shower. A multi-jet bath that alternates hot and cold water, often used after mud wraps and other body treatments.

temazcal. Maya meditation in a sauna heated with volcanic rocks.

Thai massage. Deep-tissue massage and passive stretching to ease stiff, tense, or short muscles.

thalassotherapy. Water-based treatments that incorporate seawater, seaweed, and algae.

Vichy shower. Treatment in which a person lies on a cushioned, waterproof mat and is showered by overhead water jets.

Watsu. A blend of shiatsu and deep-tissue massage with gentle stretches—all conducted in a warm pool.

(opposite) The Tides Riviera Maya

PHOTO CREDITS

1, Douglas Peebles / eStock Photo. 2, Christian Goupi / age fotostock. 5, PBorowka/Shutterstock. **Chapter 1: Best Beaches on the East Coast:** 6-7, Ellen Rooney / age fotostock. 10, BRUCE HERMAN/ Mexico Tourism Board. 11, Jim Lopes/Shutterstock. 12, BVI Tourist Board. 13 (left), Gary Blakeley/ iStockphoto. 13 (right), Bruce Herman/Mexico Tourism Board. 14, Philip Coblentz/Brand X Pictures. 15 (left), Jeff Greenberg/age fotostock. 15 (right), sebastien burel/iStockphoto. 16, Jerry and Marcy Monkman/EcoPhotography.com/Aurora Photos. 17 (left), Andy Jackson / Alamy. 17 (right), John Gray Restaurant Group. 18, Philip Coblentz/Digital Vision. 19, Richard Cummins / SuperStock. **Chapter 2: Best Beaches on the West Coast:** 20-21, Valhalla | Design & Conquer, Fodors.com member. 22, zschnepf/Shutterstock. 23 (left), Brent Reeves/Shutterstock. 23 (right), RonGreer.Com/Shutterstock. 24, alysta/Shutterstock. 25 (top), Lowe Llaguno/Shutterstock. 25 (bottom), Brett Shoaf/Artistic Visuals. 26, Robert Holmes. 27 (top), Eric Foltz/iStockphoto. 27 (bottom), Scott Vickers/iStockphoto. 28, jonrawlinson/Flickr. 29 (top), tylerdurden1/Flickr. 29 (bottom), Dieter Karner/Flickr. 30, John Elk III / Alamy. 31 (top), Janine Bolliger/iStockphoto. 31 (bottom), Lise Gagne/iStockphoto. 32, iStockphoto. 33, iofoto/Shutterstock. 34 (top), Evan Meyer/iStockphoto. 34 (center), Kyle Maass/iStockphoto. 34 (bottom left), iStockphoto. 34 (bottom right), Lise Gagne/iStockphoto. 35, Tom Baker/Shutterstock. 36 (top), CURAphotography/Shutterstock. 36 (center), Michael Almond/iStockphoto. 36 (bottom), Yoshio Tomii / SuperStock. 37 (top), iStockphoto. 37 (bottom), Lise Gagne/iStockphoto. 38 (top), Ross Stapleton-Gray/iStockphoto. 38 (center), Jay Spooner/iStockphoto. 38 (bottom), TebNad/Shutterstock. 39 (top), Jay Spooner/iStockphoto. 39 (bottom), Lise Gagne/iStockphoto. 40, David M. Schrader/Shutterstock. 41 (top), Loren Evans/iStockphoto. 41 (bottom), Bart Everett/iStockphoto. 42, Andy Z./Shutterstock. 43 (top), Stephen Goodwin/iStockphoto. 43 (bottom), hawkeye978/Shutterstock. 44, spirobulldog, Fodors.com member. 45 (top), Robert Crow/Shutterstock. 45 (bottom), Caitlin Mirra/ Shutterstock. 46, zschnepf/Shutterstock. 47 (top), James Saunders/Shutterstock. 47 (bottom), zschnepf/ Shutterstock. 48, kwest/Shutterstock. 49 (top), Scott David Patterson/Shutterstock. 49 (bottom), Laszlo Dobos/Shutterstock. **Chapter 3: Best Beaches in Hawai'i:** 50-51, eStock Photo / Grant Studios. 52, Oahu Visitors Bureau. 53 (left), Luis Castañeda/age fotostock. 53 (right), Kaua'i Visitors Bureau. 54, J.D.Heaton/Picture Finders/age fotostock. 55 (top), Photo Resource Hawaii / Alamy. 55 (bottom), Blaine Harrington/age fotostock. 56, SuperStock / age fotostock. 57 (top), Alexander Hafemann/iStockphoto. 57 (bottom), Jay Spooner/iStockphoto. 58, Cornforth Images / Alamy. 59 (top), Vlad Turchenko/Shutterstock. 59 (bottom), Bonita R. Cheshier/Shutterstock. 60, Johnny Stockshooter / age fotostock. 61 (top), James M. House/Shutterstock. 61 (bottom), Russ Bishop / age fotostock. 62-64 and 65 (top), Douglas Peebles. 65 (bottom), iStockphoto. 66, Photo Resource Hawaii / Alamy. 67 (top), Photo Resource Hawaii / Alamy. 67 (bottom), SuperStock/age fotostock. 68, Mark A. Johnson / Alamy. 69 (top), Photo Resource Hawaii / Alamy. 69 (bottom), Dallas & John Heaton/age fotostock. 70, Tony Reed / Alamy. 71 (top), Photo Resource Hawaii / Alamy. 71 (bottom), Reimar Gaertner / age fotostock. 72, SuperStock / age fotostock. 73, HVCB/Ron Dahlquist. 74 and 76, Pacific Stock/SuperStock. 77 (top), photo75/iStockphoto. 77 (bottom), Joe West/Shutterstock. **Chapter 4: Best Beaches on the East Coast:** 78-79, Stuart Westmorland / Alamy. 80, Kevin Tavares/Shutterstock. 81 (left), Chee-Onn Leong/ Shutterstock. 81 (right), rpongsaj/Flickr. 82, Jeff Greenberg / age fotostock. 83 (top), Chee-Onn Leong/ Shutterstock. 83 (bottom), atalou/Flickr. 84, Michael Czosnek/iStockphoto. 85, SuperStock / age fotostock. 86 (left), Maine State Museum. 86 (right), David Cannings-Bushell/iStockphoto. 87, Paul D. Lemke/iStockphoto. 88, Michael Rickard/Shutterstock. 89 (left), Robert Campbell. 89 (top right), Casey Jordan. 89 (bottom right), Dave Johnston. 90 (top), Doug Lemke/Shutterstock. 90 (center), Jason Grower/Shutterstock. 90 (bottom), Kenneth Keifer/Shutterstock. 91 (top), Pat & Chuck Blackley / Alamy. 91 (center), Doug Lemke/Shutterstock. 91 (bottom), liz west/wikipedia.org. 92-93, Kindra Clineff. 94, Raymond Forbes / age fotostock. 95 (top), Lori Froeb/Shutterstock. 95 (bottom), Walter Bibikow / age fotostock. 96, David Lyons / Alamy. 97 (top), greenbk/Flickr. 97 (bottom), Blaine Harrington III / Alamy. 98, Nantucket Historical Association. 99, Michael S. Nolan / age fotostock. 100, Kindra Clineff. 101 (top and bottom right), Kindra Clineff. 101 (center), Penobscot Marine Museum. 101 (bottom left), Random House, Inc. 103, Jeff Greenberg / age fotostock. 104, Susan Tansil/Flickr. 105 (top), Tomás Fano/Flickr. 105 (bottom), Rick Berk/Flickr. 106, Nrbelex/Flickr. 107 (top), Genista/ Flickr. 107 (bottom), jiashiang/Flickr. 108, Pat & Chuck Blackley/Alamy. 109 (top), dchousegrooves/ Flickr. 109 (bottom), rpongsaj/Flickr. 110, Christian Kieffer/Shutterstock. 111 (top), Cellular Immunity/Flickr. 111 (bottom), geopungo/Flickr. 112, Michelle Malven/iStockphoto. 113 (top), DoxaDigital/ iStockphoto. 113 (bottom), Isabelle Carpenter/iStockphoto. 114, Tatiana Gribanova / Alamy. 115 (top), Andrew Neil Dierks, Neil Dierks Photography/iStockphoto. 115 (bottom), Kayann Legg/iStockphoto. 116, Denise Kappa/Shutterstock. 117 (top), rockhounds_5/Flickr. 117 (bottom), Stacie Stauff Smith Photography/Shutterstock. 118, Zach Holmes / Alamy. 119 (top), Sebastien Windal/Shutterstock. 119 (bottom), Brandon Laufenberg/iStockphoto. **Chapter 5: Best Beaches in Florida and the Gulf Coast:** 120-21, Cheryl Casey/Shutterstock. 122, Cogoli Franco/SIME/eStockphoto. 123 (left), Cheryl Casey/Shutterstock. 123 (right), Ivan Cholakov/Shutterstock. 124, Cheryl Casey/Shutterstock. 125 (top), Jeff Kinsey/Shutterstock. 125 (bottom), Cheryl Casey/Shutterstock. 126, Visit Florida. 127 (top), Tom Hirtreiter/Shutterstock. 127 (bottom), Deborah Wolfe/Shutterstock. 128, St. Petersburg/Clearwater Area CVB. 129 (top), Visit Florida. 129 (bottom), Graca Victoria/Shutterstock. 130, Travelshots.com / Alamy. 131 (top), jeff gynane/iStockphoto. 131 (bottom), Visit Florida. 132, Greg Vaughn/Pacific Stock/photolibrary.com. 133, Visit Florida. 134 (top), Ernest Hemingway Photograph Collection, John F. Kennedy Presidential Library and Museum, Boston. 134 (bottom) and 135 (top), Visit Florida. 135 (bottom), George Peters/iStockphoto. 136, Michael Zegers/photolibrary.com. 139, Andrew Woodley / Alamy. 140, Masa Ushioda / Alamy. 141 (top), Stephen Frink Collection / Alamy. 141 (bottom), Denny Medley/Random Photography/iStockphoto. 142, Nicholas Pitt / Alamy. 143 (top), Christina Dearaujo/Flickr. 143 (bottom), Claudette, Fodors.com member. 144, Jeff Greenberg / age fotostock. 145 (top), Flickr. 145 (bottom), murray cohen/iStockphoto. 146, Nick Greaves / Alamy. 147 (top), Ingolf Pompe 77 / Alamy. 147 (bottom), Visit Florida. 148, PBorowka/Shutterstock. 149 and 150 (top), Douglas Rudolph. 150 (bottom), Visit Florida. 151, M. Timothy O'Keefe / Alamy. 152 (top), Bob Care/Florida Keys News Bureau. 152 (bottom), Julie de Leseleuc/iStockphoto. 153 (top), Visit Florida. 153 (bottom), Charles Stirling (Diving) / Alamy. 154 (top), Visit Florida. 154 (bottom), Gert Vrey/iStockphoto. 155, Scott Wilson, FKCC Student. 156, Jeff Greenberg / age fotostock. 157 (top), divemasterking2000/Flickr. 157 (bottom), The Pug Father/Flickr. 158, Robert Francis / age fotostock. 159 (top), laszlophoto/Flickr. 159 (bottom), WhitA/Flickr. 160, Patrick Ray Dunn / Alamy. 161 (top), Philip Lange/Shutterstock. 161 (bottom), Karl Kehm/iStockphoto. **Chapter 6: Best Beaches in the Bahamas:** 162-63, Reinhard Dirscherl / age fotostock. 164 and 165 (left), Staniel Cay Yacht Club. 165 (right), Island Effects/iStockphoto. 166, Firecrest Pictures / age fotostock. 167 (top), Dolphin Encounters Limited/wikipedia.org. 167 (bottom), Ramona Settle. 168, Alvaro Leiva / age fotostock. 169 (top), Ramona Settle. 169 (bottom), Letizia Spanò/Shutterstock. 170, Macduff Everton/Atlantis. 171 (bottom left), Richard Riley/Atlantis. 171 (top right), Macduff Everton/Atlantis. 171 (center right), livingonimpulse/Flickr. 171 (bottom right), Seth Browarnik. 172, Tim Aylen/Atlantis. 173 (top left), Ron Starr/Atlantis. 173 (top center and right), Jeffrey Brown/Tallgrass Pictures LLC/Atlantis. 173 (bottom), Macduff Everton/Atlantis. 174 (left), Fred Hsu/wikipedia.org. 174 (right), Ron Starr/Atlantis. 175, Ramona Settle. 176, DEA / A VERGANI / age fotostock. 177 (top and bottom), The Bahamas Ministry of Tourism. 178, Gregory Pelt/Shutterstock. 179 (top), Mangrove Mike/Flickr. 179 (bottom), Knumina/Shutterstock. 180, Ellen Rooney / age fotostock. 181 (top), The Bahamas Ministry of Tourism. 181 (bottom), Bahamas Tourism Board. 182, Staniel Cay Yacht Club. 183 (top), Ramona Settle. 183 (bottom), Staniel Cay Yacht Club. 184, Greg Johnston/Cape Santa Maria Beach Resort. 185 (top), The Bahamas Ministry of Tourism. 185 (bottom), Ray Wadia/The Bahamas Ministry of Tourism. **Chapter 7: Best Beaches in the Northern Caribbean:** 186-87, Stuart Pearce / age fotostock. 188, Philip Coblentz/Digital Vision. 189 (left), Morales/age fotostock. 189 (right), Angelo Cavalli/age fotostock. 190, The Ritz-Carlton, Grand Cayman. 191 (top), Allister Clark/iStockphoto. 191 (bottom), Cayman Islands Department of Tourism. 192, RENAULT Philippe / age fotostock. 193, Walter Bibikow / age fotostock. 194, RIEGER Bertrand / age fotostock. 195 (top and bottom) and 196-97, The Dominican Republic Ministry of Tourism. 198, Steve Sanacore/Sandals Resorts. 199 (top), newphotoservice/shutterstock. 199 (bottom), Chee-Onn Leong/Shutterstock. 200, Miranda van der Kroft/Shutterstock. 201, Chee-Onn Leong/shutterstock. 202, Tramonto / age fotostock. 203, Brittany Somerset. 204 (top left and bottom left), Tim-Duncan/wikipedia.org. 204 (right), http://wbrisco.skyrock.com/2372275215-JAH-RASTAFARI.html. 205, Dave Saunders / age fotostock. 206, Doug Pearson / age fotostock. 207 (left), NawlinWiki/wikipedia.org. 207 (center), Philippe Jimenez/wikipedia.org. 207 (right), wikipedia.org. 208, Julie Schwietert. 209 (top), blucolt/Flickr. 209 (bottom), Pavelsteidl/wikipedia.org. 210, Marlise Kast. 211, Katja Kreder / age fotostock. 212-14, Ramona Settle. 215, Jochen Tack / age fotostock. **Chapter 8: Best Beaches in the Eastern Caribbean:** 216-17, Saint Barth Tourisme. 218, U.S. Virgin islands Dept. of Tourism. 219 (left and right), Philip Coblentz/Digital Vision. 220, Neil Emmerson / age fotostock. 221 (top), Steve Geer/iStockphoto. 221 (bottom), toddneville/Flickr. 222-23, Rick Strange / age fotostock. 224, John Miller / age fotostock. 225 (top), World Pictures / age fotostock. 225 (bottom), Steve Geer/istockphoto. 226, Kreder Katja / age fotostock. 227 (top), Ellen Rooney / age fotostock. 227 (bottom), World Pictures / age fotostock. 228, Eric Sanford / age fotostock. 229, Joseph C. Dovala / age fotostock. 230 (top), Randy Lincks / Alamy. 230 (bottom), iStockphoto. 231 (top), Doug Scott / age fotostock. 231 (bottom), Slavoljub Pantelic/iStockphoto. 232, Doug Scott / age fotostock. 234, Giovanni Rinaldi/iStockphoto. 235-36 and 237 (top), Walter Bibikow / age fotostock. 237 (bottom), Ingolf Pompe 8 / Alamy. 238, wikipedia.org. 239, Tristan Deschamps/F1 Online/age fotostock. 240, Guy Thouvenin /

age fotostock. 241 (top), Pack-Shot/Shutterstock. 241 (bottom), Luc Olivier for the Martinique Tourist Board. 242, Barbacha|Nicolas BOUTHORS/wikipedia.org. 243, GARDEL Bertrand / age fotostock. 244, Karl Weatherly / age fotostock. 245 (top), Robert P Cocozza/iStockphoto. 245 (bottom), Jonathan Pozniak. 246, Michael DeHoog/Cheryl Andrews Marketing Communications. 247 (top), maggiejp/Flickr. 247 (bottom), World Pictures / age fotostock. 248, Philip Coblentz/Digital Vision. 249, Helene Rogers / age fotostock. 250, drewmon, Fodors.com member. 251 (top and bottom) and 252-53, St Maarten Tourist Bureau. 254, Ken Brown/iStockphoto. 255 (top), cnabickum/Shutterstock. 255 (bottom), Juneisy Q. Hawkins/Shutterstock.**Chapter 9: Best Beaches in the Southern Caribbean:** 256-57, Benjamin Howell/iStockphoto. 258, SuperStock/age fotostock. 259 (left), Grenada Board of Tourism. 259 (right), Harry Thomas/istockphoto. 260, Famke Backx/iStockphoto. 261 (top), angelo cavalli / age fotostock. 261 (bottom), fmbackx/istockphoto. 262, martinique/Shutterstock. 263, Paul D'Innocenzo. 264, Barbados Tourism Authority/Jim Smith. 265 (top), Barbados Tourism Authority. 265 (bottom), Barbados Tourism Authority/Loralie Skeete. 266, Ingolf Pompe / age fotostock. 267, Barbados Tourism Authority/Mike Toy. 268, travelstock44 / age fotostock. 269 (top), Walter Bibikow / age fotostock. 269 (bottom), Harry Thomas/iStockphoto. 270, Philip Coblentz/Digital Vision. 271 (top), Curaçao Tourism. 271 (bottom), Stuart Pearce / age fotostock. 272, Angels at Work/shutterstock. 273, Walter Bibikow / age fotostock. 274, PetePhipp/Travelshots / age fotostock. 275 (top), Steven Allan/iStockphoto. 275 (bottom), shaggyshoo/Flickr. 276, Benjamin Howell/iStockphoto. 277 (top), Corinne Lutter/iStockphoto. 277 (bottom), Christian Horan. 278, Hauke Dressler / age fotostock. 279 (top), Jason Pratt/Flickr. 279 (bottom), Christian Goupi / age fotostock. 280, Jason Pratt/Flickr. 281, SuperStock/age fotostock. 282, Michael Newton / age fotostock. 283 (top), PHB.cz (Richard Semik)/Shutterstock. 283 (bottom), ARCO/R Kiedrowski / age fotostock. 284, Gierth, F / age fotostock. 285, Medioimages/philip coblentz. 286, Blacqbook/Shutterstock. 287, Blaine Harrington / age fotostock. 288 (top and bottom), Blacqbook/Shutterstock. 289, Peter Adams / age fotostock. **Chapter 10: Best Beaches in Mexico:** 290-91, ESCUDERO Patrick / age fotostock. 292, Joao Virissimo/Shutterstock. 293 (left), BRUCE HERMAN/Mexico Tourism Board. 293 (right), Mauricio Ramos/Mexico Tourism. 294, FRILET Patrick / age fotostock. 295 (top), Kevin Hutchinson/Flickr. 295 (bottom), Santi LLobet/Flickr. 296, Brian Florky/Shutterstock. 297 (top), MAISANT Ludovic / age fotostock. 297 (bottom), Victor Elias / age fotostock. 298, LEROY Dominique / age fotostock. 299, Adalberto Rios Szalay / age fotostock. 300 (top), Pieter Folkens. 300 (bottom), Michael S. Nolan/age fotostock. 301, Ryan Harvey/Flickr. 302, James Gritz / age fotostock. 303 (top), Terrance Klassen / age fotostock. 303 (bottom), Elena Elisseeva/Shutterstock. 304, Blaine Harrington / age fotostock. 305 (top), YinYang/iStockphoto. 305 (bottom), RussBowling/Flickr. 306, SuperStock/age fotostock. 307 (top), Esparta/Flickr. 307 (bottom), miguelão/Flickr. 308, Witold Skrypczak / age fotostock. 309 (top), GARDEL Bertrand / age fotostock. 309 (bottom), Agathe B/Flickr. 310, SuperStock/age fotostock. 311 (top), JesusAbizanda/Flickr. 311 (bottom), Rob Inh00d/Flickr. 312, Alaskan Dude/Flickr. 313 (top), idreamphoto/Shutterstock. 313 (bottom), lecates/Flickr. 314 and 316 (left), Banyan Tree Hotels & Resorts. 316 (right), Rosewood Hotels & Resorts. 317 (left), Viceroy Hotel Group. 317 (right), George Apostolidis. 318, Fairmont Hotels & Resorts. 319 (left), Marriott International. 319 (right), Palace Resorts. 320, George Doyle/iStockphoto. 321, Viceroy Hotel Group.

WRITER CREDITS

Vanessa Geneva Ahern (New York); Shelley Arenas (Southwestern Washington); Christopher Baker (Puerto Rico); Carol Bareuther (British Virgin Islands, U.S. Virgin Islands); Liz Biro (North Carolina); John Blodgett ("Maine's Lighthouses"); Carissa Bluestone (Seattle); Cheryl Crabtree (California's Central Coast, Monterey Bay Area, "The Ultimate Road Trip: California's Highway 1"); Georgia de Catona (Los Cabos); Larry Dunmire ("A Whale's Tale"); Jennifer Edwards (Northeast Florida); Mary Erskine (South Carolina); Teri Evans (Miami & Miami Beach); Bonnie Friedman (Maui); Nicholas Gill (Puerto Rico); Michele Joyce (Acapulco, Oaxaca); Kevin Kwan (Eleuthera & Harbour Island); Gary McKechnie (Florida Panhandle, "Gone Fishin'"); Christine Pae (San Diego); Troy Petenbrink (Delaware); Lisa Hamilton (California's Northern Coast); Lynne Helm (Fort Lauderdale & Broward County, "Under the Sea"); Justin Higgs (The Abacos); Marlise Kast (Cancún, Puerto Rico, Riviera Maya); Steve Larese ("A Whale of a Tale"); Elline Lipkin (Los Angeles); Lynda Lohr (British Virgin Islands, U.S. Virgin Islands); Maribeth Mellin (Cozumel); Elise Meyer (Anguilla, St. Barthélemy, St. Maarten/St. Martin); Pete Nelson (Maryland); Deston S. Nokes (Oregon Coast); Jane Onstott (Mexico Pacific Coast Resorts, Puerto Vallarta, "Spaaah!"); Chad Pata (O'ahu); Paris Permenter & John Bigley (Jamaica); Rena Havner Phillips (Alabama); Alice Powers (Virginia); Vernon O'Reilly Ramesar (Aruba, Bonaire, Curaçao, Trinidad & Tobago, "Carnival in Trinidad"); Laura Randall (Orange County, California); Michael Ream (Mississippi); Jessica Robertson ("Atlantis"); Heather Rodino (Puerto Rico); Laura V. Scheel (Cape Cod, Maine, Martha's Vineyard, Nantucket); Ramona Settle (Southern Out Islands, Turks & Caicos Islands); Jordan Simon (Antigua, Cayman Islands, St. Kitts & Nevis); Eileen Robinson Smith (Charleston and Hilton Head, SC; Dominican Republic; Guadeloupe; Martinique); Roberta Sotonoff (St. Maarten/St. Martin); Kim Steutermann Rogers (Kaua'i); Paul Rubio (New Jersey); Holly S. Smith (Seattle Environs, Northwestern Washington, San Juan Islands, Olympic Peninsula); Mary Thurwachter (Palm Beach & Treasure Coast); Christina Tourigny (Tampa Bay Area); Christine Van Dusen (Georgia); Joana Varawa (Lāna'I, Moloka'i); Chelle Koster Walton (Lower Florida Gulf Coast; Florida Keys; Grand Bahama Island; Andros, Bimini & the Berry Islands); Sharon Williams (Southern Out Islands); Katie Young Yamanaka (Big Island); Jane E. Zarem (Barbados, Genada, St. Lucia, St. Vincent & the Grenadines)

NOTES

NOTES

FODOR'S 535 BEST BEACHES
Editor: Douglas Stallings

Editorial Contributors: Linda Cabasin, Joanna Cantor, Robert I. C. Fisher, Debbie Harmsen, Maria Teresa Hart, Heidi Johansen, Kelly Kealy, Alexis Crisman Kelly, Rachel Klein, Josh McIlvain, Molly Moker, Jess Moss, Jennifer Paull, Cate Starmer, Amanda Theunissen, Eric Wechter

Production Editor: Evangelos Vasilakis
Maps & Illustrations: Ed Jacobus, *cartographer;* Bob Blake, Rebecca Baer, *map editors;* William Wu, *information graphics*
Design: Fabrizio La Rocca, *creative director;* Guido Caroti, Siobhan O'Hare, *art directors;* Tina Malaney, Nora Rosansky, Chie Ushio, Ann McBride, Jessica Walsh, *designers;* Melanie Marin, *senior picture editor*
Cover Photo: (Saltwhistle Bay Off Mayreau, Grenadines): Karl Weatherly/Corbis
Production Manager: Steve Slawsky

1st Edition

ISBN 978-1-4000-0505-5

ISSN 2155-2339

SPECIAL SALES
This book is available at special discounts for bulk purchases for sales promotions or premiums. Special editions, including personalized covers, excerpts of existing books, and corporate imprints, can be created in large quantities for special needs. For more information, write to Special Markets/Premium Sales, 1745 Broadway, MD 6-2, New York, New York 10019, or e-mail specialmarkets@randomhouse.com.

AN IMPORTANT TIP & AN INVITATION
Although all prices, opening times, and other details in this book are based on information supplied to us at press time, changes occur all the time in the travel world, and Fodor's cannot accept responsibility for facts that become outdated or for inadvertent errors or omissions. So **always confirm information when it matters**, especially if you're making a detour to visit a specific place. Your experiences—positive and negative—matter to us. If we have missed or misstated something, **please write to us**. We follow up on all suggestions. Contact the 535 Best Beaches editor at editors@fodors.com or c/o Fodor's at 1745 Broadway, New York, NY 10019.

PRINTED IN CHINA

10 9 8 7 6 5 4 3 2 1